HUMAN SECURITY IN AFGHANISTAN

Reconstructing an Alternative Notion of Security for Afghanistan in the South Asian Security Paradigm

Arpita Basu Roy

MAULANA ABUL KALAM AZAD INSTITUTE OF ASIAN STUDIES,
KOLKATA

PENTAGON PRESS

Human Security in Afghanistan: Reconstructing an Alternative Notion of Security for Afghanistan in the South Asian Security Paradigm
Arpita Basu Roy

ISBN 978-81-8274-740-1

First Published in 2014

Published by
PENTAGON PRESS
206, Peacock Lane, Shahpur Jat,
New Delhi-110049
Phones: 011-64706243, 26491568
Telefax: 011-26490600
email: rajan@pentagonpress.in
website: www.pentagonpress.in

Printed at Aegean Offset Printers, Greater Noida, U.P.

Dedicated to
Ma and Baba

Contents

Preface

It is often argued that every Afghan deserves a life free from poverty and fear, conducted in security and dignity but the reality, however, is that millions of Afghans have no such rights, nor equitable opportunities to fully develop their human potential, even after a decade of international military and humanitarian intervention in the country. After years of war, the problem lies in creating a political, social, environmental, economic and cultural system that together give Afghans the building blocks of survival, livelihood and dignity. Poverty, hunger, population structures, natural resource degradation, adequate water and sanitation all are pertinent issues in this context. It is a disturbing fact that if Afghanistan fails in its nation-building after more than a quarter-century of violent conflict, the impact will be devastating, rendering the country again vulnerable to divisiveness and instability.

Much is said about the need to create work opportunities for the Afghans and to build Afghan capacity. Nevertheless, very little has been said about the mechanics of doing so or discerning the differing views that exist within the Afghan community. The international donor community has put great emphasis on "ownership"—meaning leadership and control—of reconstruction efforts by the country itself. The degree to which Afghans feel a part of what is at stake in their country and to what has been achieved so far is unclear. Some argue that the people and government of Afghanistan are increasingly taking the lead and that the international community is moving toward a supporting role, while others argue just the opposite is taking place. Some are concerned that not enough aid gets directly to the people and that Afghans see little improvement in their lives. It is recognised by many that Afghans are a critical piece of the puzzle in their country's success. Finding ways to empower Afghans in Afghanistan emphasizes the importance of an integrated approach and one that builds needed capacity on multiple levels.

Human Security should be the paradigm for international engagement , it is often argued , and in Afghanistan as it is evident, military solutions don't seem to have a long term impact on the region. A concept of human security that emerged from a post-Cold War, multi-disciplinary understanding of security involving a number of research fields, including development studies, international relations, strategic studies, and human rights, is an emerging paradigm for understanding global vulnerabilities. The proponents of this paradigm challenge the traditional notion of national security by arguing that the proper referent for security should be the individual rather than the state. Human security holds that a people-centered view of security is necessary for national, regional and global stability.

The United Nations Development Programme's 1994 Human Development Report is considered a milestone publication in the field of human security, with its argument that insuring "freedom from want" and "freedom from fear" for all persons is the best path to tackle the problem of global insecurity. Human security is defined as the protection of "the vital core of all human lives in ways that enhance human freedoms and fulfilment". Human security means protecting fundamental freedoms. It means protecting people from critical and pervasive threats and situations. It means using processes that build on people's strengths and aspirations.

Human security is far more than the absence of violent conflict as it encompasses human rights, good governance and access to economic opportunity, education and health care. It is a concept that comprehensively addresses both "freedom from fear" and "freedom from want". Is the international community through the UN system really moving forward? In the United Nations Missions Statement, the UN Country team pledged to "... work together toward the overarching goal of human security and peace building in Afghanistan, placing people at the centre of United Nations Development Assistance Framework ..." (UNDAF). The idea was to support the national priorities of Afghanistan and dedicate to collaborating with national and international counterparts to ensure long-term peace, stability and prosperity in the country. Although operating at the margins of security discourse and policy, the idea of human security is of growing significance in UN. Human security comes in two basic packages, one concerned with multiple aspects of human well being and the other more directly focussed on the protection of individuals and communities in situations of violent conflict.

The impact of an assertive United States after September 11th and the anti-terrorism agenda have undercut several aspects of the human security approach. Nevertheless, several ideas associated with human security are having a seminal influence on security discourse, state practice and the normative basis of regional order. This study is an attempt to dwell on this vast and unfathomable territory of human security challenges facing Afghanistan and South Asia. It is proposed, and rightly so, by scholars such as Prof Amitabh Acharya that as the concept of human security itself is people-centric, so should be research and dissemination efforts about it. If the UN, the Human Security Trust Fund and individual countries are to effectively promote human security, they might want to invest more on research and dissemination from "bottom-up", by increasing the engagement of common people and the civil society.

This study was undertaken as a project for the Maulana Abul Kalam Azad Institute of Asian Studies (MAKAIAS), Kolkata. The author is indebted to the Institute, its former Director, Prof Hari Vasudevan and the Executive Council for approving the project in the first place and for providing the support extended during the period that the study was conducted. I am extremely thankful to Dr. Sreeradha Datta, Director, MAKAIAS for extending necessary support during the concluding stages of the work. I am also thankful to the some of my colleagues whose feedback have been fundamental to my work. The library staff of Azad Institute has been particularly cooperative and I thank all of them.

A large part of the work on IR theory has been conducted in the University of Cambridge. I express my gratitude to the Pavate Foundation and the University of Karnataka for awarding me the Pavate Fellowship in International Studies, 2010 thereby enabling me to undertake this work at the Department of Politics and International Studies (POLIS), University of Cambridge. My gratitude to the academic and administrative staff of POLIS for their cooperation. Sidney Sussex College has been my home in Cambridge. Special thanks to the Master, Fellows and staff of the college for making me feel at home. The love, guidance and support of Prof James Mayall, my academic mentor at

Cambridge and Mrs. Avril Mayall has been primary to this work and I shall always remain indebted to them. Special thanks also to Stephan and Leslie. I also wish to express my gratitude to Shri. Krishnan Srinivasan for his invaluable support and guidance.

Parts of the study have been presented in seminars and the comments and suggestions emerging from the discussions have been particularly useful. In this connection I would like to mention my discussions with people like Shah Mahmood Miakhel, USIP; Jamal Rehman, Advisor to the Chief of Staff on Foreign and Culture Affairs; Abdul Rehman Ulfat Mahmoodi, RRR/IDG Officer, UNDP; Sayed Mohammad Shah, Afghan Research and Evaluation Unit (AREU); Aunohita Mojumdar, Freelance Journalist, Kabul; Dr. Maqsudul Hasan Nuri, Acting President Islamabad Policy Research Institute (IPRI); Mariam Safi, Head of Research , Centre for Conflict and Peace Studies; Sanaullah Tasal, Baccha Khan Center for Peace and Conflict Resolution and Officer; Vafo Niyetbakov, Senior Specialist, Department of External Policy and Economic Development, Strategic Research Center, Tajikistan. I have also immensely benefitted with my interactions with people like Ahmad Wali Masoud, Founding Director, Ahmad Shah Masoud Foundation, Mohammad Ashraf Rasooli, Minister Advisor to the President, General Abdul Khadi Khalid , Former Deputy Minister of Interior, IRA, Latif Pedram, Member of Parliament, IRA, Aziz Arianfar, Director, Center of Afghanistan Studies (Germany). I thank my contacts in Afghanistan whose feedback have been vital to this work. Research publications and policy papers published by the AREU and APPRO have been particularly useful for this work.

It is my duty to extend my heartfelt thanks to my parents who have been extremely helpful and cooperative, my daughter Ahana whose love has been my source of sustenance and to Ayan, who, in many different ways has taught me that I should not deviate from my academic predilection.

ARPITA BASU ROY

List of Tables

Introduction

The concept of security in International Relations (IR) has largely changed, rather expanded in the post cold war period. In the conventional formulation, security was conceived about how states uses power to administer threats to their territorial integrity, their independence, and their domestic political order, primarily from other states. This classical national security formulation has been criticised on various grounds. The classical formulation seemed too unilateralist in its emphasis on force in a world where there are weapons of mass destruction and where nations are knitted together on various issues. The idea behind expanding the notion of security was that a unilateralist notion of security must give way to cooperative security and that it merely restricts the scope of security to military threats from other states. Rival states, it is argued, may deploy other kinds of threats against each other's territorial integrity and domestic political order. These may include environmental, economic, and cultural threats. In addition, threats to territorial integrity and political order must be reckoned not just from other states but also from various non-state actors and even natural catastrophes. This much more expanded notion of security, which broadens the instruments and sources of threat, may be called comprehensive security. A third and more elemental critique of security even suggests that security cannot be restricted to the well being of the state. From this perspective, implicit in the classical formulation of security is the protection and welfare of the state, whereas what is central—or should be central—is the protection and welfare of the individual citizen or human being. A conception of security that is centered above all on the sanctity of the individual may be called human security. Human security is a relatively new concept, now widely used to describe the complex of interrelated threats associated with civil war, genocide, displacement of populations and terrorism. Human security and national security should be—and often are—mutually reinforcing.

The new concept of Human Security considers its primary goal to be the protection of individuals over the state. It is argued that both as an academic concept and a political agenda this concept can reinforce, and can underline ongoing developments in international law - and has the potential to become a new organising principle of international relations. The concept unifies fields of policy and analysis that have conventionally been kept separate: humanitarianism and development on the one hand, and international security on the other. But secure states do not automatically signify secure peoples. Protecting citizens from enemy attack may be a necessary condition for the security of individuals, but it is certainly not a sufficient one. A new approach to security was, therefore, needed because the analytic frameworks that have traditionally explained wars between states—and prescribed policies to prevent them—are largely irrelevant to violent conflicts within states. The latter now make up more than 95 per cent of armed conflicts. Proponents of the 'broad' concept of human security argue that the threat agenda should include hunger, disease and natural disasters because these kill far more people than war, genocide and terrorism combined. Human security policy, they argue, should seek to protect people from these threats as well as from violence. More than merely territorial security, human security includes food security, job security, health security, community security, personal security and environmental security.

As argued first in the UNDP global Human Development Report of 1990, the concept of "human development" has been conceived first and foremost as an alternative vision to the prevailing development paradigms of the time. The human development paradigm, established in 1990 by Mahbub ul Haq, Amartya Sen, Frances Stewart, Paul Streeten and others, set itself apart from previous development theories by arguing that economic growth does not automatically trickle down to improve people's well-being, while approaches such as basic needs do not hand over decision-making to beneficiaries themselves. The human development concept thus advocates putting people back at centre stage, both as the means and ends of development. By emphasising the diversity of human needs, human development was thus conceived as an alternative to pure economic development and straightjacket policy prescriptions.

In the same way that traditional economic development paradigms had failed to address the broader concerns of people, traditional "security" discourses are no longer adaptable enough to address the new threats to the safety and well-being of people within states. With a combination of new global trends, the rise of non-state actors, and new types of non-military threats to the internal stability of states and people within them, the traditional concept of "security" as a realist pact between nations became obsolete at the beginning of the 21st Century. If, in the past, existential threats were assumed to emanate from external sources, and security mainly focused on protecting the state and its sovereign territory from external attacks, new non-military threats such as poverty, infectious diseases, environmental disasters, massive population movements and drugs—all of which travel without a passport—have now become part of the "security" agenda.

The study of security has always been a central concern in the academic disciplines of international relations (IR) reflecting the discipline's birth in the profound and shocking violence of World War I (1914-1918). The issue area of security subsequently dominated the intellectual pre-occupations of students of international relations, particularly in the aftermath of World War II and through nearly half-century of the Cold War. The subject of security studies as it developed in its orthodox form during the Cold War was constructed in the image of political realism. Today the Critical Security Studies (CSS) is trying to rethink the common sense of this orthodoxy from the bottom up while exposing the extent to which "political realism is part of the problem in world politics rather than being the problem-solver". (Ken Booth, 2005). Critical perspective on security is a recognition of the idea that security is essentially a derivative concept whose features vary according to the assumptions of different political theories. CSS argues that the mainstream security studies during half a century of the Cold War derived from a combination of Anglo-American, statist, militarised, masculinised, top-down, methodologically positivist, and philosophically realist thinking, all shaped by the experiences and memories of the inter-war years and World War II and the perceived necessities of the Cold War. The aim of critical approaches is to challenge the conceptualisation of security derived from such a worldview. This according to CSS requires rethinking security from the bottom up in two senses. In the first place, investigating what security might mean in theory and practice from perspectives on politics that do not start from the same political, methodological, philosophical and historically contextual perspectives as those associated with the ideology of political realism. And second, thinking about security from the perspective of those people(s) without power-those who have been traditionally silenced by prevailing structures. Booth defines Critical Security as an issue-area study, developed within the academic discipline of international politics, concerned with the pursuit of critical knowledge about security in world politics. Security is conceived comprehensively, embracing theories and practices at multiple levels of society, from the individual to the whole human species.

Critical theory links the discussion of security with the wider analysis of community and emancipation in the belief that advances in communicative action can often play a vital role in solving or reducing human conflicts and is opposed to the statist and realist paradigm. A simple and straight-forward approach would be to regard security as involving the "absence of threats" and underpinned by appropriate form of political community (Linkalater, 2005). The concept of Human Security is upheld by the CSS. CSS underscore the uselessness of states in providing security to individuals. It can be argued that while states may pose as a threat to minorities and indigenous people, adopt reckless foreign policy thereby threatening people and might also be a source of insecurity to one another, yet the concept of binding a larger group of states in the form of regional cooperation to provide human security to individual would be a preferred solutions to the problems.

Therefore there are two implications of the human security discourse- one is humanitarian which focuses on development and the other is terrorism and counterinsurgency doctrine. On the one hand, the concept of Human Security (HS) has led to healthy debates in terms of linkages between freedom from fear and freedom from want. It has also extended the debate over security from State to individuals and communities as actors concerned with, and responding to, new security threats to human welfare and wellbeing. The debate on Human Security also has important implications for international development and development studies. If, as Amartya Sen argues, 'development can be seen as a process of expanding the real freedoms that people enjoy', then Human Security is a critical component in ensuring the foundations of development. It also underlines the interdependencies between human rights and development. However, the concept is not well understood both conceptually and in terms of effective policies and evidence-based programs in an Asian context, more so in the South-Asian context. Thus it is important to take an initiative to mobilize extensive academic interest, exchange among development studies programmes and development organisations in Asia in constructing an Asian perspective on development and Human Security. One has to look at the practical implications of the concept of human security in terms of issues/ problems and policy/program implementation from an Asian regional perspective.

There is a widely held assumption in military and foreign policy circles that development assistance is an important "soft power" tool to promote stabilisation and security in fragile states.[1] A Feinstein International Center Report shows how counterinsurgency doctrine in particular emphasizes the importance of humanitarian and reconstruction assistance (often in the form of "Quick Impact Projects" or QIPS) in "winning hearts and minds," which in turn is thought to promote stabilisation by undermining support for insurgents and/or terrorist organisations. This assumption is having a major policy impact on how development assistance is apportioned and spent, and provides an important rationale for the growing 'securitisation' of development assistance. Given how widespread the assumption is, and given its major impact on aid and counterinsurgency policies, there should be empirical evidence that supports the assumption of a causal link between reconstruction assistance, "winning hearts and minds," and improved security or stabilisation.[2] Thus a clarification of the relationship between aid and security and human security and insurgency is another area of concern. In the context of South Asia where problems of insurgency and terrorism has assumed large proportions, the importance of the human security doctrine needs to be evaluated.

For a long time, in the field of "high politics" issues of human security found it difficult to expand. Afghanistan was defined largely as a "humanitarian emergency" to be treated with charity argues Rubin.[3] Regional states argued repeatedly that the failure to rebuild Afghanistan and provide its people with security and livelihoods threatened its neighbors. Since 1998, an increase in what we may, in retrospect, call relatively small acts of terror traced to the al-Qa'ida organisation, did place Afghanistan on the global security agenda. But the means chosen to address that threat — sanctions against the Taliban, combined with humanitarian exceptions, with no reference to the reconstruction of the country — showed that those setting the international security agenda had not drawn the connection between the terrorist threats to their own security and the threats to human security faced daily by the people of Afghanistan.[4]

Decades of conflict in Afghanistan have led to an environment which is physically, socially, economically, and politically insecure. Protracted conflict has fractured and strained the social fabric of the country. A whole generation has grown up amid pervasive tension and insecurity, and all dimensions of violence, whether physical, psychological, structural, or cultural, are evident in Afghan society. Traditional security threats to the people of Afghanistan are both direct (violence, killings, etc.) and indirect. The latter emerge from a weakened state capacity and challenges to the legitimacy of institutions outside the capital, or from the withdrawal of international aid agencies from dangerous but needy zones. Afghanistan's conflict which has all the characteristics of a transnational war has thrusted upon its citizens insecurity caused by violence, lawlessness, torture, killing, rape, expulsions, displacement and looting. Statistics are few and far between, but one study estimated that "excess mortality," in the demographer's phrase, had amounted to the loss of nearly one tenth of Afghanistan's population between 1979 and 1987. As researchers have pointed out, the many causes of traditional insecurity in Afghanistan can be classified under five categories: warlordism, the narco-trade, groups that threaten the peace process, regional interference and crime. At the same time, conflict has caused widespread poverty, having devastated the rural economy on which the majority of Afghans depend, and crippled local government infrastructure for the delivery of essential services.

The security situation remains extremely fragile in Afghanistan, and is in danger of jeopardising progress made to date since the Bonn Process was initiated in December 2001. Indeed, security is often quoted as the primary issue that concerns Afghans above all others. Security challenges in Afghanistan and the sources of insecurity are varied. It deals with the different dimensions of security that includes economic, health, environmental, personal, community and political security to collectively address the issue of human security. Surveys of community perceptions of security in Afghanistan showed that Afghans' understanding of security, encompasses not just physical safety, but also livelihood security. Afghans continue to face multiple security threats. They continue to feel threatened by commanders, despite the formal disarmament process, and cited conflicts over land and property, bribery and corruption and police brutality amongst their key concerns. "Freedom from fear" is a concern in several provinces and the fiercely intensified insurgency causes harm to the lives, livelihoods and daily affairs of the average Afghans. On the other hand, the majority of Afghans feel relatively safe in their families and communities, they face a range of threats to their well-being. The Taliban are not, as is sometimes portrayed, the sole or even predominant threat to Afghans. Rather, the picture is more complex where warlords, criminals, international forces, drug traffickers, and the police all present varying degrees of threat, which are of different types and are variously configured in different localities.

Non-traditional and human security threats like poverty, unemployment and diseases remain an important cause of insecurity and are interconnected to bigger problems like terrorism, insurgency, arms and drugs trafficking. Hence, the relevance of this framework of human security in the context of Afghanistan. The unequal distribution of wealth, other forms of inequality and the prevailing poverty are major challenges to the economic security of Afghanistan. Afghanistan's economy has recovered significantly in the recent years. While reliable data is not available, anecdotal evidence suggests that economic growth so far has done little to alleviate the extent of inequality, whether it is related to income, gender or geographical location. High level of indebtedness and the staggering opium economy equaling 38.2 per cent of the country's official GDP are serious concerns to economic security.

The collapse of the state resulted in an inadequate health care system, further restricted access to health care services, particularly for the poor. Life expectancy in Afghanistan, 44.5 years at birth, is at least 20 years lower than all of its neighbouring countries and 6.1 years lower than the averages of the Least Developed Countries. It is also significantly lower than any of the post-conflict countries except the three African nations mentioned above. Infant and maternal mortality rates are among the highest in the world. Afghanistan also has the highest rates of tuberculosis in its region, and is one of 22 highly TB-burdened countries in the world, with an estimated annual risk of infection that reaches 2.55 per cent. Malaria is another prevalent public health threat that is on the rise in more than 60 per cent of the country, with over 13 million people at risk. The annual incidence is estimated to be two to three million cases. A large number of other health insecurities are related to water, stemming from poor hygiene and inadequate access to safe supplies. Over 60 per cent of Afghans use unsafe drinking water. The World Health Organisation (WHO) estimates indicate that 95 per cent of Afghans have been affected psychologically by years of conflict, and one in five suffers from mental health problems, like anxiety, depression, psychosomatic problems such as insomnia, and other symptoms of post-traumatic stress disorder.

In Afghanistan, environmental insecurity is a major concern. Water and air quality is equally poor. Access to safe drinking water is dismal. Natural capital, i.e., water, land, forest and biodiversity is under a long-term decline. Environmental degradation, and poor access to clean and safe drinking water and sanitation, are major environmental security threats to people. Man-made and natural threats to the environment have been caused by erosion, the felling of trees, the destruction of watersheds and desertification. The impact on people has been considerable. Limited access to land resources and the scarcity of water for agricultural use, combined with lack of access to a diverse diet, are some indications suggesting that people's capacity to cope with these threats has been depleted. The lack of available energy services correlates closely with many poverty indicators, while urban dwellers are exposed to many toxic and carcinogenic air pollutants. There is an immediate need to install sound environmental management practices by designing and implementing a policy through a participatory process.

Principal personal insecurities comprise physical violence by armed militia; torture by security forces or violent attacks by the Taliban or street gangs. Hostage-taking and domestic violence against women, abuse or rape, violence against children such as child abuse, abduction, child labour and prostitution. Drug abuse is another aspect of personal security. Gender insecurities persist in Afghanistan despite the achievements of the past few years in opening up schools and public spaces to women in the form of constitutional guarantees (Constitution, 2004) and reservation of seats in the parliament. Nevertheless, only one to two per cent of women in Afghanistan have identity cards, and 98 per cent have no formal papers that serve as proof of citizenship or identity. A traditional mentality continues to hold back women's participation in new political and economic opportunities. According to the National Risk and Vulnerability Assessment (NRVA), 2005, female-headed households have the highest incidence of poverty of all the vulnerable categories. Children remained at the forefront of the victims of the conflict in Afghanistan. More than 300,000 may have perished during the conflict, while grave physical and emotional scars afflict generations of Afghans who have known nothing but war. According to a 1998 UNICEF study, among more than 300 children aged eight to 18 in Kabul, 72 per cent experienced the death of a family member between 1992 and 1996.

The main threats to human security in Afghanistan are identified as chronic and pervasive poverty and poor livelihoods, poor health and nutrition, massive population displacements, a degraded environment and distrust in dysfunctional state institutions. Key human rights problems can be summarised as repression by armed groups, ethnic discrimination, political intimidation, and abuses related to land rights, the right to movement and the right to participate. Power in Afghanistan, its authority is challenged by a number of competing factions. Within this environment, a principle threat is the lack of job security, the result of two decades of negative growth and the failure of the recent recovery to trickle down far enough to provide jobs and alleviate poverty. After more than two decades of war and internecine violence, the backdrop to the lack of security is a culture of impunity that has become the norm rather than the exception in Afghanistan. The "security dilemma" for Afghans consists of the privatisation of security and a general augmentation of a military mentality in the country, both of which are severely detrimental to peace-building.

Food insecurity also threatens livelihoods both in terms of quantity and quality, despite recent improvements. A recent Ministry of Health/ Center for Disease Control/UNICEF survey indicated that an estimated 37 per cent of households have been displaced largely to urban centres in order to cope with food insecurity. After so many years of conflict, Afghanistan's education system had become the worst in the world. An estimated 80 per cent of the country's 6,870 schools were damaged, if not completely destroyed. Higher education enrolments are some of the lowest in the world. There are regional as well as rural–urban disparities in the provision of education, combined with a huge gender gap. The quality of education is severely affected by the lack of qualified teachers both in primary, and secondary schools, and the very low salaries in the profession.

Of the causes for poverty in rural regions, drought is identified as the main source, affecting more than half the population. Other sources include pest infestations, epidemic diseases such as malaria; and economic shifts such as market price fluctuations. Surprisingly, violence as a cause of poverty was reported by only two to five per cent of the rural population. The impact of years of discrimination against women, coupled with prevailing poverty and insecurities, has meant that Afghan women have some of the worst social indicators in the world today. Maternal mortality rates in Afghanistan are 60 times higher than for women in industrial countries. Seventy per cent of people affected by tuberculosis are women. The feminisation of poverty, serious malnutrition, exclusion from public life, gender based violence, rape, lack of basic health facilities, illiteracy, forced marriage and routine denial of justice are some of the human security concerns of Afghan women.

In many countries emerging from war, overt armed conflict may come to an end while low-level violence continues for many years, involving former factions, demobilised combatants, bandits or militias. Military and diplomatic measures, though important, are unlikely by themselves to secure a democratic transition. The manner in which the reconstruction is structured (needs assessed, resources allocated, partners chosen, implementation carried out, results monitored) can either carry nation-building forward rapidly, or destroy its very foundations. Sustained peace in Afghanistan is not guaranteed despite the early successes in state-building that have now led to elections. Human security still needs to advance a long way. The breakdown of institutions has left the population vulnerable to the whims of peace-spoilers and their private militias, who can easily raise and sustain an army from among impoverished populations. Rebuilding institutions will be a core task. To be most effective, this must follow a regional model strongly reflecting the country's history, and strive not only to satisfy the immediate needs of individuals, but also to develop capacities for self-sufficiency and empowerment. Over the long term, the goal of Afghanistan should not be simply to create a basic development or democracy agenda, but to use these concepts as a means to prevent conflict and provide human security as a necessary public good. An important dimension of the work have focussed on whether substantial changes have occurred since the overthrow of the Taliban regime in 2001

The events on September 11, 2001, also showed the dangers Afghanistan can pose not only to neighboring countries but also to the whole world, to allow so-called humanitarian emergencies or failed states to fester. A US administration that came to power denouncing efforts at "nation-building" and criticising reliance on international organisations and agreements, has now proclaimed that it needs to assure a "stable Afghanistan" to prevent that country from ever again becoming a haven for terrorists. The US, along with every other major country, has committed itself to supporting the reconstruction of Afghanistan within a framework designed by the United Nations.

The Agreement on provisional arrangements in Afghanistan pending the re-establishment of permanent government institutions — to give the Bonn Agreement its full and accurate title—resulted directly from this new level of commitment and political will by both Afghans and major powers. Most reports on this agreement treat it as a peace agreement, like those that have ended armed conflicts elsewhere. But in Bonn the UN did not bring together warring parties to make peace. In Bonn the UN brought together Afghan groups opposed to the Taliban and al-Qa'ida, some possessing power and others various forms of legitimacy, notably through the person of the former king of Afghanistan. The task they set themselves was the central one of protecting human security: starting the process of establishing—or, as the Afghans insisted, in recognition of their long history, re-establishing—permanent government institutions. This agreement thus differs from many others, which, as critics have noted, sometimes amounted to the codification of de facto power relations, no matter how illegitimate. This agreement does recognize power, especially in the allocation of key ministries to the relatively small group that already controls them in Kabul. In most respects, however, this agreement attempts to lay a foundation for transcending the current rather fragile power relations through building institutions. It also provided for an international security force, one of whose major purposes is to ensure the independence of the administration from military pressure by power-holding factions.

Building these Afghan institutions will constitute the core task of protecting human security in Afghanistan. The Agreement provides a framework. But implementation in such a war-torn and devastated society will largely depend on how the international donors and the UN system approach the task of reconstruction. As donors, agencies, and NGOs rush in, they risk losing sight of the central task: building Afghan institutions owned by and accountable to the people of Afghanistan. There is a real risk that, as the actors in the reconstruction market bid for locations in the bazaar that is opening in Afghanistan, they may harm, hinder, or even destroy the effort to build Afghan institutions. Donors and agencies seeking to establish programs need to find clients, and it is often easier to do so by linking up directly with a de facto power on the ground. Such uncoordinated efforts have reinforced clientelism and warlordism in Afghanistan for years in the absence of a legitimate authority, but they will now have to come to an end. Programs will have to be coordinated to assure that they work together to reinforce the capacities and priorities of Afghan institutions.

The complexity of pursuing human security objectives through military means is clearly evident upon an examination of the international effort in Afghanistan. The practice, so far, in Afghanistan have not been consistent with the stated valuation of human security and the protection of Afghan civilians. The failure to protect human security is twofold: first, international forces have inadequately addressed the threat posed to civilians by the Taliban insurgency and associated terrorist groups. Second, the tactics employed by international military forces have failed to adequately discriminate between civilians and combatants and have directly resulted in increasing numbers of civilian casualties. These failings indicate that there is sufficient violation of the emergent international doctrine of human security, and serious questions to the validity of official claims that the international community are protecting the human security of civilians in Afghanistan. Moreover, it is argued that the effective application of the principles of human security to the conduct of counterinsurgency (COIN) by international military forces would greatly improve the likelihood of success in the long-term Afghan state-building project.

Human security provides the conceptual bridge capable of linking military tactics with the broader strategic objectives being pursued by the international community in Afghanistan. Application of the principles of human security is a means by which the deficiencies of past military practice may be redressed, and which will likely result in greater success for both the state-building and counterinsurgency aspects of the Afghan mission. An international military operation grounded on human-centric principles, primarily preservation of the lives of Afghan civilians, is more likely to realize success in its ultimate goal of winning the support of the Afghan people and reducing their cooperation with and toleration of the Taliban-led insurgency. While effective counterinsurgency and human security are not synonymous, they are synchronous, meaning that the successful application of one is likely to result in advancements towards or satisfaction of the other. As described by recent changes to American counterinsurgency doctrine: "the cornerstone of any COIN effort is establishing security for the civilian populace. Without a secure environment, no permanent reforms can be implemented and disorder spreads." Strategies in any sector that improve human security will contribute towards the efficacy of counterinsurgency, and effective COIN will result in improved human security for the Afghan people. When combined, the application of human security principles to the execution of counterinsurgency will result in the most likely satisfaction of the objectives of both.

The study seeks to justify the adoption of the functional approach which primarily emphasizes the common index of need of the nation states. There are many such needs which cut across national boundaries and an effective beginning could be made by providing joint government for them. Mitrany in 1944 argued that, if nations are to achieve a promising social foundation for their political independence, they need many things in the way of material and technical help and service which are beyond their means and experience. Seen in this light, the functional approach implies not merely a change of political devise but a change of political outlook. It should help to shift the emphasis from political issues which divide, to those social issue in which the interest of peoples is plainly akin and collective.

It is rational to cooperate when there are common interests among states. Although it is another matter how states can overcome the uncertainty about their partner's objectives and fear of defection. The basic argument for any kind of regional cooperation revolves around the idea of potential gains for the people of the region. On the other hand, the price of non-cooperation could also be large, lost economic opportunities, a heavy toll extracted from the spread of disease, natural disasters and environmental destruction, as well as conflict and insecurity. Theoretically, it can be argued that states are rational egoists who care for their absolute gains although they realize common interest. Neo-liberal or interest-based theories of International relations which have come to represent the mainstream approach to power differentials argue that international regimes help states realize their common interest although they portray states as rational egoists who care only for their absolute gains. Neo-liberals have drawn heavily on economic theories of institutions that focus on information and transactions of interests that underlie different types of regimes and that affect the likelihood of a regime being created in the first place.

In the case of this region involving Afghanistan, cooperation would ease the barriers posed by the new borders between the republics and allow people to connect throughout the region and beyond with trade and investment; linked infrastructure; shared water and energy; common environmental, health and disaster protection; and a free flow of ideas and knowledge. In the case of Central Asia, the region faces real opportunities. It is today surrounded by some of the most dynamic of the world's economies. The people of the region enjoy commonalities of history, culture and language, conflict among the new nations has been avoided and new avenues for trade and access to world markets and knowledge are opening up.

Afghanistan's human security threat constitute a larger regional threat because it can be argued that lack of human security remains one of the major causes of regional threats like insurgency, terrorism, arms trafficking, drugs trafficking which have trans-national connotation. In order to address these interconnected problems, states need to cooperate in a regime to tackle the issue. Regional institutions should be developed within regional organisations like the SAARC. After decades of instability, Afghanistan faces new challenges, yet has an opportunity to realize its potential as a "land bridge" between Central Asia, South Asia and the West Asian region. At the 14th South Asian Association for Regional Cooperation (SAARC) summit, President of Afghanistan H.E. Mr Hamid Karzai asserted that "Afghanistan's political and economic isolation must never be repeated. Instead, enhanced economic cooperation must be pursued for the sake of regional economic and political stability". Similarly, Foreign Minister H.E Dr Rangin Dafdar Spanta also outlined at the SAARC Council of Ministers meeting that "Afghanistan is deeply interested in trans-border transport networks, energy corridors and freer flow of people and ideas".

Through various declarations like the Good Neighbourly Relations Declaration of 2002, the Dubai Declaration of 2003, the Berlin Agreements of 2003, the Bishkek Conference of 2004, the Kabul Conference of 2005 and the Delhi Conference of 2006, countries of the region have accepted the centrality of Afghanistan for economic cooperation and integration between Central, South and West Asian regions. There is a need to institutionalise regional cooperation within the government ministries, with the neighbours and with the donor community. It can be argued that regional organisations should build the capacity of institutions to deal with the human security threats because the ability of humanitarian disaster, instability and poverty to create displacement and migration, promote illicit trans-border economies and provide support for terrorist networks, have revealed that all countries and regions are radically interdependent and interconnected.

There are several questions that the research propose to address. These may be summed up as follows: What are the competing Security paradigms in contemporary International Relations and whether the human security paradigm is gaining precedence in security discourses? What are the multiple security threats facing contemporary Afghanistan? How are human security threats a pressing problem for Afghanistan as well as the region? What are the various approaches to deal with the human security threats and has the overthrow of the Taliban regime helped in changing the human security scenario? How functionalism/institutionalism can act as an effective approach in combating the threats emanating from human security crises? Why is it important to study the issue in a regional context and evolve regional solutions (institutions) to tackle the problem?

The study is exploratory in nature. Both secondary and primary information was used in the study. Secondary information was collected for building the historical context of the problem, and preparing the analytical framework. Existing literature, published UN, government documents and documents of other international organisations and institutions at the levels of all the stakeholders was searched for such information.

Since the study involved many questions that needed first hand information, primary data was collected from the study universe. In other words, the stakeholders were approached for their perspective on the ground realities. Ideally, primary information should be collected by formulating missions to the area for studying the communities through standard methods of social sciences including participatory appraisal and case study. Since an extensive study tour in Afghanistan, the proposed study universe, was not possible due to security reasons therefore primary data was collected from reliable agencies working and collecting data from the study universe. Collection of documents and interaction with the academia to learn more about the security discourses was attempted at the University of Cambridge, London

School of Economics and SOAS, London. The Department of Politics and International Studies, University of Cambridge and the Central Library University of Cambridge, Prof James Mayall's personal collection of documents and books on IR theory provided ample scope to work on the security discourses. The Pavate Fellowship on International Studies, 2010 helped me in acquiring ample materials on the same. This was complemented by additional information gathered by visits to the universe and its neighborhood and through observation of the universe and the functioning of different government offices and non-governmental organisations (NGOs) and regional actors involved in the security situation in Afghanistan. Data was also collected by using research techniques such as interviews with the help of semi-structured research schedules of several actors from Afghanistan and its neighborhood.

The first chapter of the book is an evaluation of the security discourses in International Relations Theory. It is on the alternative voices in international relations. It shows how dissident voices in IR theory have rejected the established views and replaced them with alternatives which together constitute the post-positivist challenge. It however brings forth the reality that no single theoretical approach is a winner in IR SRP. All theoretical traditions and alternative approaches are actively employed in the discipline today. The situation is a reflection of the necessity of different approaches to capture different aspects of complicated historical and contemporary realities. It shows how Constructivism as a self-identified perspective into ISS was largely a consequence of the general IR debate in the early 1990s between the so-called rationalist and the reflectivist approaches. It shows how Post-colonialism forms a composite but powerful intellectual and critical movement which renews the perception and understanding of modern history, cultural studies, literary criticism, and political economy. Finally it shows where exactly the discourse of human security fits and how it becomes relevant within the area of humanitarian intervention.

Human security provides the conceptual link capable of connecting military tactics with the broader strategic objectives being pursued by the international community in Afghanistan The second chapter on "Human Security Issues in Afghanistan's Reconstruction" shows the overall human security needs in the country in the issues of health, education, environment, community and politics and argues that the application of the principles of human security is a means by which the deficiencies of past military practice may be redressed, and which will likely result in greater success for both the state-building and counterinsurgency aspects of the Afghan mission.

This third chapter seeks to argue in favour of a non-traditional security regime in South Asia by highlighting the menacing food insecurity situation in Afghanistan and placing it within the broader framework of South Asian Security. The focus of the chapter would directly concern Afghanistan, the new entrant to SAARC, a country menacingly threatened by the problem of food security and poverty. Decades of conflict in Afghanistan have led to an environment which is physically, socially, economically, and politically insecure. Protracted conflict has fractured and strained the social fabric and economic infrastructure of the country. A whole generation has grown up amid pervasive tension and insecurity, and all dimensions of violence, whether physical, psychological, structural, or cultural, are evident in Afghan society. The underlying connections between food insecurity and the lack of opportunities and livelihoods to the regional threats like terrorism and insurgency are imbedded in the theme.

The fourth chapter talks of Urban Vulnerabilities in contemporary Afghanistan. This chapter discusses the trends and vulnerabilities in urban spaces in 'post-conflict' Afghanistan. Vulnerability has been defined as "the exposure to contingencies and stress, and difficulties coping with them" and the term "vulnerability" has been developed as a recognised conceptual framework and analytical approach to address marginality and poverty through means other than economic terms alone. The number of urban residents in Afghanistan in the post-2001 period has risen dramatically due to migration from the rural areas and repatriation from neighbouring lands, leaving the international donor community and the local government to increasingly look at ways to address the challenges of urban planning and poverty. Vulnerability has thus two sides: an external side of risks, shocks and stress to which an individual or household is subject; and an internal side which is defencelessness, meaning a lack of means to cope without damaging loss." The chapter argues that Afghanistan's urban poor has little or no access to basic services and social infrastructure because of a result of limited resources, combined with the authorities' unwillingness and lack of capacity to serve effectively. It analyses on the heterogeneity of urban poverty and show how some households manage to achieve longer-term well-being while others endure perpetual poverty. Further, it shows that urban vulnerability is not necessarily linked to informal settlements, which often enjoy relatively good access to services and security of tenure due to the backing of powerful patrons. While lack of services has long been recognized as a major problem in urban Afghanistan, investments in safe water supply, sanitation, shelter and pollution-free environment have largely been insufficient. By highlighting such crises of urbanization the chapter argues for democratic representation and grassroots governance.

There are pressing environmental needs in Afghanistan. The fifth chapter talks about natural resources as a reconstruction agenda and the primary argument here is that effective natural resource management and recovery is an essential part of Afghanistan's secure future. It is increasingly recognised by the international community that natural resources and the environment have a determining influence on peace and security and these issues can also contribute to a relapse into conflict if they are not properly managed in post-conflict situations. It argues that natural resource reconstruction could be done in cooperation with neighbours through the exchange of data and expertise, and building of professional and inter-sectoral relations through a regional cooperative regime.

The work culminates in the idea that real participation in the process of amelioration of grievances would reduce the incentive to participate in activities that impedes the development of the region. The Sixth and the concluding chapter of the work argues for developing a human security regime in South Asia. The institutions created on specific issues will be secular (not based on primordial identities) and temporary thus would never jeopardize the legitimacy of the state. Further, accountable functioning of the functional institutions would add strength to the nation-states' ability to deliver and would thus facilitate the integration of various primordial identities into the national mainstreams of the nation states they are part of.

NOTES

1. Paul Fishstein and Andrew Wilder, "Winning Hearts and Minds? Understanding the Relationship between Aid and Security", Feinstein International Center Report, January 2012, http://sites.tufts.edu/feinstein/program/winning-hearts-and-minds-understanding-the-relationship between aid-and-security>
2. Ibid
3. Barnett Rubin, "Afghanistan and threats to Human Security", *After September 11*, A Social Science Research Council Essay Forum, http://essays.ssrc.org/10yearsafter911/afghanistan-and-threats-to-human-security/
4. Ibid.

1

Alternative Voices in International Relations and Constructing the Notion of Security

Security has remained at the heart of the International Relations (IR) academic project and as observed by Ken Booth, it has been so ever since David Davies founded the world's first university chair in the subject back in 1919. However, in the following decades how security should be operationalised, remained narrow, fixed, and uncontested until recently. The orthodox view of security has been that the theory and practice of security in world politics should be synonymous with statism (the idea that the sovereign state should be the highest focus of loyalty and decision-making), strategy (the manipulation of military power and force), and stability (the promotion of order in the 'anarchical society'). Therefore, this trinity identified the referents, selected the threats and determined legitimate knowledge.[1]

For several decades, the predominance of the realist paradigm had silenced every other paradigm. It was the security of the state against external dangers which was to be achieved by increasing military capabilities that remained the primary focus of this line of thought. This focus on a state-centric definition of security grew out of realist assumptions of a sharp boundary between domestic 'order' and international 'anarchy', a 'state of nature' where war is an ever-present possibility.[2] It was believed that, given the lack of an international authority with the power to curb others' aggressive ambitions, states must rely on their own capabilities for the achievement of security. Realists have nevertheless accepted that such behaviour by the states lead to what can be called a "security dilemma",[3] i.e., what is justified by one state as legitimate security-enhancing measures are likely to be perceived by others as a threatening military build-up. Such a situation leads to destabilising arms races which in turn reduces overall security of the system and its member-states. For realists, whatever stability does exist in such a world can be attributed to balance of power. The escalation of arms race between the Soviet Union and the USA could be cited as a classic case of security dilemma, yet the tight bipolarity produced a balance which for some scholars like Waltz assured a considerable measure of security.

The obsession with the concept of 'security' defined in terms of national interest and power remained unquestionable as long as the world reflected the neo-realist description of it. There were challenges to the claim of supremacy of realism/neo-realism to ultimate knowledge about international system. This time to time challenge to realism/neo-realism prevented it from attaining a status of a robust theory in IR. In response to such challenges there emerged a series of theoretical formulations which can be called realist/neo-realist 'scientific research programme'. At the core of this realist/neo-realist research programme lays the hypothesis that 'state is the ultimate actor in international relations'. This core is protected by a set of auxiliary hypotheses describing/prescribing international situations and the behaviour of states in those situations. The sudden end of the Cold War removed the reference point on which most, if not all, realist/neo-realist assumptions rested. The weak challenge of the Cold War period gained renewed vigour and brought the core of the realist/neo-realist research programme under question. The route the challenging paradigms took to attack the realist/neo-realist research programme was the notion of security. The state-centric notion of security was challenged by numerous formulations in various ways creating a Kuhnian crisis in IR theory. The following section discusses the changing notion of security along with the evolution of the discipline of IR.

Various critiques of established traditions by alternative approaches are sometimes identified as post-positivism. The dissident voices in IR theory have rejected the established views and replaced them with alternatives and together they constitute the post-positivist challenge to the realist/neo-realist dominance of international theory.[4] As Steve Smith says, "In the last few years a number of powerful attacks on realism have been mounted by scholars from a diffuse grouping of positions...there are four main groupings involved in this challenge. The first one comes from critical theory. A second strand of thought has developed...under the general heading of historical sociology...The third grouping comprises feminist writers...Finally there are those writers concerned to develop postmodern readings of IR".[5]

Critical theory is focussed on the works of Robert Cox, Mark Hoffman, and Andrew Linklater.[6] For the critical theorists, knowledge of the world is always to be understood within a context of interests. According to them, problem-solving positivism needs to be replaced by critical theory, aware of the political interests it represents, and with an overt commitment to emancipation. "Critical Theory" in the narrow sense designates several generations of German philosophers and social theorists in the Western European Marxist tradition known as the Frankfurt School.[7] According to these theorists, a "critical" theory may be distinguished from a "traditional" theory according to a specific practical purpose: a theory is critical to the extent that it seeks human emancipation, "to liberate human beings from the circumstances that enslave them".[8] Because such theories aim to explain and transform *all* the circumstances that enslave human beings, many "critical theories" in the broader sense have been developed. They have emerged in connection with the many social movements that identify varied dimensions of the domination of human beings in modern societies. In both the broad and the narrow senses, however, a critical theory provides the descriptive and normative bases for social inquiry aimed at decreasing domination and increasing freedom in all their forms.[9]

Under the broad heading of historical sociology, from the historical research of Michael Mann[10] and Charles Tilly[11] to the very specific studies of social revolutions by Theda Skocpol,[12] the historical sociologists show that the state, made by war in many cases, is the product of interaction between internal forces and an external setting. Its findings represent a significant undermining of the neo-realists. Leading historical-comparative sociologist in the US during mid-1960s into the 1980s, pre-dominantly Barrington Moore, Jr., Charles Tilly, and Theda Skocpol based their "theoretical insights" on Karl Marx, Weber and even Alexis de Tocqueville.

The point here is that, historical sociologist show that the state, made by war in many cases, is the product of the interaction between internal forces and an external setting. This undermines realist, and especially neo-realist claims of the power of the external setting in determining state behaviour, and of the functional equivalence of states, whatever their internal makeup and regardless of their location in time and space. Post-positivists are not united by what they agree upon but by what they oppose. At times, they are incompatible and cannot be seen as easily combinable. What they reject however is the simplistic philosophy of science that underlines most positivistic scholarship in international theory.

Set against this background, the discipline of International Relations is marked by great opportunity as well as crises. The subject finds itself in an intellectual and historical context as a well-established academic discipline, with an institutional emplacement and a substantial specialist, theoretical, and analytic, literature with considerable intellectual attraction. The traditional and alternative theories constitute the main analytical tools and concerns of contemporary IR. The subject developed through a series of debates between different theoretical approaches and these debates were shaped and influenced by the major economic and political problems and contemporary world events. They were also influenced by methodological developments in other areas of scholarship.

This kind of broader interest about the discipline within social sciences has been stimulated by processes accompanying or following from the end of the Cold War. From the 1990s there is an unprecedented interest, political, and intellectual, in the subject matter of IR. It was also from the mid 1990s that other issues started gaining importance. Ecology, migration, and communications constitute three such instances which represent transnational issues that goes beyond the competence or domain of individual states and they involve political and ethical questions.

No single theoretical approach is a winner in IR Scientific Research Programme (SRP). All theoretical traditions and alternative approaches are actively employed in the discipline today. The situation is a reflection of the necessity of different approaches to capture different aspects of a complicated historical and contemporary realities. World politics is not dominated by one single issue or conflict; on the contrary it is shaped and influenced by different issues and conflicts. It also reflects that different scholars also prefer particular theories for reasons that reflect their personal values and world views. More fundamental questions relate to whether "new" issues simply represent "old" problems presented in a new guise. Or has the international community in the post-Cold War period devised new techniques or strategies for solving problems?[13]

Constructivism: Constructing a New Notion of Security

Corresponding to this development in IR theory, IR security studies also started witnessing changing notions of security. Constructivism as a self-identified perspective into International Security Studies (ISS) was largely a consequence of the general IR debate in the early 1990s between the so-called rationalist and the reflectivist approaches. They shared a rejection of the static material assumptions that dominated and instead emphasised the social dimensions of IR and the possibility for change. Constructivism is based on the general notion that international relations are socially constructed. To construct something is an act which brings into being a subject or object that otherwise would not exist. Social phenomenon such as states, alliances or international institutions, are not thought to exist independent of human meaning and action. The central themes of change, sociality, and processes of interaction point to the added value of constructivism within a field that has emphasised generalisation across time, materiality, and rational choice.

The term constructivism was introduced to IR by Nicholas Onuf (1989) to refer broadly to a range of postpositivist perspectives, which shared a critique of the static assumptions of mainstream IR theory. However, scholars have since made a distinction between 'conventional' constructivism, and more critical variations, including poststructuralism. Conventional constructivism is said to occupy the middle ground between rationalism and poststructuralism. By adopting a positivist epistemology, constructivists have gained considerable legitimacy, such that their debate with rationalists has come to occupy an important place in the discipline.

Constructivism adds a social dimension that is missing from rationalist approaches. What is rational is seen as a function of legitimacy, defined by shared values and norms within institutions or other social structures rather than purely individual interests. Constructivists have questioned the individualist ontology of rationalism and instead emphasise a social ontology. As fundamentally social beings, individuals or states cannot be separated from a context of normative meaning which shapes who they are and the possibilities available to them. Structures not only constrain actors they also constitute identities. The individual or state can also influence their environment as well as being influenced by it, through a process of interaction and mutual constitution.

Constructivists emphasise social cognition where intersubjective meanings have some independent status as collective knowledge not merely the aggregation of individual beliefs. Although a closer look at the role of individual cognition and rationality in constructivism suggests this difference is less stark. There is a tension between conventional constructivism and that with its roots in the linguistic turn, particularly regarding consistency. These inconsistencies arise from the combination of a social ontology with an epistemology that rests on a separation between an external world and the internal thought processes of individuals.

Consistent constructivism rests on a longer lineage, outside of IR, with a genealogy that intersects with, but is distinct from, poststructuralism. Constructivism is, from this perspective, first and foremost an epistemological position, heavily indebted to the 'linguistic turn'. The linguistic turn builds on the notion that we cannot get behind our language to compare it with that which it describes. Language is bound up in the world rather than a mirror of it.

Positivist epistemology however rests on a correspondence theory of language, that is, objects are assumed to exist independent of meaning and words act as labels for objects in this reality. Hypothesis testing is then a method of comparing scientific statements about the world with the world to see whether they correspond. Consistent constructivism is based on an understanding of language and action as rule-based. This approach to language requires that we 'look and see' how language is put to use by social actors as they construct their world. As such it is less concerned with the intentions of individuals than the intention expressed in social action. For example, the 'intention' of individuals engaged in ethnic cleansing in the former Yugoslavia could not be separated from a world in which neighbours had become 'dangerous others'. Intention and action were defined in a public language by socially constituted actors. This approach also highlights problems apparent in the frequent emphasis on causality of conventional constructivism and the conflation of reason and cause. The competition to identify the 'true' cause or intention usually devolves into a battle of interpretations. Reasons, however, can be given in public language and make actions possible, such as the presence of Weapons of Mass Destruction (WMD) in Iraq, whether they were believed or not. This suggests we should focus less on the desire for ultimate truth and more on social fact that the action happened and then how this became possible.[14]

Although the constructivists were critical about the realist view of security politics and inter-state relations, they did not exclusively advocate an expansion of the referent object beyond the state or outline a theory that went beyond the military—political sector. But there were other proponents of the widening approach which called for the expansion of the referent object beyond the state. These approaches can be listed as: Post-colonial Approach, Human Security, Critical Security Studies, and Feminism. With this widening of the referent object also came the widening of the sectors or areas to which security analysis should be applied, adding development, environment, economics, and social-welfare issues.

Post-Colonialism

"Post-colonialism" loosely designates a set of theoretical approaches which focus on the direct effects and aftermaths of colonisation. It also represents an attempt at transcending the historical definition of its primary object of study towards an extension of the historic and political notion of "colonising" to other forms of human exploitation, normalisation, repression, and dependency. Post-colonialism forms a composite but powerful intellectual and critical movement which renews the perception and understanding of modern history, cultural studies, literary criticism, and political economy. "Post-colonialism" appeared in the context of decolonisation that marked the second half of the 20th century and has been appropriated by contemporary critical discourse in a wide range of domains mapped by at least half a dozen disciplines.

Post-colonial International Security Studies overlapped with social theory and historical sociology, and hence with critical constructivism, in pointing to the need for conceptualisations of security that acknowledged the specificity of the Third World. Drawing on the work of Charles Tilly, Keith Krause held that the state-centric concept of security advocated by traditional realist approaches was based on a particular European history of state formation. The European state was built on an understanding of security as oriented towards external threats, and rested upon 'a strong identification of the security of the state with the security of its citizens'. Therefore, this understanding of security implied that state-centric conceptions of security provide neither an analytic nor a normative position from which to identify the threats that regimes may pose to their own citizens. The failed states literature discussed that these states lacked in many respects certain essential features of the western state. The post-colonialists would argue that these failures are a result of "the after-effects of the unequal encounter with western colonialism"[15] and that there is a recurring economic, social, and military unequal relationship between the west and the rest.

Reformulating Realism: Defending the Realist/Neo-Realist SRP

Realist re-visions of security often analyse security in terms quite similar to the post-1945 era but adapted to the post-Cold War world. Assuming that it is not possible for the US to act alone, it acknowledges the importance of co-operative collective security mechanisms among great powers. Such concepts also advocate that there should be attempts by the west to create regional power balances in unstable areas in the other parts of the world. In fact, William Odom (1992) equates security with a new Pax Americana in which US military dominance in key strategic regions keeps the peace. He urges that US military forces should increase their capabilities for rapid interventions.[16] Such realist re-analysis did nothing to move beyond the ethno-centrism of earlier national security studies as it equated security with order and international boundary maintenance to be achieved by the preservation of a hierarchical international system in which the great powers act as world's policemen.

The most important re-examination of security from a neo-realist perspective while attempting to getting beyond a military, state-centric focus was Barry Buzan's landmark study *People, States, and Fear.* It was among the first to systematically probe the conceptual inadequacies of a "simple-minded" notion of security, state-centric in focus, often indistinguishable from power, and very close to the policy imperatives of a Cold War rivalry that very suddenly disappeared.[17] For Buzan, rethinking security involved an exploration of different referent objects of security, where individual along with the state became equally important, if not more important. Buzan's ideas also involved abandoning the overriding concern with military security that dominated the Cold War mindset in favour of a broadened notion of security which encompassed five distinct 'issue sectors': military, political, economic, societal, and environmental. Calling himself a 'liberal realist' and having broadened his definition of security, Buzan makes a case for the need of a new field of international security studies which in contrast to the traditional national security approach, would take as its starting point this multi-dimensional definition of security. The multi-sectoral approach pioneered by Buzan opened the way for the so-called Copenhagen School where issues were designated as existential threats, called for emergency action, and legitimised the use of extraordinary means. It tried to break free of the "sovereignty-bound political lexicon" that dominated both realist and liberal theories of security.

Although Buzan examines security from the perspective of the individual and the international system as well as of the state, he concludes that the most important and effective provider of security is likely to remain the sovereign state. Answering the questions raised by scholars who say that states can sometimes be a source of threat rather than a source of security, Buzan says the evolution towards stronger states, more typical of the west, will result in a greater degree of security for the individual. He feels that a movement towards 'mature anarchy' whereby the states are becoming stronger and co-evolving with interdependent global market economy would ultimately contribute towards greater international security.

Some critics, however criticise Buzan's claim that strong western democracies are successful security providers for all their citizens. And groups like women and minorities, whose economic security is often compromised when military security takes over may not agree with Buzan's argument. Peripheral states may also have problems accepting Buzan's liberal assumptions that their economic security can be improved by greater interdependence with the world economy. Moreover, environmental security, the least developed dimension of security in Buzan's work, may be at odds with the continued economic development of states and the world economy required for progress towards mature anarchy.[18]

But, according to William Bain, the study of security in the contemporary world affairs shows a considerable degree of disarray- that makes it impossible to speak of a coherent field of study that is organised around a clear set of problems, settled methods of inquiry and an established sense of purpose. There seems to be no agreement on the questions that merit scholarly attention and there is no reliable way of separating authentic security issues from non-security issues. It is troublesome, as he rightly says, to obtain agreement on the proper referent object of security, be it states, classes, systems, societies, identities, groups, individuals, or some combination thereof.[19]

The partial, if not total success of these alternative theoretical formulations in challenging the core hypothesis of the realist/neo-realist SRP and noticeable success in forcing a modification of the notion of security may not have resulted in loss of state's ontological status, but it has made profound impact on the discourse of security, which now stands deepened, broadened, and expanded. If not anything, the single merit of a notion of security with deepened meaning, broader understanding and expanded scope is its relevance to a large part of the world, particularly to the developing world like South Asia. As part of such deepening and broadening of the concept we analyse the concept of Human Security.

Human Security: Definition, Conceptualisation

A straightforward expansion of security to include development was made with the United Nations Development Programme's concept of Human Security, launched in 1994.[20] Human Security has the advantage of being promoted from a strong institutional base and, like Common Security in the early 1980s, combines political-activist and academic agendas. The original UNDP formulation opted for an expansion of security along several dimensions. The 'logic of security' should be broadened beyond territorial defence, national interests, and nuclear deterrence to include 'universal concerns' and the prevention of conflicts, but also crucially a global co-operative effort to eradicate poverty and underdevelopment. The referent object was shifted from the nation-state to that of the 'people', and to be 'people-centred' was to be 'concerned with how people live and breathe in a society, how freely they exercise their many choices, how much access they have to markets and social opportunities—and whether they live in conflict or in peace'. This approach implied a radical widening of the types of threats and sectors to which security was applicable include, food, health, the environment, population growth, disparities in economic opportunities, migration, drug trafficking, and terrorism.[21]

Dr. Mahbub ul Haq first drew global attention to the concept of human security in the United Nations Development Programme's 1994 Human Development Report and sought to influence the UN's 1995 World Summit on Social Development in Copenhagen. The UNDP's 1994 Human Development Report's definition of human security argues that the scope of global security should be expanded to include threats in seven areas: Economic security requires an assured basic income for individuals, usually from productive and remunerative work or, as a last resort, from a publicly financed safety net. In this sense, only about a quarter of the world's people are presently economically secure. While the economic security problem may be more serious in developing countries, concern also arises in developed countries as well. Unemployment problems constitute an important factor underlying political tensions and ethnic violence.

Food security requires that all people at all times have both physical and economic access to basic food. According to the United Nations, the overall availability of food is not a problem, rather the problem often is the poor distribution of food and a lack of purchasing power. Food security problems have been dealt with at both national and global levels in the past. However, their impacts are limited. According to UN, the key is to tackle the problems relating to access to assets, work, and assured income (related to economic security).

Health Security aims to guarantee a minimum protection from diseases and unhealthy lifestyles. In developing countries, the major causes of death are infectious and parasitic diseases, which kill 17 million people annually. In industrialised countries, the major killers are diseases of the circulatory system, killing 5.5 million every year. According to the United Nations, in both developing and industrial countries, threats to health security are usually greater for poor people in rural areas, particularly children. This is mainly due to malnutrition and insufficient supply of medicine, clean water or other necessity for healthcare.

Environmental security aims to protect people from the short- and long-term ravages of nature, man-made threats in nature, and deterioration of the natural environment. In developing countries, lack of access to clean water resources is one of the greatest environmental threats. In industrial countries, one of the major threats is air pollution. Global warming, caused by the emission of greenhouse gases, is another environmental security issue.

Personal security aims to protect people from physical violence, whether from the state or external states, from violent individuals and sub-state actors, from domestic abuse, or from predatory adults. For many people, the greatest source of anxiety is crime, particularly violent crime. Community security aims to protect people from the loss of traditional relationships and values and from sectarian and ethnic violence. Traditional communities, particularly minority ethnic groups are often threatened. About half of the world's states have experienced some inter-ethnic strife. The United Nations declared 1993 the Year of Indigenous People to highlight the continuing vulnerability of the 300 million aboriginal people in 70 countries as they face a widening spiral of violence.

Political security is concerned with whether people live in a society that honours their basic human rights. According to a survey conducted by Amnesty International, political repression, systematic torture, ill treatment or disappearance was still practised in 110 countries.[22] Human rights violations are most frequent during periods of political unrest. Along with repressing individuals and groups, governments may try to exercise control over ideas and information.

Since then, human security has been receiving more attention from the key global development institutions, such as the World Bank. Tadjbakhsh,[23] among others, traces the evolution of human security in international organisations, concluding that the concept has been manipulated and transformed considerably since 1994 to fit organisational interests.

Human security could be said to further enlarge the scope for examining the causes and consequences of underdevelopment, by seeking to bridge the divide between development and security. Too often, militaries didn't address or factor in the underlying causes of violence and insecurity while development workers often underplayed the vulnerability of development models to violent conflict. Human security springs from a growing consensus these two fields need to be more fully integrated in order to enhance security for all.

It is argued that security and development are deeply interconnected.[24] Human security forms an important part of people's well-being, and is therefore an objective of development. An objective of development is "the enlargement of human choices". Insecurity cuts life short and thwarts the use of human potential, thereby affecting the reaching of this objective. Lack of human security has adverse consequences on economic growth, and therefore development. Some development costs are obvious. For example, in wars, people who join the army or flee can no longer work productively. Also, destroying infrastructure reduces the productive capacity of the economy. Imbalanced development that involves horizontal inequalities is an important source of conflict. Therefore, vicious cycles of lack of development which leads to conflict, then to lack of development, can readily emerge. Likewise, virtuous cycles are possible, with high levels of security leading to development, which further promotes security in return.

Further, it could also be said that the practice of human development and human security share three fundamental elements.[25] First, human security and human development are both people-centred. They challenge the orthodox approach to security and development, i.e., state security and liberal economic growth, respectively. Both emphasise people are the ultimate ends but not means. Both treat human as agents and should be empowered to participate in the course. Second, both perspectives are multidimensional. Both address people's dignity as well as their material and physical concerns. Third, both schools of thought consider poverty and inequality as root causes of individual vulnerability.

Despite these similarities, the relationship with development is one of the most contested areas of human security. "Freedom from fear" advocates, such as Andrew Mack, argue that human security should focus on the achievable goals of decreasing individual vulnerability to violent conflict, rather than broadly defined goals of economic and social development. Others, such as, Tadjbakhsh and Chenoy, argue that human development and human security are inextricably linked since progress in one enhances the chances of progress in another while failure in one increases risk of the failure of another.[26]

The application of human security is highly relevant within the area of humanitarian intervention, as it focusses on addressing the deep rooted and multi-factorial problems inherent in humanitarian crises, and offers more long-term resolutions. In general, the term humanitarian intervention generally applies to when a state uses force against another state in order to alleviate suffering in the latter state. These principles on humanitarian intervention are the product of a debate pushed by United Nations Secretary General Kofi Annan. He placed a challenge before the international community to find a new approach to humanitarian intervention that responded to its inherent problems.[27] In 2001, the International Commission on Intervention and State Sovereignty (ICISS) produced the "The Responsibility to Protect", a comprehensive report detailing how the "right of humanitarian intervention" could be exercised. It was considered a triumph for the human security approach as it emphasised and gathered much needed attention.[28]

The report illustrates the usefulness of the human security approach, particularly its ability to examine the cause of conflicts that explain and justify humanitarian intervention. In addition, it could also act as a paradigm for identifying, prioritising, and resolving large transnational problems, one of the fundamental factors that act as stimuli for humanitarian intervention in the first place. However, human security still faces difficulties concerning the scope of its applicability, as large problems requiring humanitarian intervention usually are built up from an array of socio-political, cultural, and economic problems that may be beyond the limitations of humanitarian projects.[29] On the other hand, successful examples of the use of human security principles within interventions can also be found.

Human security draws its inspiration from the human rights tradition. Some ideas and concepts of human security is fundamental to the human rights tradition. Both approaches use the individual as the main referent and both argue that a wide range of issues (i.e., civil rights, cultural identity, access to education, and healthcare) are fundamental to human dignity. A major difference between the two models exists in their approach to addressing threats to human dignity and survival. Whilst the human rights framework takes a legalistic approach, the human security framework, by utilising a diverse range of actors, adopts flexible and issue-specific approaches, which can operate at local, national or international levels.

Human security addresses the neglect of gender concerns under the traditional security model. Traditional security's focus on external military threats to the state has meant that the majority of threats women face has been overlooked. By focussing on the individual, the human security model aims to address the security concerns of both women and men equally. Women are often the worst victims of violence and conflict: they form the majority of civilian deaths; the majority of refugees; and, are often the victims of cruel and degrading practices, such as rape. Women's security is also threatened by unequal access to resources, services, and opportunities. Human security seeks to empower women, through education, participation, and access, as gender equality is seen as a necessary precondition for peace, security and a prosperous society.[30]

Norway, Canada, and Japan were the first states to adopt Human Security and have linked the concept with the 'pre-eminent progressive values of the 1990s: human rights, international humanitarian law, and socio-economic development based on equity'. The Canadian government has also provided funding for the Canadian Consortium on Human Security, 'an academic-based network promoting policy relevant research on human security'.[31] Taking a constructivist perspective that combines interests and ideas, Suhrke holds that this progressive conception of Human Security suited Canadian aspirations for a middle-power status and Norwegian ambitions about a UN Security Council seat in 2001-2003. These aspirations and ambitions coalesced with global structural shifts in the 1990s that made more room for normative foreign policies based on humanitarian concerns.[32]

Critics of the concept argue that its vagueness undermines its effectiveness[33] that it has become little more than a vehicle for activists wishing to promote certain causes; and that it does not help the research community understand what security means or help decision makers to formulate good policies.[34] Critical advocates of Human Security have either tied it to a Critical Security Studies agenda or linked it to neo-liberal economics. What is crucial about the Human Security debate is that it shows the value of institutionalisation. Although Human Security did articulate a very broad agenda, it also provided the reason for a diversity of political actors seeking to boost support for development issues and humanitarian foreign policies.

Human security has gained importance in the current world as the nature of threats have changed from those of the traditional to those primarily owing to intolerance, viz., religious and ideological intolerance and terrorism, racism, competition for regional or global supremacy and arms race. The other threats food scarcity and diseases, environmental hazards, and natural calamities. A human security perspective asserts that the security of the state is not an end in itself. Rather, it is a mean of ensuring security for its people. In this context, state security and human security are mutually supportive. Building an effective, democratic state that values its own people and protects minorities is a central strategy for promoting human security.

NOTES

1. Ken Booth, "Realities of Security: Editor's Introduction", *International Relations*, Vol. 18, No. 1, March 2004, Sage Publications, p. 5.
2. K.N. Waltz, *Theory of International Politics*, Addison-Wesley, Reading, Mass, 1979, p. 102.
3. John H. Herz, "Idealist Internationalism and the Security Dilemma", *World Politics*, Vol. 2, 1950, pp. 157-80.
4. Yosef Lapid, 'The third debate: on the prospects of international theory in a post-positivist era', *International Studies Quarterly*, 33(3), pp. 235-54.
5. Steve Smith, 'The Self-Images of a Discipline', in K. Booth and S. Smith (eds), *International Relations Theory Today*, The Pennsylvania State University Press, University Park, Pennsylvania, 1995.
6. Andrew Linklater's works include *Critical Theory and World Politics: Citizenship, sovereignty, and humanity*, Routledge, 2007, *International Relations: Critical Concepts in Political Science*, Routledge, 2000, *Beyond Realism and Marxism: Critical Theory and International Relations*, Macmillan Press, 1990, *New Horizons in Politics: Essays with an Australian Focus*, (edited with Hugh V. Emy), Allen and Unwin, 1990, *Men and Citizens in the Theory of International Relations*, Macmillan Press, 1982.
7. Critical theory precisely denotes the theoretical work of the Frankfurt Institute for Social Research (or Frankfurt School), becoming the International Institute for Social Research at Columbia University, New York, in 1933 when the Frankfurt Institute was closed by the Nazi regime and its members—mainly Jewish and Marxist—were forced to leave Germany. Although using the tern social research in its title, and carrying out some projects involving the collection of data from surveys, the Institute is mainly known for, and was primarily concerned in, the formulation of theories by which to understand the predicament of human society and its development. This is conditioned by the failure of revolution in Germany in 1918-1919—contrary to the idea that revolution should succeed in industrialised societies—and, above all, the rise of fascism in Europe from the 1920s onwards. In the darkest of times, when political hope was remote, emphasis moved to culture, and the structures of social organisation. Among key contributors to critical theory are Theodor W Adorno, Herbert Marcuse, and Max Horkheimer (the Institute's Director), and its associates—not employed at the Institute but who published material in its journal, *Zeitschrift für Sozialforschung* (Journal for social research) and in other ways engaged with the Institute and its aims—Walter Benjamin and Ernst Bloch. After 1945, Hannah Arendt extends the concern for liberation developed in the Institute's work. In Germany after 1945, Jürgen Habermas and Axel Honeth are seen as continuing the project of critical theory. But, in a looser sense, the term is sometimes (if inaccurately) used for French post-structuralism. There are, still, interesting possibilities to compare the work of

French theorists, such as, Michel Foucault and Gilles Deleuze with that of the Frankfurt school. The issues of power and agency might be central to such work, but, too, the interest in everyday life (from Henri Lefebvre and Michel de Certeau) is another, less examined but important area. (Critical Spaces: 'Introduction to Critical Theory' by Malcolm Miles, http://www.criticalspaces.org.uk/paper1.html).

8. M. Horkheimer, *Critical Theory*, Seabury Press, New York, 1982, p.244.
9. 'Critical Theory', *Stanford Encyclopedia of Philosophy*, 2005, http://plato.stanford.edu/entries/critical-theory/
10. Michael Mann, *Incoherent Empire*, Verso, London, 2003.
11. Charles Tilly, *Coercion, Capital and European States, AD 990-1990*, Blackwell, Oxford, 1990.
12. Theda Skocpol, *States and Social Revolutions*, Cambridge University Press, Cambridge, 1979.
13. Brian White, Richard Little, and Michael Smith, *Issues in World Politics*, Palgrave, New York, 2001, p.15.
14. Timothy Dunne, Milja Kurki and Steve Smith, *International Relations Theories: Discipline and Diversity*, Oxford University Press, 2007.
15. J. Sharp, *Geographies of Postcolonialism*, Sage Publications, Glasgow, 2008.
16. William Odom, 'Military lessons and US forces', G. Allison and G. Treverton (eds.), *Rethinking America's Security: Beyond Cold War to New World Order*, W.W. Norton, New York, 1992, pp.337-48.
17. Barry Buzan, *People, States, and Fear: An Agenda for International Security Studies in the Post-War Era*, 2nd edition, Lynne Rienner, Boulder, 1991.
18. S. Dalby, 'Security, Modernity, Ecology: The Dilemmas of Post-Cold War Security Discourse', *Alternatives*, Vol. 17, No.1, Winter, 1992, pp. 95-134.
19. William Bain (ed.), 'Introduction', *The Empire of Security and the Safety of the People*, Routledge, Oxon, 2006, p. 2.
20. United Nations Development Programme (1994): Human Development Report.
21. Buzan and Hansen, *op cit*, p.203.
22. "Human Security", *Wikipedia*, http://en.wikipedia.org/wiki/Human_security
23. S. Tadjbakhsh, "Human Security In International Organizations: Blessing or Scourge?", *The Human Security Journal*, Vol. 4, Summer 2007.
24. Frances Stewart, "Development and Security", Centre for Research on Inequality, Human Security, and Ethnicity (CRISE), Working Paper 3, University of Oxford, London, 2004
25. Sabina Alkire, "A conceptual Framework for Human Security", Centre for Research on Inequality, Human Security, and Ethnicity (CRISE), Working Paper 2, University of Oxford, London, 2003.
26. Tadjbakhsh & Chenoy, *Human Security: Concepts and Implications*, Routledge, London, 2006.
27. ICISS, "The Responsibility to Protect: Report of the International Commission on Intervention and State Sovereignty", International Development Research Council, Ottawa, 2001.
28. Some of its main principles are as follows: the protection of individual welfare is more important than the state. If the security of individuals is threatened

internally by the state or externally by other states, state authority can be overridden. Addressing the root causes of humanitarian crises (e.g., economic, political or social instability) is a more effective way to solve problems and protect the long-term security of individuals. Prevention is the best solution. A collective understanding of the deeper social issues along with a desire to work together is necessary to prevent humanitarian crises, thereby preventing a widespread absence of human security within a population (which may mean investing more in development projects).

29. N. Thomas and W.T. Tow, "The Utility of Human Security: Sovereignty and Humanitarian Intervention", Sage Publications, Vol. 33(2), 2002, pp. 177-192.
30. K. Haq, 'Human Security for Women,' in M. Tehranian, (ed.), *Worlds Apart: Human Security and Global Governance*, I.B. Tauris Publishers, London, 1999, p. 96.
31. This network since 2002 has been publishing the *Human Security Bulletin* (www.humansecurity.info)
32. Astri Suhrke, 'Human Security and the Interests of the State', *Security Dialogue*, Vol. 30, No. 3, 1999, pp. 265-276.
33. Roland Paris, "Human Security—Paradigm Shift or Hot Air?", *International Security*, Vol. 26, No. 2, 2001.
34. For a comprehensive analysis of all definitions, critiques and counter-critiques, see Tadjbakhsh, Shahrbanou & Chenoy, Anuradha M. *Human Security: Concepts and Implications*, Routledge, London, 2006.

2

Human Security Issues in Afghanistan's Reconstruction

As discussed in the chapter 1, the end of the Cold War changed the way the concept of security was understood previously. In the classical formulation, security is about how states use force to manage threats to their territorial integrity, their autonomy, and their domestic political order, primarily from other states. A fundamental critique of this concept of security goes to suggest that security cannot be restricted to the well being of the state rather what should be central—is the protection and welfare of the individual citizen or human being. A conception of security that is centred above all on the sanctity of the individual may be called human security. Human security is a relatively new concept, now widely used to describe the complex of inter-related threats associated with civil war, genocide, displacement of populations, and terrorism. Human security and national security should be—and often are—mutually reinforcing.

A new approach to security was needed because the analytic frameworks that have traditionally explained wars between states—and prescribed policies to prevent them—are largely irrelevant to violent conflicts within states. The latter now make up more than 95 per cent of armed conflicts. All proponents of human security agree that its primary goal is the protection of individuals. Proponents of the 'broad' concept of human security argue that the threat agenda should include hunger, disease, and natural disasters because these kill far more people than war, genocide, and terrorism combined. Human security policy, they argue, should seek to protect people from these threats as well as from violence. More than merely territorial security, human security includes food security, job security, health security, community security, personal security, and environmental security.

Given the regional and international interest in Afghanistan's security and development, it is unsurprising that political expedience exerts a major influence on the country's policy agenda. In too many cases, this has led to programmes and strategies that are largely divorced from the interests and experiences of ordinary Afghans.[1] It is often ignored that human security threats like poverty, unemployment, and diseases remain an important cause of insecurity and are interconnected to bigger problems like terrorism, insurgency, arms, and drugs trafficking. This connect makes the paradigm of human security relevant in the context of Afghanistan. The chapter would argue that Human Security provides the conceptual bridge capable of linking military tactics with the broader strategic objectives pursued by the international community in Afghanistan. Application of the principles of human security is a means by which the deficiencies of past military practice may be redressed, and which will likely result in greater success for state-building, reconstruction, and counterinsurgency aspects of the Afghan mission. However, with the military drawdown of forces expected to be over by 2014 and uncertainties related to the scenarios that may evolve the chapter would critique the international approach to peace building in Afghanistan which has been primarily military in nature. Despite billions of dollars in international aid, the state institutions remained fragile and unable to provide good governance, deliver basic services to the majority of the population or guarantee human security. It would provide an evaluation of certain human security issues like food, education, health, and environment to highlight the areas which could have become focus areas. By way of conclusion, the chapter would argue that an international military operation grounded on human-centric principles, primarily preservation of the lives, livelihoods, and social development of Afghan civilians, could have led to the realisation of success in its ultimate goal of winning the support of the Afghan people and reducing their co-operation with and toleration of the insurgency.

Because of its potential the concept of human security has become a new paradigm for security, development, and justice in international relations. Since it was first proposed in the 1990s, there has been an endless debate between its proponents and critics, and even among its advocates, over the meaning and utility of the concept. By designating the individual rather than the state as the referent object of security, human security is emerging as a framework that can serve as a means to evaluate threats, foresee crises, analyse causes of discord, and propose solutions entailing a redistribution of responsibilities.[2]

Afghanistan's Reconstruction Needs

Afghanistan displays distinctiveness—one in terms of the protracted nature of its conflict and its tendency to transform and secondly the sudden change brought about in the country in the post 9/11 period. The Afghan War, like many protracted conflicts, displays a remarkable tendency to mutate in character. This has been particularly evident in the year 2001, following an extraordinary series of events.[3] Over the last two and a half centuries. Afghanistan has sustained many attacks. The latest has been the post-1979 phase during which the country has been ravaged by war like never before. The Soviet intervention in 1979, which continued till 1980s, the internal conflict of the 1990s, the turmoil during the Taliban regime and the US intervention after the catastrophe of September 11, 2001 shook Afghanistan appallingly.[4] The problem of drawing lessons from the Afghan conflict is further complicated by the fact that the war is anything but over. The Taliban have been driven from power, but many of the ex-Taliban have been dispersed, strong enough to resurface anytime.[5] The reconstruction needs of Afghanistan at such juncture is overwhelming.

Building the State

One of the greatest challenges in Afghanistan in 2001 was to rebuild appropriate state instrumentalities.[6] The task is a much larger one than simply assembling a 'government', for the Afghan state ceased to exist years ago. Ever since the Bonn Agreement signed on December 5, 2001, there has been a new effort at rebuilding state institutions. An 'Interim Administration' chaired by Hamid Karzai entrusted the duty of ensuing the process, and the Bonn Agreement specified the steps which would follow and culminate in the holding of a free and fair election by June 2004. The aim of the process is to reconstitute basic state functions and win them sufficient legitimacy to sustain them in the long run. Building up a war-torn nation does not merely require scaling up of relief for physical reconstruction. To rebuild a war-torn nation several diverse interconnected strategies were required: support for livelihoods, small communities, demobilised soldiers, women, people with disabilities, cultural heritage, and structures- all were vital to the assistance and reintegration of different war-affected groups.[7] Moreover, the range of changes brought about by conflict needs to be identified and incorporated in any rehabilitation strategy. Therefore, there is an acute need for reliable and up-to-date base-line data, as a basic pre-requisite for defining needs and also for planning, designing, and evaluating reconstruction interventions. Without doubt, any effort at nation building during this transitional phase will require the efficient tackling of spoilers like warlords and other irritants. Politically neutral spaces have to be created for civil society to mature and contribute positively to any ongoing peace negotiations or processes. Civilians have to take control effectively in order to contribute to the nation-building process and the international community should provide the assistance necessary required for such reconstruction.

Whether democracy is a suitable option for Afghanistan is a matter of debate. While some scholars have rejected the idea as mere fantasy,[8] other have stressed on its importance because ordinary Afghans should have this basic right[9] to get access to a mechanism for changing their rulers without bloodshed. Elite stability is a major requirement, as different elements within the elites should hold firmly to the commitments that they accepted in Bonn, and for those groups who were not present at the Bonn meeting as the viable path forward. If the levels of trust were low there is always a danger that the process will unravel.[10]

While everyone recognised the need to create an effective national army and civilian police force because it is an important requirement for blooming civilian life, the problems of corruption and nepotism might hamper the process of impartial service and justice. In a system struggling to overcome the delirious effects of more than two decades of war, corruption and nepotism serves as alluring sources of income for the newly appointed government officials.

Security

Security is a major threat to the reconstruction process. Warlords, a majority of whom posed themselves as Taliban opponents and were sponsored by the USA during and before the US attack on Afghanistan may attempt to destabilise the country and act as spoilers to the Bonn process. Bribing them by paying huge dividends might lead to other related problems and crushing their power completely might be a difficult process for a fragile state structure at hand. According to Sultan Barakat, overt armed conflict might come to an end in countries emerging from war while low-level violence continues for many years, involving former factions, demobilised combatants, bandits or militias. The growing tensions between different warlords who form part of the new government also form a disturbing feature of the contemporary political situation in Afghanistan. Unidentified gunmen in Kabul assassinated Vice President Haji Abdul Qadir in July 2002, while President Karzai narrowly escaped an assassination in Kandahar on 5 September, 2002. Moreover security related problems might threaten any reconstruction and development activity like infrastructure building or formation of human social capital. "The interim administration of Hamid Karzai needs much more support and resources to bring peace and safety to the Afghan people", says IRC president George Rupp. "Unless there were dramatic security improvements in Afghanistan, reconstruction efforts will be stymied, the Bonn peace process risks collapse, free, and fair elections may never be realised and a return to anarchy and civil war becomes increasingly likely".[11]

Barakat[12] also highlights the ideas of two schools of thought concerning the timing of reconstruction and development activities. The first is that, peace is a pre-condition for reconstruction and development. The second is that, through the initiation of reconstruction and development activities at an appropriate time during the conflict, the seeds of long-term recovery will be sown. The second is the more acceptable theory world-wide provided the challenges of rebuilding itself is approached as a national project, accessible to public discussion and participation, set to heal inter-community wounds and restore dignity, trust, and faith in the system.

Infrastructure Development and Rehabilitation of the Environment

Physical infrastructure is of very high cost and is an area where large mistakes can be made if the policy and institutional framework is not fully thought out. Rebuilding of the country's infrastructure constitute a major challenge of reconstruction as the country is almost totally shattered. In a land locked country like Afghanistan, the road network provides vital communication and transport services. The entire road network provides vital communication and transport services, unlike what has been reported by UNDP in 1993 (6%). National roads, that encircle the major centres of Afghanistan, and also connects it to neighbouring countries, were concrete and asphalt surfaced and covered some 2500 kilometers. Rehabilitation of national loans is a top priority to ease humanitarian delusion and to provide the basics for subsequent economic recovery. Labor intensive methods should be employed in this rehabilitation work to aid the demobilisation efforts as explained by Rudie Hager. These approaches can be based on international experience as compiled by the International Labour Organization (ILO). The financing needs to be on a grant basis so as not to provide a debt-burden to post-conflict Afghanistan.

Agriculture has been the backbone of the Afghanistan economy and, as Rudie Hager explained, agriculture can be recovered to play this role again. Almost half of the irrigation systems require rehabilitation and a program should be made for addressing the needs with the *Kariz* system, Afghanistan system of underground channels, being first. A water allocation policy is needed and the concerned ministry, as Ambassador Toreng already mentioned, in the upcoming government would need to be effective in negotiating water rights with neighbouring countries. Cost recovery should be introduced but as it will only likely cover O&M, the rehabilitation work on the irrigation system would need to be on a grant basis. Labour-intensive approaches should be employed to provide employment to local Afghans. Participatory needs assessment is required at the municipal, community, and household levels, taking into account the physical, legal, and financing options with regard to urban development. Needs assessment should cover both housing and urban services.

Afghanistan has a high-energy potential, both—hydropower and natural gas, in production. Electricity generation is both hydro and diesel based and is currently operating at a fraction of the previous capacity. The rehabilitation of the generation, transmission, and distribution systems is badly needed and once completed, attention will need to focus on further developing the available hydropower. Telecommunications systems have been largely destroyed. There is probably little sense in going back to try and restore the fixed line systems, but rather to the quickly set in place a network of satellite based communications for national and international calls, augmented by a cell phone system with pre-paid cards for local calls. These require private sector opportunities, but need appropriate policy and regulatory framework.

Afghanistan's environment has suffered greatly from war and drought related damages. Forest coverage has fallen by more than 50 per cent and rehabilitation is the key need. Pistachio industry is endangered. Environment needs to be seen as a cross-cutting issue in all sectors' planning activities. While rehabilitation will certainly be focussed on the community-level, policy, and institutional development must precede rehabilitation efforts. The policy and institutional framework may need to be greatly different from what had previously existed, for example, where private sector will now be the leading provider.

Restoration of Social Services and Women's Rights

Education: Education had to be seen as a priority, both in the reconstruction and in subsequent development stages. The most urgent need at the time was to attempt to recover "normalcy". This implies restarting a formal education system, accessible to all, including women. Many poor Afghans however resist the idea of sending both boys and girls to school.[13] A first step in this direction is the training of teachers and other personnel. An information gathering system, enabling the updating of the curriculum was also a priority. In turn, lack of adequate physical infrastructure constitutes another key constraint.

There should be supporting community-based schools as well as implementing peace and social education programs for children, teachers, and adults including production and dissemination of materials and magazines on these themes. The establishment of night schools for working children and adults might be useful. Crucial to this process of improving the education system is building capacity of the Ministry of Education both physical, organisational, and technical. All programs in this area should be designed according to the three main principles. First, education and learning opportunities were a human right for all; secondly, a variety of delivery options should exist, to make education readily available to hard-to-reach areas, and disadvantaged groups. Finally, education should be seen an instrument contributing to the development and unity of the country.

Health Services Delivery in Afghanistan: The health system was in great need of reconstruction and rehabilitation. It is furthermore necessary to building new and better systems, given the impact of 23 years of war. Other punctual sources of concern include the depletion of human resources caused by neglect of training institutions, brain drain, and restriction of female medical education, and the deterioration of the management system. These weaknesses become more severe given the increased vulnerability of the population due to the effects of drought and war.[14]

There should be an integrated primary Health Care and multi-sectoral approach (i.e., one addressing water and sanitation, transport as well as health services). This approach should ensure that essential public health services were available to all Afghans. It should also be very flexible and should focus on capacity building, both by strengthening management structures, and through human resources development. Finally, it recommended that a management advisory group needs to be established to assist government in equitable allocation of resources.

The Role of Women in the Reconstruction of Afghanistan

The promotion of women's rights in Afghanistan was seen as a central priority, however, the deeply entrenched cultural attitudes on gender-related issues seemed to be a deterrent. It was believed by donors that Afghanistan will not reach its full potential until Afghan women were given this right to exercise and develop their full potential. There was a need for designing a mechanism to empower women by joining their voices and efforts. A legal framework enforcing women's rights was also imperative. It was recognised that in the short run, awareness, advocacy and education should be facilitated and promoted. In the longer-term, women should become involved in the public sector, they should have property rights, and their formal education should be promoted. Most importantly, a proposal of engaging women in the political discussion by incorporating a Senior Gender Advisor in Mr. Brahimi's team[15] was proposed thereby contribute to another key priority, i.e., to ensure women's participation at the decision-making structures/political set-up of the future Afghan government. However, the imposing importance of tradition and culture which has given its women a traditional secondary position seemed to be a real disadvantage for the women.

Water and Sanitation

Approximately 75 per cent of Afghans were in urgent need of clean water. The capacity of agencies of the Government of Afghanistan has been seriously degraded by 23 years of war. In order to address this and other major concerns, the creation of a national water authority seemed vital. Critical among the policy issues that need to be addressed were:

A national and legal framework should be established. Regulatory practices should be based on existing structures. Comprehensive and standardised data and past and current water and sanitation interventions should be compiled. The ownership of ground water needs to be clarified and enforced. This is critical for the sustainability of any initiative.

Private Sector Development

There were several pre-requisites for the successful establishment of private sector commerce and industry in Afghanistan. The key principle is to build a sustainable economic environment based on private enterprise, thus limiting and minimising the extent and duration of external aid. For the longer-term stability and an open economy allowing Afghanistan to trade easily and freely with the rest of the world is a necessity. Moreover, for the next 10 to 15 years Afghanistan is not going to have the required revenue to sustain a large state structure.[16]

For creating an environment for investment and allowing freedom to do business, there should be a required set-up. The financial environment needs to be sound with the banking system, institutional mechanisms, and regulatory governance firmly in place and adequate information flow between potential investors and opportunities. There should be guidelines for doing business and guidelines for foreign investors with proper infrastructure and adequate transport and communications linkages. Moreover, commercial infrastructure like offices and hotels should be built up. And there should be a secure environment whereby political, physical, legal/financial, external (border) security should be ensured. With so many pre-requisites required for the private sector to operate and most of them sadly lacking at present, private sector development remains a big challenge.

Afghanistan's Human Security

Afghans, largely victims of "humanitarian emergency", found no voice in the sphere of 'high politics' for a long time. Although, it was understood that the failure to rebuild Afghanistan and provide its people with security and livelihoods threatened the region yet nothing substantial was done to address the threat. Since 1998, an increase in what we may, in retrospect, call relatively small acts of terror traced to the al-Qa'ida organisation, did place Afghanistan on the global security agenda. But the means chosen to address that threat—sanctions against the Taliban, combined with humanitarian exceptions, with no reference to the reconstruction of the country—showed that those setting the international security agenda had not drawn the connection between the terrorist threats to their own security and the threats to human security faced daily by the people of Afghanistan.

Decades of conflict in Afghanistan have led to an environment which is physically, socially, economically, and politically insecure. Protracted conflict has fractured and strained the social fabric of the country. A whole generation has grown up amid pervasive tension and insecurity, and all dimensions of violence, whether physical, psychological, structural, or cultural, are evident in Afghan society. Traditional security threats to the people of Afghanistan are both direct (violence, killings, etc.) and indirect. The latter emerge from a weakened state capacity and challenges to the legitimacy of institutions outside the capital, or from the withdrawal of international aid agencies from dangerous but needy zones. Afghanistan's conflict which has all the characteristics of a transnational war has thrusted upon its citizens insecurity caused by violence, lawlessness, torture, killing, rape, expulsions, displacement, and looting. Statistics are few and far between, but one study estimated that "excess mortality", in the demographer's phrase, had amounted to the loss of nearly one tenth of Afghanistan's population between 1979 and 1987. As researchers have pointed out, the many causes of traditional insecurity in Afghanistan can be classified under five categories: warlordism, the narco-trade, groups that threaten the peace process, regional interference, and crime. At the same time, conflict has caused widespread poverty, having devastated the rural economy on which the majority of Afghans depend, and crippled local government infrastructure for the delivery of essential services.

The security situation remains extremely fragile in Afghanistan, and is in danger of jeopardising progress made to date since the Bonn Process was initiated in December 2001. Indeed, security is often quoted as the primary issue that concerns Afghans above all others. Security challenges in Afghanistan and the sources of insecurity are varied. It deals with the different dimensions of security that includes economic, health, environmental, personal, community, and political security to collectively address the issue of human security. Surveys of community perceptions of security in Afghanistan showed that Afghans' understanding of security, encompasses not just physical safety, but also livelihood security. Afghans continue to face multiple security threats. They continue to feel threatened by commanders, despite the formal disarmament process, and conflicts over land and property, bribery and corruption and police brutality amongst their key concerns. "Freedom from fear" is a concern in several provinces and the fiercely intensified insurgency causes harm to the lives, livelihoods, and daily affairs of the average Afghans. On the other hand, the majority of Afghans feel relatively safe in their families and communities, they face a range of threats to their well-being. The Taliban are not, as is sometimes portrayed, the sole or even pre-dominant threat to Afghans. Rather, the picture is more complex where warlords, criminals, international forces, drug traffickers, and the police all present varying degrees of threat, which are of different types and are variously configured in different localities.

Non-traditional and human security threats like poverty, unemployment, and diseases remain an important cause of insecurity and is interconnected to bigger problems like terrorism, insurgency, arms, and drugs trafficking. Hence, the relevance of this framework of human security in the context of Afghanistan becomes important.

Economic Security

The unequal distribution of wealth, other forms of inequality and the prevailing poverty are major challenges to the economic security of Afghanistan. Afghanistan's economy has recovered significantly in the recent years. While reliable data is not available, anecdotal evidence suggests that economic growth so far has done little to alleviate the extent of inequality, whether it is related to income, gender or geographical location. Human poverty in Afghanistan is a multidimensional problem that includes inequalities in access to productive assets and social services; poor health, education, and nutritional status; weak social protection systems; vulnerability to macro- and micro-level risks; human displacement; gender inequities, and political marginalisation. Some groups and/or households, such as women, the disabled and Kuchi nomads, are more vulnerable to poverty. High level of indebtedness and the staggering opium economy equaling 38.2 per cent of the country's official GDP are serious concerns to economic security.

Situation of Chronic Conflict and Political Instability (SCCPI) have generic features that generate specific vulnerabilities. SCCPIs have a number of common characteristics. These include a state with weakened or absent institutions, strong parallel or non-formal economies, existence of, or high susceptibility to violence, forced displacement of people, the denial of basic human rights to sections of the community and high vulnerability of livelihoods to external shocks and existence of serious poverty.[17]

Livelihoods—and the people who depend on them—become vulnerable when options become limited and/or when resources to support livelihoods systems are compromised or lost altogether. Diversity in livelihoods options is reduced in SCCPIs when, for example, agriculture lands are mined, economies contract, and generate widespread unemployment or labour is diverted due to forced migration or conscription. Resources to support livelihood systems are similarly limited by these and other threats, including the depletion of stocks and savings, the disposition of essential productive assets and loss from theft and looting.

In SCCPIs, individuals and households are vulnerable to a range of specific hazards ranging from food insecurity, diseases, conscription, asset stripping, physical assault, arbitrary detention, and forced displacement. The rich and the powerful may be able to manipulate economies to their advantage but usually to the disadvantage of the poor and marginalised. All these dimensions are present in Afghanistan. Vulnerabilities in Afghanistan are consequently complex and multiple, and understanding and responding to them requires a careful analysis of context and scale.

The phases of the conflict over the last 25 years combined with drought have been major structural determinants of livelihood changes. One such phenomenon is the movement of people. Though migration has historical roots in Afghanistan, forced movements of whole or parts of households have set in place a longer-term dynamic that is leading to multi-locational households and mobile livelihoods. This has served to blur the distinction between rural and urban and promote financial flows across space, both urban to rural and rural to urban. Though these changes can be generalised, an analysis of household vulnerabilities and responses to such forced migration must be understood in context and examined with respect to socio-economic status, gender, and ethnicity, the contingency of history, location, and household assets. Similarly, the response of households in a context of war and a black market economy confounded with drought have resulted in multi-layered livelihood changes that have not been well understood or described. Before the drought households diversified into low-risk activities in order to maintain asset bases and assure food security in what was a high-risk environment.[18]

If improved livelihood outcomes are an objective, they must be specifically addressed by design, implementation, and evaluation. Livelihoods are dynamic and complex realities; their composition cannot be assumed or taken for granted. Livelihood diversity has increased and the range of vulnerabilities is vast, deep, and potentially expanding, even as Afghanistan in fragile "post-conflict" era. There is a need to address these concerns systematically.

Health Security

In 2002, after the collapse of the Taliban regime, only 9 per cent of Afghans had access to basic health services; 25 per cent of children died before age five; 42 per cent of child deaths were due to preventable causes; and the country had only 460 low-functioning health facilities.[19] Life expectancy in Afghanistan, 44.5 years at birth, is at least 20 years lower than all of its neighbouring countries and 6.1 years lower than the averages of the Least Developed Countries. It is also significantly lower than any of the post-conflict countries except the three African nations mentioned above. Infant and maternal mortality rates are among the highest in the world. Afghanistan also has the highest rates of tuberculosis in its region, and is one of 22 highly TB-burdened countries in the world, with an estimated annual risk of infection that reaches 2.55 per cent. Malaria is another prevalent public health threat that is on the rise in more than 60 per cent of the country, with over 13 million people at risk. The annual incidence is estimated to be two to three million cases. A large number of other health insecurities are related to water, stemming from poor hygiene and inadequate access to safe supplies. Over 60 per cent of Afghans use unsafe drinking water. The World Health Organisation (WHO) estimates indicate that 95 per cent of Afghans have been affected psychologically by years of conflict, and one in five suffers from mental health problems like anxiety, depression, psychosomatic problems, such as, insomnia, and other symptoms of post-traumatic stress disorder.

In the immediate post-conflict period in Afghanistan, health services throughout the country were in a deplorable state. At that time, the Afghanistan Research and Evaluation Unit (AREU) published a monograph entitled, *The Public Health System in Afghanistan*, which reported that "the ratio of basic health centres to population ranged from approximately one per 40,000 in the central and eastern regions, to one per 200,000 in the south". It also drew attention to the severe shortage of health personnel and a "grossly deficient, even absent, infrastructure".[20] For the most part, healthcare was provided by NGOs, many of which had not established relations (formal or informal) with what was then a very fragile transitional government. Where health services were available at all, the level and quality of delivery varied considerably and there was no policy framework within which NGOs could operate. Instead, healthcare was "delivered on a project basis by many distinct, relatively uncoordinated service providers".[21]

Four major constraints to achieving an efficient and effective national health system: lack of managerial and service delivery capacity within the Ministry of Public Health (MoPH); lack of physical infrastructure and qualified personnel; poor distribution of financial and human resources; and, uncoordinated and undirected efforts of the NGOs. MoPH (Ministry of Public Health) has made considerable progress in making the Basic Package of Health Service (BPHS) accessible to most Afghans.[22] Independent evaluations show improvements in quality of care, the health management information system shows consistent and significant increases in a number of indicators, and the management capacity of MoPH has improved.[23]

Today, about 67 per cent of Afghans have access within two hours walking distance to primary health care services; child mortality has been reduced by a quarter; there are 1,710 quality health care facilities; more than 90 per cent of Afghan children have been immunised against polio; TB cases are down 60 per cent; and Afghanistan has more attendants for birthing mothers. Gloria Steele, USAID's Acting Administrator for Global Health, called these improvements "tremendous". "More than three decades of war has put Afghanistan near the bottom of development indicators", Afghanistan still has the highest fertility and infant and under five mortality in Asia. Maternal mortality in Afghanistan is the second highest in the world, and it remains one of only four polio endemic countries and one of 22 TB high burden countries".[24]

Looking to the future, there are a number of challenges facing the Government at central, provincial, and community levels, including full integration of the Grants and Contracts Management Unit (GCMU) and strengthening the technical and managerial competence in other essential departments of the Ministry; maintenance of the level of technical assistance; strengthening linkages between central, provincial, and district levels; defining roles and responsibilities of the Provincial Health Offices and, increasing access and quality, especially in remote areas.

Environmental Security

The legacy of conflict that has plagued Afghanistan and its people for nearly 30 years has damaged not only the country's society and institutions, but also its environment.[25] Water and air quality is poor. Access to safe drinking water is dismal. Natural capital, i.e., water, land, forest, and biodiversity is under a long-term decline. Environmental degradation, and poor access to clean and safe drinking water and sanitation, are major environmental security threats to people. Man-made and natural threats to the environment have been caused by erosion, the felling of trees, the destruction of watersheds and desertification. The impact on people has been considerable. Limited access to land resources and the scarcity of water for agricultural use, combined with lack of access to a diverse diet, are some indications suggesting that people's capacity to cope with these threats has been depleted. The lack of available energy services correlates closely with many poverty indicators, while urban dwellers are exposed to many toxic and carcinogenic air pollutants. There is an immediate need to install sound environmental management practices by designing and implementing a policy through a participatory process.

Long-term consequences of war and over-exploitation of Afghanistan's once rich natural resources has created grave environmental threats. The main impacts are the depletion and overuse of important resources (forests, biodiversity, water), which exacerbates the stressful socio-economic conditions and the impact of natural hazards; reduced access to natural resources; erosion of the rule of law; collapse of traditional governance systems and processes; pollution with toxic rocket fuel, spilled oil and land mines, making essential land, and pastures unsafe to use.[26] Moreover surface and groundwater scarcity and contamination, massive and ongoing deforestation, desertification of important wetlands, soil erosion, air pollution, and depleted wildlife populations. In addition, the prolonged lack of water and the rapid disappearance of half of the country's forest and woodland cover turned thousands of people into environmental refugees. This has led to increased population pressure on over-burdened urban areas and could generate new small-scale conflicts over access to scarce resources. National capacity to address these problems is severely limited as a result of the collapse of local and national forms of governance and resource management.[27] In fact, the most serious issue in Afghanistan is the long-term environmental degradation caused, in part, by a complete collapse of local and national forms of governance.[28]

Environmental degradation has a large scale impact on the population. Almost 80 per cent of the country's population (19 million people) live in rural areas. That portion of the population relies heavily on productive natural resources, which makes it extremely vulnerable to the impacts of local, and global phenomena (such as droughts, natural disasters, climate change and desertification) and the degradation of natural resources through erosion and pollution of soil and water. The influx of returning refugees, sheer population growth, and the creation of new environmental refugees and internally displaced persons—as a result of droughts, natural disasters, climate change, and desertification—exert additional stress on natural resources. Afghanistan's fast growing urban centres are not free from the impact of environment. Populations in the urban pockets consume increasing amounts of agricultural goods and energy. Due to over-population in many urban areas and the high concentration of pollution sources, such as, cars and industries, the residents suffer from severe air pollution, poorly organised collection and disposal of waste, lack of sanitation, and access to safe drinking water. There is also a shortage of green open spaces.[29]

Climate change, the resulting melting of mountain glaciers, severe droughts and poor management of water resources are threatening water security.[30] Water is key to the health and well-being of people, and essential to maintaining agricultural productivity which is at the heart of the Afghan economy. The first State of Environment (SOE) Report for Afghanistan, produced by the National Environmental Protection Agency (NEPA) with assistance from the United Nations Environment Programme (UNEP), point out that both surface and groundwater resources have been severely affected by the drought, as well as by uncoordinated and unmanaged extraction. It has been pointed out that in many cases, deep wells have been drilled without considering the long-term impacts on regional groundwater resources, including traditional *karez* systems (underground water canals). Water resources across the country are also threatened by contamination from waste dumps, chemicals, and open sewers. Many of the country's wetlands are completely dry and no longer support wildlife populations or provide agricultural inputs. For example, UNEP found that over 99 per cent of the Sistan wetland, a critically important haven for waterfowl, was completely dry.[31]

Furthermore, wind-blown sediments were in-filling irrigation canals and reservoirs, as well as covering roads, fields and villages, with an overall effect of increasing local vulnerability to drought. Improved water resource management will, in many regions, be an essential first step in rebuilding rural communities and improving human health. Maintaining water quality and quantity should be the overriding goal of all land-use planning activities and integrated water basin planning should be implemented across the country.

Afghanistan's irrigated land and gardens (3 million hectares) account for the bulk of agricultural produce. An additional 3.5 million hectares are used for non-irrigated production, which is dependent on rainfall. Together they play a major role in the country's economy, with agriculture accounting for more than half of GDP. Similarly more than 80 per cent of the population is engaged in agriculture, including livestock-raising. The country is consequently extremely vulnerable to water shortages. About 20 cubic kilometres is used for irrigation and drinking per year. This includes 85-90 per cent of water taken from surface sources, and 10-15 per cent from below the ground. Agriculture uses almost 99 per cent of the water, primarily from rivers and streams, followed by springs, *kareze*, shallow and deep aquifers. The assessment is that the use of water is likely to increase in the coming years due to growing demand from agriculture but also from urban centres and industries.

The total irrigated area has fluctuated over the past 30 years. By the mid-1970s, Afghanistan was almost self sufficient for its food supply. Nearly 3.3 million hectares were cultivated using various methods of irrigation, representing approximately 85 per cent of the country's total crop production. This has dropped to about two million hectares due to unrest and war, droughts, flood damage, aggravated by the failure to operate and maintain irrigation systems at a community and national level. The total area under irrigation is increasing again, but as much as a third of the total available land previously irrigated is not being cultivated due to water shortages. As a result the irrigation infrastructure has seriously deteriorated, and many farmers returning to their land cannot secure a reliable water supply to resume farming. Some provinces that rely heavily on ground water for irrigation—such as Ghazni, Helmand, and Uruzgan—are particularly vulnerable, with drought and water shortages impacting directly on livelihoods.

The mountains of Afghanistan have always served as a natural storage facility and source of water. In fact, more than 80 per cent of Afghanistan's water resources originate in the Hindu Kush Mountains. Unfortunately, drought and warming of air temperatures have reduced the size of the glaciers in Afghanistan. Major glaciers in the Pamir and Hindu Kush have considerably shrunk, while smaller ones have been reported to have completely vanished. A severe drought in 2001 further prevented the feeding of the Sistan wetlands by the Helmand river, and unfortunately by 2003, satellite images showed that 99 per cent of the Sistan wetlands were dried up. As a result, much of the Sistan basin's natural vegetation has died, and an increase in soil erosion has occurred, as well as the spread of sand on to roads, fields, and settlements. Waterfowl were also severely affected as the Sistan wetlands were very important to the birds. In the mid 1970s, there were close to 150 different species of waterfowl that were identified in the area, few to none remain today.

Nationwide, the majority of Afghan households do not have access to safe drinking water. Because of unsafe sanitary facilities, water contamination is a major issue in Afghanistan. Many water sources are contaminated with harmful bacteria, such as, *E. Coli* which sickens and kills many people, especially children and the elderly. Valuable water resources are polluted as a result of the disposal of industrial and domestic liquid wastes. It's common for household discharge and street waste to end up in streams. Moreover, in some bodies of water, the amount of hazardous chemicals fail hygienic standards. Even in the capital of Kabul, there are places where the water quality is so poor that it is unsafe for consumption. A Water Law has been developed and will hopefully address the pollution, and water quality standards, however, it is only in a draft form and still in the legislative pipeline. The government must put together a plan to ensure safe drinking water for its citizens, as well as assess and develop adaptation plans for the impacts of climate change on Afghanistan's water resources.

Agriculture in Afghanistan uses almost 99 per cent of the water resources. The reduction and loss of Afghanistan's glaciers, drought, war related damage to the irrigation systems it does have, poor management, waste, pollution, and the fact that over 80 per cent of Afghans are engaged in agriculture and livestock-raising, makes the country extremely susceptible to water shortages. The three largest river basins in Afghanistan are the Indus, Amu Darya, and Helmand. The most irrigated provinces are Balkh, Kunduz, and Jowzjan. The least irrigated provinces are Laghman, Kunar, and Bamiyan. The rich mineral resources of Afghanistan (gas, coal, copper, gold, rare metals), currently unexploited, could be the focus of major investment and development once stability and investment conditions improve. However, this could also bring adverse environmental and social impacts, if such projects are not designed and implemented within a proper, modern regulatory framework.

Following the convening of the Loya Jirga in 2002, a mandate for environmental management was included in the new transitional governmental structure. For the first time in the history of the country, a ministerial–level body was established to support conservation of the environment and sustainable development of Afghanistan's natural resources which has evolved into a National Environmental Protection Agency (NEPA). One of the first tasks was to identify the most pressing environmental needs. In co-operation with the United Nations Environment Programme (UNEP), NEPA embarked on post-conflict environmental assessment during late 2002.[32] Together with Afghan authorities, local communities, and international and national experts, UNEP and NEPA carried out a series of assessment missions in 35 rural locations and 38 urban sites. This work culminated in 2003 with the publication of UNEP's Post-Conflict Environmental Assessment of Afghanistan. Increasing consumption of these resources has consequences, such as, climate change and biodiversity loss, which will challenge the security of the nations all over the world. Natural security ultimately means sufficient, reliable, affordable, and sustainable supplies of natural resources for the economy.

Personal Security

Principal personal insecurities comprise physical violence by armed militia; torture by security forces or violent attacks by the Taliban or street gangs. Hostage-taking and domestic violence against women, abuse or rape, violence against children, such as, child abuse, abduction, child labour, and prostitution. Drug abuse is another aspect of personal security. Gender insecurities persist in Afghanistan despite the achievements of the past few years in opening up schools and public spaces to women in the form of constitutional guarantees (Constitution, 2004) and reservation of seats in the parliament. Nevertheless, only one to two per cent of women in Afghanistan have identity cards, and 98 per cent have no formal chapters that serve as proof of citizenship or identity. A traditional mentality continues to hold back women's participation in new political and economic opportunities. According to the National Risk and Vulnerability Assessment (NRVA), 2005, female-headed households have the highest incidence of poverty of all the vulnerable categories. Children remained at the forefront of the victims of the conflict in Afghanistan. More than 300,000 may have perished during the conflict, while grave physical and emotional scars afflict generations of Afghans who have known nothing but war. According to a 1998 UNICEF study, among more than 300 children aged eight to 18 in Kabul, 72 per cent experienced the death of a family member between 1992 and 1996.

Community Security

The main threats to human security in Afghanistan are identified as chronic and pervasive poverty and poor livelihoods, poor health and nutrition, massive population displacements, a degraded environment, and distrust in dysfunctional state institutions. Key human rights problems can be summarised as repression by armed groups, ethnic discrimination, political intimidation, and abuses related to land rights, the right to movement and the right to participate. Power in

Afghanistan, its authority is challenged by a number of competing factions. Within this environment, a principle threat is the lack of job security, the result of two decades of negative growth and the failure of the recent recovery to trickle down far enough to provide jobs and alleviate poverty. After more than two decades of war and internecine violence, the backdrop to the lack of security is a culture of impunity that has become the norm rather than the exception in Afghanistan. The "security dilemma" for Afghans consists of the privatisation of security and a general augmentation of a military mentality in the country, both of which are severely detrimental to peace-building. As the state is unable to hold the monopoly over military.

Food insecurity also threatens livelihoods both in terms of quantity and quality, despite recent improvements. A recent Ministry of Health/ Centre for Disease Control/UNICEF survey indicated that an estimated 37 per cent of households have been displaced largely to urban centres in order to cope with food insecurity. After so many years of conflict, Afghanistan's education system had become the worst in the world. An estimated 80 per cent of the country's 6,870 schools were damaged, if not completely destroyed. Higher education enrolments are some of the lowest in the world. There are regional as well as rural–urban disparities in the provision of education, combined with a huge gender gap. The quality of education is severely affected by the lack of qualified teachers both in primary, and secondary schools, and the very low salaries in the profession.

Of the causes for poverty in rural regions, drought is identified as the main source, affecting more than half the population. Other sources include pest infestations, epidemic diseases, such as, malaria; and economic shifts, such as, market price fluctuations. Surprisingly, violence as a cause of poverty was reported by only two to five per cent of the rural population. The impact of years of discrimination against women, coupled with prevailing poverty and insecurities, has meant that Afghan women have some of the worst social indicators in the world today. Maternal mortality rates in Afghanistan are 60 times higher than for women in industrial countries. Seventy per cent of people affected by tuberculosis are women. The feminisation of poverty, serious malnutrition, exclusion from public life, gender based violence, rape, lack of basic health facilities, illiteracy, forced marriage, and routine denial of justice are some of the human security concerns of Afghan women.

Political Security

In many countries emerging from war, overt armed conflict may come to an end while low-level violence continues for many years, involving former factions, demobilised combatants, bandits or militias. Military and diplomatic measures, though important, are unlikely by themselves to secure a democratic transition. The manner in which the reconstruction is structured (needs assessed, resources allocated, partners chosen, implementation carried out, results monitored) can either carry nation-building forward rapidly, or destroy its very foundations. Sustained peace in Afghanistan is not guaranteed despite the early successes in state-building that have now led to elections. Human security still needs to advance a long way. The breakdown of institutions has left the population vulnerable to the whims of peace-spoilers and their private militias, who can easily raise and sustain an army from among impoverished populations. Rebuilding institutions will be a core task. To be most effective, this must follow a regional model strongly reflecting the country's history, and strive not only to satisfy the immediate needs of individuals, but also to develop capacities for self-sufficiency and empowerment. Over the long term, the goal of Afghanistan should not be simply to create a basic development or democracy agenda, but to use these concepts as a means to prevent conflict and provide human security as a necessary public good.

The Problem

The events on September 11, 2001, also showed the dangers Afghanistan can pose not only to neighbouring countries but also to the whole world, to allow so-called humanitarian emergencies or failed states to fester. A US administration that came to power denouncing efforts at "nation-building" and criticising reliance on international organisations and agreements, has now proclaimed that it needs to assure a "stable Afghanistan" to prevent that country from ever again becoming a haven for terrorists. The US, along with every other major country, has committed itself to supporting the reconstruction of Afghanistan within a framework designed by the United Nations.

The Agreement on provisional arrangements in Afghanistan pending the re-establishment of permanent government institutions—to give the Bonn Agreement its full and accurate title—resulted directly from this new level of commitment and political will by both Afghans and major powers. Most reports on this agreement treat it as a peace agreement, like those that have ended armed conflicts elsewhere. But in Bonn the UN did not bring together warring parties to make peace. In Bonn, the UN brought together Afghan groups opposed to the Taliban and *al-Qa'ida*, some possessing power and others various forms of legitimacy, notably through the person of the former king of Afghanistan. The task they set themselves was the central one of protecting human security: starting the process of establishing—or, as the Afghans insisted, in recognition of their long history, re-establishing—permanent government institutions. This agreement thus differs from many others, which, as critics have noted, sometimes amounted to the codification of *de facto* power relations, no matter how illegitimate. This agreement does recognise power, especially in the allocation of key ministries to the relatively small group that already controls them in Kabul. In most respects, however, this agreement attempts to lay a foundation for transcending the current rather fragile power relations through building institutions. It also provided for an international security force, one of whose major purposes is to ensure the independence of the administration from military pressure by power-holding factions.

Building these Afghan institutions will constitute the core task of protecting human security in Afghanistan. The Agreement provides a framework. But implementation in such a war-torn and devastated society will largely depend on how the international donors and the UN system approach the task of reconstruction. As donors, agencies, and NGOs rush in, they risk losing sight of the central task: building Afghan institutions owned by and accountable to the people of Afghanistan. There is a real risk that, as the actors in the reconstruction market bid for locations in the bazaar that is opening in Afghanistan, they may harm, hinder, or even destroy the effort to build Afghan institutions. Donors and agencies seeking to establish programs need to find clients, and it is often easier to do so by linking up directly with a *de facto* power on the ground. Such uncoordinated efforts have reinforced clientelism and warlordism in Afghanistan for years in the absence of a legitimate authority, but they will now have to come to an end. Programs will have to be co-ordinated to assure that they work together to reinforce the capacities and priorities of Afghan institutions.

Observations

Understandably, Afghanistan's reconstruction needs at the start of 2001 were enormous. A joint study by the Asian Development Bank, the UNDP and the World Bank, prepared for a Ministerial Meeting in Tokyo on January 21-22, 2002, produced estimates of the costs of reconstruction which, over a ten-year period, ranged from a basic figure of $14.6 billion to a high of $18.1 billion.[33] The challenge still remains as to how to co-ordinate the use of funds and how to participate in capacity building. The lessons of previous experiences of aid in Afghanistan and development assistance elsewhere must be considered for the success of a reconstruction policy. Making the outcome of this political process in Afghanistan integrated into a major reconstruction plan was very challenging. Without a coherent vision for Afghanistan any reconstruction programme for opportunistic interests like gaining access to Central Asian oil and gas supplies and controlling the drug trade was likely to fail. Reconstruction had to essentially be a continuous and a prolonged process of negotiation between diverse internal interest groups and between them and political actors. It can be argued that for a sustained peaceful settlement, the country must be seen in its regional context and not just its relationship with powerful western neighbours. Hence, sincerity and goodwill of the neighbouring countries is an essential pre-requisite for sustained peace, security and therefore economic reconstruction. Subsequent chapters would focus on why there should be a regional security framework and how it can help in regional peace-building.

NOTES

1. Paula Kantor and Adam Pain, *Rethinking Rural Poverty Reduction in Afghanistan*, Afghanistan Research and Evaluation Unit (AREU) Policy Note, October 2011
2. Amitav Acharya, Subrat K Singhdeo and M Rajaretnam, *Human Security: From Concept to Practice: Case Studies from Northeast India and Orissa*, World Scientific Books, 2011
3. Sultan Barakat, 'Setting the scene for Afghanistan's reconstruction: the challenges and critical dilemmas', *Third World Quarterly*, Vol. 23, No. 5, October 2002, pp. 801-816.
4. Amin Saikal, *Modern Afghanistan; A History of Struggle and Survival*, I.B. Tauris, London and New York, 2004.
5. Anthony H. Cordesman, *The Lessons Of Afghanistan: War Fighting, Intelligence and Force Transformation*, Vanguard Books, Lahore, 2003, p.1.
6. William Maley, 'The Reconstruction of Afghanistan', Ken Booth And Tim Dunne (eds.), *Worlds in Collision: Terror and the Future of Global Order*, Palgrave,

Macmillan, 2002, p.185.

7. Alpaslan Ozerdem, 'Disarmament, demobilization and reintegration of former combatants in Afghanistan: lessons learned from a cross-cultural perspective', *Third World Quarterly*, no.1, pp.961-975.
8. Marina Ottaway and Anatol Lieven, 'Rebuilding Afghanistan; Fantasy versus Reality', *Policy Brief, Carnegie Endowment for International Peace*, hington, DC, January 2002.
9. N.15, p.186.
10. Ibid.
11. 'International Aid, Advocacy Groups Urge Expanded Nato Role To Stabilise Afghanistan', International *Rescue Committee IRC* Web Page: News, June 17, 2003.
12. *Op cit*, n. 3, p.808.
13. Jason Eskenazi, 'Learning In A Harshland: Scenes From Afghanistan's Schools', Culture, *www.eurasianet.org*, 16 July 2003.
14. Afghanistan has one of the highest rates of maternal and infant deaths in the world, and presents a extremely high proportion of illness and death due to communicable diseases such as measles, cholera, tuberculosis, malaria, meningitis, hepatitis, typhoid, childhood respiratory infections, diarrhoea.
15. In fact, it later confirmed that this proposal will be supported by UNDP, UNICEF, and UNIFemme.
16. Ahmed Rashid expressed this view in an interview with Narmeen Shaik of Asia Source, March 21, 2002. *Asia Source*, July 16, 2003.
17. J. Schafer, Overview of issues for a research programme on integrating livelihoods and political economy approaches, Overseas Development Institute (London: 2001).
18. Adam Pain and Sue Lautze, *Addressing Livelihoods in Afghanistan*, AREU Issue chapter Series, September 2002.
19. *Building Health Security in Contemporary Afghanistan*, Conference Report, May 13, 2009, www.intlhealth.fhpr.osd.mil/MultiMedia/conferencematerials/buildingafghanistanhealth.aspx
20. R.Waldman and H Hanif, The Public Health System in Afghanistan, Kabul: AREU, 2002.
21. Ibid.
22. In early 2002, MoPH and the major donors developed a Basic Package of Health Service (BPHS) that would come to form the technical foundation of the Ministry, and provided clear guidelines for infrastructure reconstruction and rehabilitation and for staffing. At the same time, MoPH and its international partners agreed that the BPHS could be managed and expanded more effectively and efficiently if the MoPH contracted with NGOs.
23. Ronald Waldman, Lesley Strong, and Dr. Abdul Wali, *Afghanistan's Health System Since 2001: Condition Improved, Prognosis Cautiously Optimistic*, AREU, Briefing chapter Series, December 2006.
24. *Op cit*, n.5.
25. UNEP and NEPA, *Afghanistan's Environment 2008*, 2008.
26. Ibid, p. 5.

27. Afghanistan's Environmental Recovery: A Post-conflict Plan for People and their Natural Resources, UNEP, August 2006.
28. Pekka Havisto, 'Introduction', *Afghanistan: Post Conflict Environmental Assessment*, UNEP, 2003.
29. *Op cit*, n 13, p.5.
30. *Op cit*, n.13, p.11.
31. *Afghanistan: Post Conflict Environmental Assessment*, UNEP, 2003.
32. Afghanistan's National Environmental Protection Agency was established in 2005. In the same year, Afghanistan's first Environmental Law was drafted and signed by President Hamid Karzai. It then went though amendments by the National Assembly and the final version was finally promulgated in early 2007. The law defines the agency's function as well as its powers. NEPA serves as Afghanistan's environmental policy-making and regulatory institution. It's role is to regulate, coordinate, monitor and enforce environmental laws. The agency is expected to play a major role in environmental protection, as well as to be the central point in dealing with the management of Afghanistan's environment so that it benefits all the citizens of Afghanistan.
33. *Afghanistan: Preliminary needs Assessment for Recovery and Reconstruction (Manila, New York and Washington DC: Asian Development Bank,* UNDP and World Bank), January 2002, p.47.

3

Addressing Food Security and Poverty, Education and Health in Afghanistan through Regional NTS Regime

Adam Smith had eloquently put it that, "No society can surely be flourishing and happy, of which the far greater part of the members are poor and miserable".[1] In recognition of this truth the international community has repeatedly affirmed its commitment to fighting poverty and hunger through a series of statements issued at international summits of heads of state culminating in The Millennium Declaration issued at the 24th special session of the United Nations General Assembly in June 2000. The Millennium Declaration consolidates the earlier commitments and contains a commitment to halve the proportion of the world's population living in extreme poverty by 2015. At the 1996 World Food Summit in Rome, 186 heads of state pledged to halve the number of undernourished people in the world by 2015. Though there are disputes over definitions and the exact numbers involved, it is safe to say that several hundred million people in developing countries live in extreme poverty and hunger. The challenge is to create conditions that allow those who are poor today to escape poverty.

This chapter seeks to argue in favour of a non-traditional security regime in South Asia by highlighting the menacing food insecurity situation in Afghanistan and placing it within the broader framework of South Asian Security. It is premised on the changing notion of security in International Relations in the post-Cold War period. From the classical notion of security that pertains to territorial security of the nation-state the focus is now wider and includes the concept of Non-Traditional Security (NTS). NTS has two implications or aspects one concerning physical violence (threat) not emanating from state such as terrorism and insurgency and the other related to individual livelihoods or human security. The focus of the chapter would directly concern Afghanistan, the new entrant to SAARC, a country menacingly threatened by the problem of food security and poverty. Decades of conflict in Afghanistan have led to an environment which is physically, socially, economically, and politically insecure. Protracted conflict has fractured and strained the social fabric and economic infrastructure of the country. A whole generation has grown up amid pervasive tension and insecurity, and all dimensions of violence, whether physical, psychological, structural, or cultural, are evident in Afghan society. The underlying connections between food insecurity and the lack of opportunities and livelihoods to the regional threats like terrorism and insurgency are embedded in the theme.

Food Security

The World Food Summit of 1996 defined food security as existing "when all people at all times have access to sufficient, safe, nutritious food to maintain a healthy and active life".[2] Commonly, the concept of food security is defined as including both physical and economic access to food that meets people's dietary needs as well as their food preferences. Food security is built on three pillars which are food availability which means sufficient quantities of food available on a consistent basis; food access which is having sufficient resources to obtain appropriate foods for a nutritious diet and food use meaning the appropriate use based on knowledge of basic nutrition and care, as well as adequate water and sanitation.

Food security is a complex sustainable development issue, linked to health through malnutrition, but also to sustainable economic development, environment, and trade. There is a great deal of debate around food security with some arguing that: There is enough food in the world to feed everyone adequately; the problem is distribution. Future food needs can—or cannot—be met by current levels of production. National food security is paramount—or no longer necessary because of global trade. Globalisation may—or may not—lead to the persistence of food insecurity and poverty in rural communities. Are households getting adequate food, is it distributed within the household and does that food fulfils the nutritional needs of most members of the family show that food security is clearly linked to health. Agriculture remains the largest employment sector in most developing countries and international agriculture agreements are crucial to a country's food security.

Food insecurity exists because of poverty, poor health of the population, lack of water and a fragile environment, gender inequity, disasters and conflict, population growth with increasing urbanisation and barriers to trade. Poor people who lack access to sufficient resources to produce or buy quality food have very small farms or use less effective farming techniques, and/or are unable to afford fertilisers and labour-saving equipment, all of which limit food production may not be able to produce enough food. Without good health, the body is also less able to make use of the food that is available. Addressing health issues will improve utilisation and availability of food. Producing sufficient food is directly related to having sufficient water. Irrigation can ensure an adequate and reliable supply of water which increases yields of most crops by 100 per cent to 400 per cent. Although only 17 per cent of global cropland is irrigated, that 17 per cent produces 40 per cent of the world's food. Increasing irrigation efficiency and limiting environment damage through salinisation or reduced soil fertility are important for ongoing food availability.

Where water is scarce and the environment fragile, achieving food security may depend on what has been called 'virtual water', that is, importing food from countries with an abundance of water. This may be a more efficient use of a scarce resource. Women play a vital role in providing food and nutrition for their families. Women's lower social and economic status limits their access to education, training, land ownership, decision making and credit and consequently their ability to improve their access to and use of food. Food utilisation can be enhanced by improving women's knowledge of nutrition and food safety and the prevention of illnesses. Increasing women's involvement in decision making and their access to land and credit will in turn improve food security as women invest in fertilisers and better seeds, labour-saving tools, irrigation, and land care.

Droughts, floods, cyclones, and pests can quickly wipe out large quantities of food as it grows or when it is in storage for later use.

Likewise, seeds can be destroyed by such environmental dangers. Conflict can also reduce or destroy food in production or storage as farmers flee to safety or become involved in the fighting. Previously productive land may be contaminated with explosive debris and need to be cleared before it can again be used for food production. Stored food, seeds and breeding livestock may be eaten or destroyed by soldiers, leading to long-term food shortages. Government spending needs to prioritise food security in the aftermath of conflict.

Population growth increases the demand for food. With most productive land already in use, there is pressure for this land to become more productive. Poor harvests and higher costs lead many poor farmers to migrate to cities to look for work. Expanding cities spread out across productive land, pushing food production further and further away from consumers. This increases the cost of all the activities associated with producing and transporting food, and decreases the food security of the poor in cities. Many poor countries can produce staples more cheaply than rich nations but barriers to trade, such as, distance from markets, quarantine regulations and tariffs make it difficult for them to compete in export markets against highly subsidised farmers in rich countries. This deprives poor farmers of income and entire countries of the agricultural base they need to develop other sectors of the economy. In addition, trade imbalances prevent poor countries from importing agricultural products that could enhance their food security.

Afghanistan faces enormous recovery needs after three decades of war, civil unrest, and recurring natural disasters. Despite recent progress, millions of Afghans still live in severe poverty with a crumbling infrastructure and a landscape that is suffering from environmental damage. This rugged, landlocked country remains one of the poorest in the world, with more than half the population living below the poverty line.[3] Nearly one-third of Afghanistan's people are food-insecure, which means they cannot get enough nutritious food to support an active, healthy lifestyle. The 2007-2008 National Risk and Vulnerability Assessment (NRVA) found that 7.4 million people—nearly a third of the population—are unable to get enough food to live active, healthy lives. Another 8.5 million people, or 37 per cent, are on the borderline of food insecurity. Around 400,000 people each year are seriously affected by natural disasters, such as, droughts, floods, earthquakes or extreme weather conditions.

Afghanistan was hit by both drought and globally high food prices in 2008, which saw the price of wheat and wheat products increase dramatically across the country. Despite prices beginning to fall in 2009, they remained higher than normal, and began to rise again in mid-2010, causing new hardship for the poorest Afghans. Insecurity is a major and growing concern. Insurgent activity and military operations have affected food security in some regions, undermined reconstruction efforts and restricted humanitarian interventions. Environmental degradation is also a severe problem. War, uncontrolled grazing, pastureland encroachment, illegal logging and the loss of forest and grass cover have worsened drought conditions and reduced agricultural productivity.

In Afghanistan, continued militancy and skirmishes leading to deaths of bread earners of the families have increased the vulnerabilities of widows and children. The latest national survey has found that 31 per cent of the country's population, suffer from food insecurity.[4] Droughts have damaged Afghan economy leading to further food insecurity. Insecurity is a major and growing concern for aid agencies in the war-torn Afghanistan. Continued insurgency and military operations have affected food security in some regions of Afghanistan, undermining reconstruction efforts and restricted humanitarian assistance in parts of the country.

International agencies like the World Food Program (WFP) is the organisation that has been implementing food programmes in Afghanistan planning to distribute food to around 7.3 million people across the country. This move is part of the urban safety in Kabul at the time of writing in seven different locations around the city and WFP distributes 50 kg of wheat to each recipient to about 600,000 people or some 100,000 families in Kabul. Another 8.5 million war-weary Afghans are on the borderline of food insecurity. WFP has been working continuously in Afghanistan since 1963, and is active in all 34 provinces. In recent years, WFP's focus has shifted from emergency assistance to rehabilitation and recovery. WFP fed more than 6.5 million people in 2010, primarily in remote, food-insecure rural areas. WFP's food assistance targets poor and vulnerable families, schoolchildren, illiterate people, tuberculosis patients and their families, returning refugees, Internally Displaced People (IDP) and disabled people—with an emphasis on vulnerable women and girls.

Developing the national education system with the incentive of school meals programmes was undertaken by the WFP. In 2010, WFP provided a daily snack of micronutrient-enriched biscuits or a hot meal to over a million children to alleviate short-term hunger and encourage school attendance. WFP also provided a take-home ration of vegetable oil to 600,000 girl students, as an incentive for their families to send them to school. This part of the food-for-education programme is aimed at closing the gender gap in Afghan classrooms in areas where female enrolment is low.

In order to provide food to vulnerable Afghans as they build or repair community assets, including roads, bridges, reservoirs, and irrigation systems. Food for training program of the WFP helped the poor acquire new marketable skills so they can earn a better living. In 2010, WFP also provided about 140,000 vulnerable people—mostly women—with food rations to support their families while participants attended classes in literacy, handicraft production, carpentry, plumbing skills, reproductive health or childcare. WFP assisted more than 1.5 million people through Food-for-Work and Food-for-Assets programmes in 2010. These projects are agreed upon in consultation with the government and local communities. WFP emergency food assistance supported over 1.8 million people affected by natural and man-made disasters in 2010. Food reached people affected by floods and landslides, as well as returning refugees and people displaced by conflict.

The nutrition programme's of this agency in Afghanistan quite effectively helped fight malnutrition among pregnant women, new mothers and children under the age of 5. This lifesaving food assistance helps women survive pregnancy in a country with one of the world's highest rates of maternal mortality. Children receive a special nutritional paste made from peanuts, which helps prevent the life-long consequences of poor nutrition during those critical years of life. WFP plans to feed some 55,000 pregnant women and nursing mothers and 62,000 children under the age of 5 in 2011. WFP has been promoting flour fortification in Afghanistan since 2004. Adding vitamins and minerals to flour helps reduce deficiencies in iron and other micronutrients, particularly important among women of child-bearing age. Eight mills around the country are now producing a total of 250 metric tons of fortified flour every day, on average.

Under a pilot Purchase for Progress (P4P) programme, WFP bought wheat directly from small-scale farmers for distribution elsewhere in the country, strengthening Afghan grain markets and small-scale producers' access to them. Through P4P, WFP has also begun partnering with Afghan factories to locally produce fortified biscuits that WFP purchases for use in its School Meals programme, and is exploring the production of other specialised foods. Under a new voucher project, beneficiaries receive vouchers instead of food rations, allowing them to buy their choice of food from participating retailers and avoiding distortion of functioning markets. After a successful pilot phase in Kabul, this project was launched in Jalalabad in February 2011. WFP plans to expand it to other cities, aiming to support some 30,000 people in 2011.

The national campaign against tuberculosis (TB) was also supported by the WFP by providing family rations to patients as an incentive to complete their eight-month treatment course at clinics across the country. WFP is assisting more than 20,000 TB patients and their families every month. The United Nations Humanitarian Air Service (UNHAS) provided safe and efficient air transport and cargo services for the humanitarian community around Afghanistan and to neighbouring countries. UNHAS carried more than 28,400 passengers and 121 metric tons of light cargo in 2010. Staff from 261 agencies made use of the air service.

The U.S. Department of Agriculture (USDA) provided technical assistance for the reconstruction of Afghanistan's agricultural sector. USDA worked in partnership with the U.S. Department of State, the U.S. Agency for International Development, the U.S. military, and the Afghan Government, as well as other organisations.[5] USDA has deployed 57 people for medium- and long- term assignments in Afghanistan since 2003. Experts have come from a variety of USDA agencies including the Foreign Agricultural Service; the Natural Resources Conservation Service; the Food Safety Inspection Service; the Animal Plant Health Inspection Service; and the Co-operative State Research, Extension, and Education Service. These experts help enable, support, and foster reconstruction of the agricultural sector, and help build the ability of the Afghan central government to support and provide services to the agricultural sector.

To effectively assist, train, and demonstrate techniques to Afghan farmers and agriculture officials, USDA PRT experts travel in the field as part of military units of 50-100 personnel with 2-3 civilian U.S. Government advisors. As members of a fully integrated U.S. government team, USDA agricultural experts have helped to install windmills to pump water for irrigation and livestock, trained veterinarians to detect and treat parasites, refurbished a university's agricultural research laboratory, stabilised eroded river banks and irrigation canals, developed post-harvest storage facilities, established nurseries and reforested areas, rehabilitated degraded orchards, and mentored provincial directors of agriculture.

Under this USAID-funded program, USDA provided technical assistance to USAID Afghanistan and the Government of Afghanistan in five critical areas: (a) livestock health, (b) sanitary-phytosanitary (SPS) issues, (c) agricultural extension, (d) conservation of biodiversity, and (e) strengthening the Afghan Government's capacity to manage and protect forests and rangelands, and watersheds. USDA provides assistance through the use of its technical specialists from various agencies within USDA as well as staff from the Land-Grant Colleges and Universities. Other program activities include long-term advisors at Kabul University and the Ministry of Agriculture, Animal Husbandry and Food, in-country technical assistance and training.

In 2003, at the request of and with funding from the U.S. Department of State, USDA helped establish the Afghan Conservation Corps (ACC). The ACC's aim is to be a massive, community-based employment program putting thousands of unemployed Afghans to work by growing and planting trees, fostering conservation of water, and controlling soil erosion. The ACC is a collaborative effort of the Afghan Government with operational and management support from the United Nations Office of Project Services (UNOPS) staff in Afghanistan. USDA has provided technical assistance to the ACC through a variety of training activities in areas of seed handling, nursery management, handling and planting of trees, soil and water conservation, and conservation education. Technical specialists have been from the USDA Natural Resources Conservation Service, USDA Forest Service, agencies within USDA as well as from Land-Grant Colleges and Universities. USAID has also provided support for USDA's work with the ACC.

In the South Asian region, the SAARC approach to the issue of Food Security is a comprehensive one aiming to develop a mix of short-term and long-term responses and regional/sub-regional projects. As

SAARC's intends to operationalise the SAARC Food Bank to provide immediate relief in food crises, the Colombo Declaration on Food Security emphasises urgency of action on multiple fronts.[6] Leaders of the South Asian States at the 15th Summit of the South Asian Association for Regional Cooperation (SAARC) held in Sri Lanka in August 2008 affirmed their resolve in their 'Colombo declaration on Food Security' to ensure region-wide food security and make South Asia, once again, the granary of the World. In order to ensure region-wide food security in South Asia, several measures were recommended including convening of a SAARC Conference of Ministers of Agriculture, operationalisation of the SAARC Food Bank and a work plan to increase food production, investment in agriculture and agro-based industries and research, sharing of technologies and best practices, etc. SAARC leaders further directed that SAARC region should forge greater co-operation with the international community to ensure food availability and nutrition security in South Asia. SAARC resolution L.15 also stresses the need for the international community to provide support, upon request, to national and regional efforts by providing the necessary assistance for increasing food production, particularly through agricultural development assistance, transfer of technology, as well as food crop rehabilitation assistance, etc.[7]

Poverty

Poverty is a multidimensional phenomenon and accordingly there is a wide variety of approaches to its measurement. Conventionally poverty has been defined in terms of income or expenditure based on the assumption that persons' material standard of living largely reflects their well-being. The poor are then identified as those with a material standard of living below a certain level. The welfare of a person can be determined by the amount of goods and services he or she consumes. Consequently, poverty can be defined as a condition of deprivation characterised by a lack of food, clothing, shelter and a possible other array of human needs. According to the relative approach, wealthier societies will have a relatively higher poverty line as the concept of deprivation is assessed with respect to a living standard that is generally considered as an acceptable minimum in a specific society at a specific time. The poverty line is then often expressed as a percentage (40-60 per cent) of a central tendency indicator (average or median) of the per-capita income or consumption distribution. Such relative conceptualisation of poverty extends beyond the basic physiological needs. In contrast to the relative approach, the absolute conceptualisation of poverty assumes it is possible to define a minimum standard of living based on a persons' physiological needs for food, water, clothing, and shelter—that is, their basic subsistence needs. Among the advantages of the absolute approach is that there are reasonably objective norms for poverty measurement, and that it allows for comparisons over time or between different groups, and it is thus well suited to monitor progress in a society that starts off from extremely low levels of material well being.[8] Poverty in Afghanistan is widespread throughout rural and urban areas. The government estimates that 42 per cent of the country's total population lives below the national poverty line. Another 20 per cent of the people live just above that line and are highly vulnerable to the risk of falling into poverty. Up to 70 per cent of Afghans are food insecure, according to the UN Food and Agriculture Organisation, and high food prices have recently pushed millions into high-risk food insecurity.

Poverty incidence is significantly associated with household size and number of children in the household. It is likely that high fertility is an important contributing factor to poverty in Afghan households. Also various characteristics of the head of household and of household members are correlated with poverty. This is particularly the case for the sex of the household head, and the head's educational attainment, employment status and industry of work. Child labour and seasonal migration are coping strategies that seem particularly to be employed by poor households, and net primary and secondary enrolment of poor children (50 and 13 per cent, respectively) is lower or substantially lower than that of non-poor children (respectively, 53 and 18 per cent). Afghan households tend to be large. They include numerous children and several generations that share the same dwelling. Agriculture is traditionally the major activity for a large portion of the population, but the sector has suffered from nearly 30 years of conflict, low investments, and natural disasters. The average size of landholdings is small, and as a result agriculture is rarely the main source of food or income. About two thirds of rural households own some livestock, and farmers also sell their labour.

Access to land is also importantly related to poverty: whereas 26 per cent of land-owning households are poor, this is the case for no less than 42 per cent of households that cultivate land on the basis of renting, sharecropping or mortgaging arrangements. Finally, the face of poverty is revealed in poor access to basic services like food, safe drinking water, improved sanitation, and electricity. The incidence of poverty is more severe in rural areas. About 45 per cent of rural people and the nomadic Kuchi people are poor, as compared to 27 per cent of the urban population.

The poorest rural people include small-scale farmers and herders, landless people, and women who are heads of households. There are an estimated 1 million Afghan widows. Their average age is 35, and 90 per cent of them have an average of four or more children. Without the protection of a husband, widows suffer from social exclusion in Afghanistan's patriarchal society. Many widows have no choice but to become beggars. Children aged five or under are the most vulnerable segment of Afghan society. As many as 50 per cent of them suffer from chronic malnutrition. The estimated 1.5 million Kuchis are nomadic herders whose livelihood depends heavily on livestock and migration patterns. As a result of conflict and insecurity, in recent years 15 per cent of Kuchi families have been forced to settle because they have lost their livestock and migration routes. They are now among the poorest households in rural areas.

There was a major inflow of refugees returning to their homes between 2002 and 2005. The flow has dwindled because of increasing insecurity, limited economic opportunities, and limited access to basic social services. For people who have resettled after as many as two decades of exile, economic, and social reintegration is a serious challenge. And internal displacement remains a problem. There are as many as 160,000 internally displaced persons, mainly in southern Afghanistan. Poverty varies significantly between provinces, from a poverty headcount of 10 per cent to more than 70 per cent. Poverty is most severe in the Northeast, Central Highlands and parts of the Southeast. The provinces of Daikundi, Badakhstan, Zabul, and Paktika represent large pockets of poverty.[9]

A basic lack of resources affects the majority of Afghans who depend on agriculture for their livelihood. There is little arable land per capita, precipitation is scarce, and climatic conditions are difficult in many parts of the country. Since 1999, recurrent droughts have severely affected the livelihoods of rural households, which had already lost many of their assets. Despite significant improvements since 2001 in governance, social services, and transport infrastructure, three decades of conflict have left most Afghans in conditions of hardship and insecurity. Much infrastructure remains to be reconstructed, and internal markets are still disrupted.

Poverty in Afghanistan is closely related to the high illiteracy rate in rural areas, where 90 per cent of women and 63 per cent of men are unable to read or write rural people's dependance on livestock and agricultural activities for at least part of their income inadequate land ownership and access to land lack of irrigation infrastructure. Many rural households are poor because they have incurred heavy debts, or because they live in remote, disadvantaged areas, or because they have lost the male head of the household. Often one or more members of the households is disabled.[10]

Table 1: Poverty Indicators in Afghanistan

Number of rural poor (million, approximate) (2010)	9,696,589.2
Poverty headcount ratio at rural poverty line (% of rural population) (2008)	37.5
Poverty headcount ratio at national poverty line (% of population) (2008)	36.0
Income share held by lowest 20% (2008)	9.0

Source: http://www.ruralpovertyportal.org/country/statistics/tags/afghanistan

Health

Decades of war and varying forms of conflict had its toll on the public health system in Afghanistan like every other sector. The health infrastructure suffered extensive damage. The situation was compounded by food insecurity, human displacement, severe droughts, drain of health personnel, and destruction of rural health infrastructure. Afghanistan had one of the worst health profiles in the World in 2002.

According to a study conducted by Afghanistan Public Policy Research Organisation (APPRO), standard health indices such as infant mortality rate (165/1000 live birth/year), maternal mortality rate (1,700/ 100,000 live birth/year), and life expectancy (46 years), are among the lowest in the world. There are also high rates of malnutrition: about half of the children under five years of age are stunted due to chronic malnutrition and up to 10 per cent have acute malnutrition. Every year there are approximately 72,000 new cases of tuberculosis with more than

15,000 deaths and over 13 million people at risk of malaria.[11] Mental health has been underlined as a main issue and there are numerous cases of depression, anxiety, and other trauma-related mental ailments (Cardozo *et al.* 2004) while disability stands at more than four per cent of the Afghan population (WHO, 2002). In 2002, the sector was described as having: grossly deficient, even absent, infrastructure; top-heavy structure with doctors who are not trained to deal with priority, community-level problems, and who lack public health expertise poorly distributed resource, health care provision delivered on a project basis by many distinct, relatively uncoordinated service providers, as opposed to health care delivered in accordance with clear and coherent national health policy, lack of practical, useful, and coordinated management system for decision-making. Significant changes have taken place since 2002.

However, hospitals and health centres are denuded of staff, equipment, power, and medicines. For a population of about 23 million people there are only about 17500 health professionals. A quarter of the doctors are in Kabul, where only seven per cent of the population live. By World Health Organisation standards a minimum of 63000 health workers are needed to provide a basic essential service. The Afghan government lacks the money to pay even basic costs and salaries, and re-establishing a viable health system will take years.

In the short term, Afghanistan will be almost entirely dependent on international aid. Although $4.6bn (£3.2bn; € 5.3bn) was pledged at the donor conference in Tokyo it is uncertain when and how much of it will be realised, or how much will filter through to the health sector. Many groups, including Physicians for Human Rights, have emphasised that more aid is needed. Currently over 70 per cent of health care is being provided by about 20 health related non-governmental organisations, many of whom have been in the country for years. Their continued presence is crucial to setting up the basic primary care services needed to tackle maternal and child mortality, communicable disease, and malnutrition, which the World Bank and United Nations have identified as priorities for action.

With many more non-governmental organisations and donors poised to start individual initiatives the importance—and difficulty—of co-ordinating their activities was underlined at a recent symposium at the London School of Hygiene and Tropical Medicine in London. Stephane Vandam, a health policy expert at the WHO, said: "The international aid and donor community have immense responsibilities to ensure that the health needs of Afghans are being addressed and the new ministry of public health is supported to assume a leadership role".

Support must avoid creating dependency. "In the rush to provide services fast for the maximum number of people, Western agencies often forget to think about the long-term impact of their interventions", Dr Willem van de Put of the Dutch based non-governmental organisation HealthNet International, told the British Medical Journal (BMJ). He added: "Initiatives controlled by Western experts frequently fail. The prime function of NGOs (Non-Governmental Organisations) working in the health sector is to support, train, and empower local health professionals, to build sustainable services, a process which takes time, patience, and sensitivity".

Maintaining security is essential to establish sustainable health services. It is particularly important in resurrecting the confidence of women doctors, nurses, and traditional birth attendants. Updating their medical and management skills and, through them, training cadres of community workers to help provide local maternal and child health services is vital. After years of oppression, violence and upheaval, cultural awareness and sensitivity are needed on the part of external agencies.

Education

Education is one of the most important aspects of human development. The Convention on the Rights of the Child—the most widely ratified human rights treaty—enshrines the right of all children to a primary education that will give them the skills they need to continue learning throughout life. Yet, a large majority of Afghan people have been denied this right, most of them women and girls. Consequently, they are bereft of many opportunities for personal development and contributions to society.

The overall indicators of education and literacy in Afghanistan reflect an education system that has performed very poorly. In addition, they invariably show very large gender gaps. Overall, only 17 per cent of the population aged 25 years and over has attended any type of formal education, and the corresponding figure for women is as low as six per cent. This manifests the lack of human capital in the country, which is required for good public administration and strong private sectors in the economy. The low literacy rates—26 per cent of the total adult population, and 12 and 39 per cent for females and males, respectively—also imply that the large majority of people is denied access to much information relevant to them and to further personal development.

Despite these extremely poor overall indicators, there are signs of strong improvement in recent years, probably since the overthrow of the Taliban regime. Although still 2.3 million primary-school age children are not attending primary school, the net primary enrolment ratio reported in the NRVA 2007/2008 is 52 per cent against 37 per cent in the 2005 round. Analysis of literacy by age also supports this sign of improvement of the education system. In the youngest age groups beyond primary school age literacy rates rise sharply.

This suggests that after decades of stagnation, male literacy increases from 30 to 62 per cent in the youngest age group, and female literacy from 10 to 37 per cent. In addition, the literacy gender gap has started to narrow, indicating that educational improvement has especially benefited girls. This effect is, however, particularly observed in urban areas; in rural areas the absolute gap between male and female literacy rates is largely maintained. The rural population lags behind in educational development to the extent that literacy rates and gender gap indicators of the youngest age groups is now at the level of the urban population at the start of the observed recent surge in literacy levels.

Afghanistan is faced with a huge challenge to meet the human right of children to receive at least primary education. This should provide them with necessary skills for life and provide the country with the human capital required to make progress to the goals it has set for development. Past performance of the education sector has resulted in a very poor overall adult literacy rate of 26 per cent and a very low educational attainment level, as only 17 per cent of the total population aged 25 and over has attended any type of formal education. In addition, the difficult access to education for girls is reflected in large gender gaps and even worse female education indicators.

Present enrolment figures are still among the worst in the world—net primary and secondary enrolment rates are, respectively, 52 and 16 per cent—but in comparison with the NRVA 2005 they show a significant improvement. Also age specific literacy rates indicate that in recent years primary school-age children have been much better served: 62 per cent of boys around age 14 are literate, compared to only 30 per cent of the 26-year old men; female literacy in corresponding ages rises from 10 to 37 per cent. These figures also imply a narrowing gender gap, especially in urban areas where the literacy rate of girls at the end of primary school age is nearly 80 per cent of that of their male age peers.

It is the task of the Afghan government to maintain this momentum and further expand educational opportunities for the new generations. This will become increasingly hard since underserved areas—especially rural areas—are usually the ones that are more difficult to penetrate with development programmes. In addition, the very high population growth will provide ever larger numbers of school-age children in the near future.

Observations

On issue like food insecurity, poverty, and education the emphasis should be on the pivotal role of regional co-operation, in this case the role of SAARC in preventing and coping with the food crisis and ensuring that people have access to food. The deep concerns and grave challenges that the recent volatility in food and fuel prices had posed for the region also calls for co-operative endeavours. It is imperative to co-operate on these issues and broaden the existing co-operative regime on Food Security with Afghanistan as a focus. Such co-operation can be highly effective in addressing the impacts of natural disasters, including floods, drought, and other events that contribute to food insecurity. Thus, effective regional institutions like early warning systems which can enhance food security by coordinating agricultural information from member States on matters, such as, expected crop yields, floods, and drought can be effective in tackling the issue. Regional and sub-regional action involving investment in effective food storage facilities/food banks and transport logistics would additionally help in dealing with any incumbent crisis. One of the limitations however is that the concept of Non-Traditional Security (NTS) is not well understood both conceptually and in terms of effective policies and evidence-based programs in an Asian context, more so in the South-Asian context. In South Asia problematic interstate relationships inhibit co-operation on various issues of Non-Traditional Security.

NOTES

1. Smith, Adam (1979, (originally 1776)), The Wealth of Nations (eds.) Andrew Skinner, Penguin Books, London.
2. Rome Declaration on World Food Security, World Food Summit, 13-17 November, 1996, Rome, Italy, http://www.fao.org/docrep/003/w3613e/w3613e00.htm, accessed 30 April 2012.
3. World Food Program, http://www.wfp.org/countries/Afghanistan/Overview.
4. Farid Behbud and Zhang Jianhua, "Over 7 million Afghans suffering from food insecurity", March 1, 2011, http://news.xinhuanet.com/english2010/indepth/2011-03/01/c_13756241.htm.
5. United States Department of Agriculture. http://www.fas.usda.gov/icd/drd/afghanistan.asp.
6. Statement by His Excellency Dr. Sheel Kant Sharma, Secretary General of SAARC, Inaugural Session, Fifteenth SAARC Summit, Colombo, 3 August 2008.
7. Sri Lanka highlights SAARC Colombo Declaration on Food Security in the Human Rights Council, September 24, 2008. Statement made by Mr. O.L. Ameerajwad, Counsellor of the Permanent Mission of Sri Lanka to the UN in Geneva, during the segment of general comments after the adoption of resolutions at the end of the 9th Session of the Human Rights Council, on 24th September 2008.
8. *National Risk and Vulnerability Assessment: A Profile of Afghanistan2007/08*. ICON-Institute, European Commission, 2009.
9. International Fund for Agricultural Development.
10. 'Rural Poverty in the Islamic Republic of Afghanistan', www.ruralpoverty portal.org/country/home/tags/afghanistan.
11. Saeed Parto, Daud Kohi, and Rozbih Mihran, "Sector Reform in Public Health, Education and Urban Services: Evidences from Herat and Kabul", APPRO Paper, Afghanistan, August 2007.

4

Urban Vulnerabilities in Contemporary Afghanistan*

Vulnerability has been defined as "the exposure to contingencies and stress, and difficulties coping with them" and the term "vulnerability" has been developed as a recognised conceptual framework and analytical approach to address marginality and poverty through means other than economic terms alone.[1] The chapter proposes to discuss the trends and vulnerabilities in urban spaces in 'post-conflict' Afghanistan. The number of urban residents in Afghanistan in the post-2001 period has risen dramatically due to migration from the rural areas and repatriation from neighbouring lands, leaving the international donor community and the local government to increasingly look at ways to address the challenges of urban planning and poverty. Vulnerability has thus two sides: an external side of risks, shocks and stress to which an individual or household is subject; and an internal side which is defencelessness, meaning a lack of means to cope without damaging loss".[2] Afghanistan being a perfect case of a Situation of Chronic Conflict and Political Instability (SCCPI) having generic features like weakened state institutions, strong parallel or non-formal economies, existence of, or high susceptibility to violence, forced displacement of people, the denial of basic human rights to sections of the community, lack of

*This chapter has been recently published in a book edited by Kingshuk Chatterjee, *Pakistan and Afghanistan : The (In)Stability Factor in India's Neighbourhood,* Knowledge World, New Delhi, 2013, pp.89-109.

livelihoods and existence of serious poverty which produce specific vulnerabilities for the people is a perfect case to study vulnerabilities in post–conflict reconstruction situation. Vulnerability has become a recognised analytical approach in research and applications dealing with uncertainty and risks, especially in terms of livelihood security.[3]

Afghanistan's urban transition is precipitating a crisis in local governance. Against an analysis of peace-building and post-conflict reconstruction, the chapter would argue that Afghanistan's urban poor has little or no access to basic services and social infrastructure because of a result of limited resources, combined with the authorities' unwillingness and lack of capacity to serve effectively. It analyses situation in the different urban spaces in Afghanistan and shows that there are determinants that shape and differentiate the situations of the poor and the vulnerable. By interpreting the various vulnerabilities as human security threats, it shows how exclusion from basic services adversely affects the capacity of the urban poor to earn adequate income and acquire the necessary human assets to have quality of life. While lack of services has long been recognised as a major problem in urban Afghanistan, investments in safe water supply, sanitation, shelter, and pollution-free environment have largely been insufficient. By highlighting such crises of urbanisation the paper, by way of conclusion, would argue for democratic representation and efficient urban management.

Peace-building in "Post–conflict" spaces

The term peace-building is broadly used and are associated with activities that go beyond crisis intervention, such as, longer-term development, and building of governance structures and institutions. The general understanding of the peace-building enterprise is largely influenced by the former UN Secretary-General Boutros Boutros-Ghali's vision and direction for peace-building in his 1992 document *An Agenda for Peace*.[4] According to this UN document, peace-building consists of a wide range of activities associated with capacity building, reconciliation, and societal transformation.[5] Experiences in various parts of the world in the mid-1990s have shown that sustained peace based on political and military stabilisation is not sufficient to end a protracted conflict based on ethnic, religious, and other primordially fuelled rivalries, in the absence of a long-term perspective of structural transformation.[6] Post-conflict peace-building is connected to peacekeeping, and often involves demobilisation and reintegration programs, as well as immediate reconstruction needs.[7] Various transformation techniques aim to move parties away from confrontation and violence, and guide them towards political and economic participation, peaceful relationships, and social harmony.[8] Such transformation is most crucial in urban spaces where reconstruction needs are maximum.

Peace-building should essentially mean a wide range of sequential activities, proceeding from cease-fire and refugee-resettlement to the establishment of a new government and economic reconstruction.[9] Peace-building in post-settlement phase entails both short-term and long-term frameworks. In the absence of local administrative structures, essential government functions are restored by international administrators or peace-keeping forces. According to Ho-Wong Jeong, the goals of peace-building will ultimately be achieved by reconstruction and reconciliation that are geared not only towards changing behaviour and perceptions but also towards social and institutional structures that can be mobilised to prevent future conflict.[10] The UN is committed to peace-building in the world because of a conviction to achieve the great objective of the charter, i.e., to maintain international peace and security, of securing justice and human rights and of promoting, in the words of the Charter, "social progress and better standards of life in larger freedom".[11]

Development cannot be easily disentangled from democracy and security.[12] "Post-conflict reconstruction" supports the transition from conflict to peace in an affected country through the rebuilding of the socioeconomic framework of the society. Wars often cause huge impacts, such as, death and injury to much of the population, massive displacement of people as refugees and Internally Displaced Persons (IDPs), widespread destruction of properties, poor institutional capacity and vulnerability to disease and crime.[13] Further, conflicts greatly reduce the security, prevent access to production facilities and erode the social capital.[14] In this context, the rebuilding of war torn urban spaces of a conflict-zone becomes very crucial.

The Afghan Context

In societies like Afghanistan, where conflict has been controlled to a certain degree, 'peace-building' also involves a complex process of negotiations, new challenges, and opportunities for social transformation particularly when the international community is an unwieldy entity with no single centre and lots of contradiction. It comprises the major world powers, with the United States as the dominant agent in some situations and as a reluctant participant in others. In Afghanistan, for instance, the US wants to have complete control over war operations but did not involve itself with peace-keeping activities like social empowerment, development or political transition. Meanwhile, the multilateral organisations that are bound by their mandates to play the dominant role in peace-keeping and state reconstruction, like the United Nations, remained the weakest and most divided of all.[15]

In Afghanistan, with the international coalition and US-backed Afghan insurgents removing the *Taliban* from power, there has been a struggle to establish a centralised and legitimate democratic government. The blueprint of nation-building in Afghanistan which has been laid down by the Bonn Agreement of 2001 faced challenges of political, economic, and social dimensions. Certain challenges had been identified by the World Bank,[16] which included the widespread destruction of infrastructure; low social indicators; prevalence of drugs and arms; delicate, uncertain and factionalised politics; legacy of a three-year drought and extremely weak administrative capacity. The poor infrastructure of the country, the continuing drought, the high number of Internally Displaced Persons and refugees in neighbouring countries, the gender inequality—all added to the enormity of the transitional challenge. The unsettled military and political environment along with the competing regional and international interests further threatens to influence the process and outcome.[17]

War-torn countries, anyway, are characterised by death and injuries of much of the people, massive displacement of people as refugees and Internally Displaced Persons (IDPs), widespread destruction of properties, poor institutional capacities, and vulnerability to disease and crimes. In a context, where conflict was controlled to a large extent, we find a large number of refugees and internally displaced settling in urban spaces. There is worldwide boom in urbanisation and Afghanistan is no exception. Out of the total settled population of Afghanistan of 25,500,100, the total urban settled population is 6,074,200 with total settled population of Kabul Province being 3,309,400.[18] Urban dwellers in the country are about 25 per cent of the total population. Most cities are currently experiencing a steady influx of returned refugees and Internally Displaced Persons (IDPs), and by 2015, the number of urban residents in Afghanistan is expected to double, growing at a rate twice as high as the average growth rate in the rural areas.

Vulnerabilities in Urban Afghanistan

The term vulnerability started being used in the late 1980s, after researchers and practitioners expressed discomfort in defining marginality and poverty solely through economic terms. Since then, vulnerability has become a recognised conceptual framework and analytical approach in research and applications dealing with uncertainty and risks, especially in terms of livelihood security. In practical terms, the concept is pre-dominant in guiding actions taken by government and Non-Governmental Organisations (NGOs) trying to identify and target recipients of their services. This study involved many questions that need first hand information, to be collected from the study universe. In other words, some stakeholders were approached in Kabul for their perspective on the ground realities of the study universe. However, the authors' various trip to the study universe helped her develop some perspectives on Kabul.

In Afghanistan, projected annual changes in "percentage urban" (1.98-2.34 per cent for Afghanistan) are above regional averages (1.16-1.42 per cent for Asia),[19] according to a study conducted in 2005.[20] This development is put down to three trends: self-generated growth (urban natural increase);[21] net in-migration fuelled by economic scarcity, unemployment, and environmental hazards (mainly droughts) in rural areas;[22] as well as refugee return flows (both assisted and spontaneous). Respondents from the United Nations High Commissioner for Refugees (UNHCR) as well as international agencies and NGOs dealing with refugees and IDPs, such as the International Organisation for Migration (IOM), emphasised that refugees and IDPs returned to their villages of origin. However, the qualitative evidence suggests that due to a lack of livelihood and other opportunities in the countryside, a significant number of assisted returnees immediately left the countryside for the city. This implies that Afghanistan's urban population may be underestimated, constituting an important area of further research. In another study conducted by AREU on Kabul, Jalalabad, and Herat what is visible is the stark similarity in the vulnerabilities of the urban poor.[23] The economy can be described as what is best known as 'coping economies' characterised by a widespread struggle for survival in a high–risk environment. In such situations, people are often found facing depleting asset bases often rely on the employment of child labour, leading to long-term negative effects on health-status and education.[24]

Also within the context of post-conflict reconstruction, housing reconstruction plays an important role in establishing the country's development and peace. Post conflict reconstruction requires repair and reconstruction of housing, social, and economic infrastructure of conflict affected countries. Reintegration of displaced people can lead the country towards development and then peace as well. However, most of housing projects are not appropriate for the beneficiaries' needs and socio-economic conditions. A sustainable housing must be appropriate to the needs of the family, suitable to the local environment and located in an area where there is employment and where services are adequate to the needs of the occupants. Informal settlements now account for the larger part of houses in Afghanistan's urban centres. Housing shortages, high rents, diminished housing stock, and the influx of returnees, internally displaced people and expatriate development workers all exacerbate the problem. The absence of an effective and coherent land management system in growing urban centres has provided opportunities for illicit dealings, whether by politicians, government officials, private militias or unscrupulous land developers.[25]

The capital of Afghanistan, Kabul, has suffered immensely from war and destruction, leaving large parts of the city in a deplorable condition. Moreover, the high influx of refugee returnees since 2001 has put additional pressure on an already overloaded service infrastructure and the limited job market. Migrants from other parts of the country have also flocked into the city, seeking employment, public services and/or agency assistance in the wake of the opportunities offered by the new government and by the many international organisations involved in security and reconstruction activities who have established offices there since December 2001. Kabul's current population is therefore quite heterogeneous, in contrast to most of Afghanistan's more homogeneous rural communities. Much of Kabul's physical infrastructure has been destroyed following decades of conflict and lack of maintenance. This has created housing shortages and service delivery backlogs resulting in, for example, a lack of clean water supply and urban traffic congestion. There is a shortage of low income housing.[26] This has encouraged the spread of informal, or squatter, settlements throughout Kabul. It is estimated that as many as half of the city's population live in squatter settlements. Moreover, the high number of international organisations in Kabul also has quite adverse effects on urban livelihoods, as due to their presence, prices in the city have increased significantly. Ecologically, life in Kabul poses the additional problem of quite harsh winters.

The citizens of Kabul are faced with sharp increase in land prices and rents, as aid, commercial, military and other organisations with international currency operating funds move into Kabul. Land speculation has led to a proliferation of high rise, high rent buildings owned by Afghan merchants and powerbrokers in sharp contrast to the city's widespread squatter settlements symbolic of the wealth disparities (and tensions) in the city. Often these new buildings are not in compliance with extant municipal zoning or building codes. There are, however, currently no effective mechanisms for the enforcement of these regulations. There are significant land tenure issues, including property disputes arising from war and regime changes.

The city of Jalalabad is the urban centre of eastern Nangarhar Province located in the junction of Kabul and Kunar rivers. Population figures are somewhat variable, ranging from 181,000 to 500,000. There is wide seasonal fluctuation in population numbers, with people moving in to temporarily escape the winter months in Kabul. In addition, the city's proximity to Pakistan results in patterns of seasonal migration, mostly in search of work abroad. There is a significant proportion of IDPs living in Jalalabad or in camps very close to the city, many of whom sought refuge in the years of war and decided to stay rather than return to their native places. Jalalabad's closeness to the border of Pakistan makes the city an important trading centre for all kinds of goods and foodstuffs. Urban vulnerability seems to be present largely in the form of food insecurity for many households, though the overall situation has been judged more favourable than in Kabul. Living conditions for the poor and vulnerable in squatter settlements and IDP camps are characterised by widespread lack of basic services like water and electricity. Livelihood strategies try to take advantage of job opportunities in Pakistan, but even more so from efforts in finding access to employment in the agricultural wage labour sector of Nangarhar District.

The city of Herat is located in western Afghanistan in close proximity to Iran and Turkmenistan. Quite similar to Jalalabad in the east, its location makes Herat an important commercial centre with significant trade relations to neighbouring countries. The city, with its very rich and ancient cultural heritage, has an estimated population of 249,000.[27] Unregulated customs duties from border traffic and a high trade volume contribute to the city's development and relative wealth. As such, a well-maintained infrastructure in Herat gives the impression of prosperity, especially when compared with other towns in Afghanistan. In spite of this, urban poverty is highly visible, especially in the numerous squatter settlements on the outskirts of town. Additionally, the city has attracted a large number of migrants from drought-affected rural areas, as well as returned refugees from Iran. This has put pressure on an already limited job market and resulted in a decrease of the price of labour and falling daily wages. As such, there is a wide difference in living standards in Herat, with a huge number of inhabitants able to take advantage of a relatively stable political situation and the position of the town on major trade routes. Yet living conditions of the urban poor and vulnerable in Herat are similar to those in Kabul or Jalalabad. Malnutrition has been observed, squatter settlements are widespread, insecure casual and daily labour function as sources of income and an overall decline in entitlements is abundant. However, Herat's proximity to Iran also provides opportunities. Labour migration of male household members is widespread and remittances from abroad are often the most important means for managing livelihoods.

Kandahar or Qandahar is the second largest city and one of the most culturally significant cities of the Pashtuns in Afghanistan, with a population of about 512,200 as of 2011. Kandahar has been the Pashtuns' traditional seat of power for hundreds of years. It is a major trading centre for sheep, wool, cotton, silk, felt, food grains, fresh and dried fruit, and tobacco. The region produces fine fruits, especially pomegranates and grapes, and the city has plants for canning, drying, and packing fruit. The region around Kandahar is one of the oldest known human settlements[28] Kandahar is Afghanistan's fast-growing southern urban hub of commerce. The area has been devastated through heavy fighting—not only during the Soviet period but also when the Americans attacked the Taliban in 2001—and many walls and homes were in ruins. This has not inhibited the return of many refugees and IDPs, however, who are living in their small compounds throughout the area along with other newly arrived squatters who seek shelter in the many destroyed structures and bunkers.

Poor urban dwellers struggle to make ends meet, with income used primarily for food, house reconstruction, and costly medical care. Sending children to school calls for additional direct costs for school supplies (notebooks, pens, pencils, books), uniforms and, in some cases, transportation (e.g., rickshaws utilised especially for girls)—an ongoing commitment on the part of parents and the household in general.[29] The amount spent on these direct costs varied considerably according to the number of children in the household enrolled in school. Under-nutrition is especially common among women and children in the poorer households and, in the case of infants, this is often accompanied by chronic diarrhoea. Drug addiction was a problem in some households, sometimes resulting in domestic violence. The following complicated example from a poor nuclear unit illustrates the links between economic problems, stress, conflict between spouses, costly health care and selling of household assets in the poorer households, adult females were also active in home-based income generation, which included sewing (four women) and embroidering (three women) for cash, along with selling eggs (one old woman). In a report published in 2005 a number of households had sold some of their physical assets—both productive and non-productive—in recent years.[30]

Stefan Schutte's study shows that for the urban context, coping economies tend to be characterised by widespread unemployment, a subsequent loss of income, insecure and expensive housing, food insecurity, and lack of long-term investment and tenure rights. Involvement in the urban coping economies of Afghanistan poses rather similar conditions for the poor and vulnerable, and these tend to be more encompassing than the differences between each city. However, there are also differences between the groups under study, with gender and physical health being important markers.

Human Security Threats in Urban Spaces

There are several risks to livelihood security in urban Afghanistan. There are risks of unemployment, loss of income, and indebtedness. Urban labour markets in Afghanistan are generally highly diversified, but for the unskilled and less literate labour force, access to opportunities is usually limited to the heterogeneous sector of informal employment. Job opportunities for unskilled persons are unreliable, irregular and subject to high seasonal variance. Most people have huge difficulties in finding constant and secure sources of income, which keeps their available cash at an erratic and low level. Naturally, common forms of coping with unemployment and irregularities of income are the employment of child labour and establishing access to credit. The former often leads to a depletion of educational levels, the latter to indebtedness. Unfortunately, several households are entrapped in a vicious cycle of having to decide between either sending their kids to school to learn or in the streets to make money, leaving very limited space for children to negotiate between school and work. Educated individuals also have difficulties in finding employment in present day Afghanistan. Their participation in cash for work activities, like picking garbage and digging ditches, is perceived as very humiliating and reveals a certain degree of despair among the educated urban population. Generally, employment opportunities for women are very limited. A kind of "cultural vulnerability" leaves little space for them. With their mobility harshly restricted, some women may manage to find work as servants, cleaning staff, or carpet weavers, but more choices hardly exist. People with less competitive power, such as, the elderly, people with disabilities and other health problems are also particularly susceptible to loss of income and indebtedness.

The question of food security is not inseparable from loss of income, because in urban areas sufficient nourishment depends on whether a household can afford to buy enough food. In the absence of subsistence production, levels of cash income, in combination with fluctuating food prices, are the most important factors influencing household supplies. However, the ample evidence of existing malnutrition. In the context of urban food security, it is the ability of an individual or household to render its endowments into effective command over food, be it via direct access or exchange relations, through mobilising resources out of social networks, through state support or through humanitarian assistance. The urban poor and vulnerable are not capable of making sufficient use of their asset base to obtain command over food, leading to the observed problems of malnutrition and hidden hunger. In the words of Drèze and Sen:

> "The life of a person can be seen as a sequence of things the person does, or states of being he or she achieves... 'Capability' refers to the alternative combinations of functioning from which a person can choose. Thus, the notion of capability is essentially one of freedom—the range of options a person has in deciding what kind of a life to lead ... poverty is, thus, ultimately a matter of capability deprivation".[31]

Employment of child labour, finding access to loans, begging and mobilising social resources are the most common strategies utilised in all three cities. Begging takes different forms. It is generally perceived as a humiliating practice, and often women and children rely upon begging as a last resort. Interestingly, in surveys conducted in three cities of Kabul, Jalalabad, and Herat women emerged as great managers of social relations and in spite of mobility restrictions, women are important managers of social relations, on which they can rely for support infrequently in case of need. These relations include not only shopkeepers, but also neighbours, extended family or friends. Bigger households may face difficulties in securing sufficient food intake for all, especially when there is a limited number of productively working household members and thus a high dependency rate. Household composition in terms of gender and health also influence income opportunities and thus levels of food security. Households headed by women, people with disabilities or elderly persons seem to be explicitly exposed to the risk of food insecurity. Functioning social networks have the potential capacity to act as critical safety nets and to help reduce food insecurity.

There are clear consequences of what food and livelihood insecurity can have on health. Loss of income and food insecurity both have negative consequences on physical and mental well-being and they compound into one another. A lack of income prevents investing in health care, which in turn may lead to illness. Poor health of the main breadwinner of a household may result in further income loss and may put livelihoods of all members of a household at risk. Facilities for health care are present in all three cities studied, though, as the ACF survey states, overall quality of public health services in Kabul is very poor and ineffective. Apart from that, access is limited, as costs of treatment either usually surpass the financial capacities of the poor and vulnerable, or facilities are located far away from the vulnerable neighbourhoods. Alternative, good quality health care in private clinics is inaccessible to the poor, as consultation fees may already exceed the daily income realised through casual labour. Without basic resources in place, many households do not attempt to seek professional medical treatment. It is more likely that people approach pharmacies directly and seek advice to their problems in order to avoid expensive prescription fees of clinics or doctors. Obtaining loans for treatment, reducing the labour force to provide constant care for household members in need and trying to mobilise social relations for support are certainly the most important coping strategies. Poor housing, lack of sanitary facilities, defective water supply or inadequate waste, and sewage disposal are some of the reasons for susceptibility to health risks. Young children and adolescents can be critically affected by insufficient nutritional intake, and combined with hard work and little recreational time, are vulnerable to deteriorating health. War victims, the disabled and women in general have a certain disposition to experience mental health problems, caused by overall worrying about household situations, problems of physical health or humiliating experiences in the past.

The legacy of conflict that has plagued Afghanistan and its people for nearly 30 years has damaged not only the country's society and institutions, but also its environment. Environmental degradation, and poor access to clean and safe drinking water and sanitation, is major environmental security threat to people. The lack of available energy services correlates closely with many poverty indicators, while urban dwellers are exposed to many toxic and carcinogenic air pollutants.[32] The main impacts are the depletion and overuse of important resources (forests, biodiversity, water), which exacerbates the stressful socio-economic conditions and the impact of natural hazards; reduced access to natural resources; erosion of the rule of law; collapse of traditional governance systems and processes; pollution with toxic rocket fuel, spilled oil and land mines, making essential land, and pastures unsafe to use.[33] Moreover surface and groundwater scarcity and contamination, massive and ongoing deforestation, desertification of important wetlands, soil erosion, air pollution, and depleted wildlife populations.

Nationwide, the majority of Afghan households do not have access to safe drinking water. Because of unsafe sanitary facilities, water contamination is a major issue in Afghanistan, including capital Kabul. Many water sources are contaminated with harmful bacteria such as *E. Coli* which sickens and kills many people, especially children and the elderly. Valuable water resources are polluted as a result of the disposal of industrial and domestic liquid wastes. In addition, the prolonged lack of water and the rapid disappearance of half of the country's forest and woodland cover turned thousands of people into environmental refugees. This has led to increased population pressure on over-burdened urban areas and could generate new small-scale conflicts over access to scarce resources. National capacity to address these problems is severely limited as a result of the collapse of local and national forms of governance and resource management.[34] In fact, the most serious issue in Afghanistan is the long-term environmental degradation caused, in part, by a complete collapse of local and national forms of governance.[35] Due to over-population in many urban areas and the high concentration of pollution sources, such as, cars and industries, the residents suffer from severe air pollution, poorly organised collection and disposal of waste, lack of sanitation, and access to safe drinking water. There is also a shortage of green open spaces.[36] Climate change, the resulting melting of mountain glaciers, severe droughts and poor management of water resources are also threatening water security.[37] Water is key to the health and well-being of people, and essential to maintaining agricultural productivity which is at the heart of the Afghan economy.[38] Many of the country's wetlands are completely dry and no longer support wildlife populations or provide agricultural inputs. For example, UNEP found that over 99 per cent of the Sistan wetland, a critically important haven for waterfowl, was completely dry.

Urban Management and Vulnerabilities

Afghanistan's urban poor suffers as a result of limited resources and has inadequate access to basic services and social infrastructure. There are determinants that shape and differentiate the situations of the poor and the vulnerable. Some households manage to achieve longer-term well-being while others endure perpetual poverty. Further, urban vulnerability is not necessarily linked to informal settlements, which often enjoy relatively good access to services and security of tenure due to the backing of powerful patrons. Exclusion from basic services adversely affects the capacity of the urban poor to earn adequate income and acquire the necessary human assets to have quality of life. While lack of services has long been recognised as a major problem in urban Afghanistan, investments in safe water supply, sanitation, shelter, and pollution-free environment have largely been insufficient for democratic representation and grassroots governance. Problems are further aggravated as it combines the authorities' unwillingness and lack of capacity to serve effectively.

Diligent management and inclusive governance is essential in 'post-conflict' Afghanistan. The fast-growing and vibrant cities of Afghanistan, which host roughly 25 per cent of the country's population, pose particular development problems but also carry significant potential for advancing social and economic well-being if they are diligently

Table 2 : Forms, Sources, and Determinants of Urban Vulnerability

Form of Vulnerability	Vulnerability to Income Failure	Vulnerability to Food Insecurity	Vulnerability to bad health	Vulnerability to social exclusion and disempowerment
Source of Vulnerability	Exposure to an unreliable and erratic labour market	Capability Deprivation Decline of entitlements	Poor living and working conditions	Powerlessness and marginalisation
Determinants of Vulnerability	Quality of health Levels of Education Household Composition Diversification of Income Sources	Vagaries of market forces Income Levels	Quality of Housing Income Levels Access to Health Care Access to Clean Water and Sanitation	Quality of intra-and inter-household relations Time and resources available to keep up social relations Social affiliation Membership in social networks

managed and inclusively governed. Urban governance needs more co-ordinated approach. Both require flexible approaches as well as enhanced co-operation between government departments as well as between those departments and city residents. This in turn entails a more collaborative and communicative approach to planning and management, both at the city and sub-city levels. Clearly this constitutes a challenge, as many current urban planners are wedded to existing and familiar approaches and practices. Further, there are few young professionals coming into the system who have capacity in new methodologies, systems, and equipment. Yet Afghanistan is blessed with a wealth of well-trained Afghan returnees who represent an opportunity for the modernisation of urban planning, management, and practice.

Urban management happens to be one of the twelve pillars of the National Development Plan of the Islamic Republic of Afghanistan. Increasingly the Afghan government is turning its attention to urban reconstruction and development and donors are beginning to respond to these challenges in a far more concerted manner. A critical focus is on the supply of infrastructure. Although this is crucial, unless urban management is effective and governance systems are sound, investments in physical development will not be sustainable or evenly spread. To this end it is important that clarity is achieved over the functional responsibilities of different levels of government and government departments.

NOTES

1. Chambers, R., "Vulnerability, Coping and Policy", *IDS Bulletin*, 1989, 20: 1-7.
2. Ibid.
3. Stefan Schutte, *Urban Vulnerability in Afghanistan: Case Studies from three cities*, Afghanistan Research and Evaluation Unit (AREU), Working Paper Series, Kabul, May 2004.
4. *An Agenda for Peace, preventive diplomacy and peace-keeping*, Report of the Secretary-General pursuant to the statement adopted by the Summit Meeting of the Security Council on 31 January 1992, A/47/277 - S/24111, 17 June 1992.
5. Boutros-Ghali, *An Agenda for Peace*, United Nations, New York, 1995.
6. The Peace-building experiences from Somalia, Liberia, Haiti, and Bosnia-Herzegovina reflect the same.
7. Michael Doyle and Nicholas Sambanis, "Building Peace: Challenges and Strategies After Civil War", The World Bank Group, http://www.worldbank.org/research/conflict/papers/building.pdf, p.3.
8. Ibid.
9. Ho-Won Jeong, *Peace-building in Post Conflict Societies: Strategy and Process*, New

Delhi: Viva Books Private Limited (first Indian reprint, Copyright Lynne Rienner publishers), 2006, p.1.

10. Ibid., p.12-13.
11. "Preamble", Charter of the United Nations.
12. Ho-Won Jeong, n.9.
13. FAO, 2005.
14. World Bank, 1998.
15. Marina Ottaway, *op. cit.*, p.20.
16. Alastair Mckechnie, Country Director: Afghanistan, *Reconstruction of Afghanistan: A World Bank Perspective*, Presentation Delivered to OECD-Development Assistance Committee, 2 May 2002.
17. Sultan Barakat, "Setting the scene for Afghanistan's reconstruction: the challenges and critical dilemmas", *Third World Quarterly*, Vol. 23, No. 5, October 2002, pp.801-816.
18. Population Estimation 2012-13, Central Statistics Organization, Islamic Republic of Afghanistan, http://cso.gov.af/en/page/6449, accessed June 26, 2012.
19. UNDESA (United Nations Department of Economic and Social Affairs*). World Urbanization Prospects: The 2003 Revision, Population Division 1*, New York: UN. 2004.
20. Jo Beall and Daniel Esser, *Shaping Urban Futures: Challenges to Governing and Managing Afghan Cities*, Afghanistan Research and Evaluation Unit, Issues Paper Series, Kabul, March 2005.
21. That is, urban births exceeding urban deaths.
22. Urban in-migration exceeding urban out-migration.
23. Stefan Schutte, Urban Vulnerability in Afghanistan: Case Studies from Three Cities, AREU Working Paper Series, May 2004, p.9.
24. Pain, A. and Goodhand, J. *Afghanistan: current employment and socio-economic situation and prospects*. In Focus Programme on Crisis Response and Reconstruction, Working Paper 8. Geneva: ILO. 2002.
25. *Op cit*, n.20.
26. Stefan Schutte, *op cit*.
27. Central Statistics Office (CSO), *Afghanistan Statistical Yearbook*, Issue No.24, Kabul, 2003.
28. Alexander the Great had laid-out the foundation of what is now Old Kandahar in the 4th century BC. Since the 1978 Marxist revolution, the city has been a magnet for groups such as the Pakistan-based Haqqani network, Quetta Shura, Hezbi Islami, al-Qaida and other terrorist groups, many of which are believed to receive support from Pakistan's ISI spy network. From late 1994 to 2001, it served as the capital of the Taliban government until they were toppled by US-led NATO forces during Operation Enduring Freedom in late 2001 and replaced by the current government of President Hamid Karzai.
29. Pamela Hunte, *Household decision-making and School Enrollment in Afghanistan, Case Study 4: District 2, Kandahar City*, AREU, Kabul, 2005.
30. One unit had sold its embroidery machine, dishes and jewellery in order to rebuild its war destroyed house; another family sold its wooden wheelbarrow (from which it used to sell things) and its dishes in order to pay off an old

outstanding debt.

31. Drèze, J. and Sen, A. *India: Economic Development and Social Opportunity.* Oxford/ New York: Oxford University Press, 1995.
32. United Nations Environment Programme (UNEP), *From Conflict to Peacebuilding: The Role of Natural Resources and the Environment*, 2009, p.5.
33. Ibid.
34. Afghanistan's Environmental Recovery: A Post-conflict Plan for People and their Natural Resources, UNEP, August 2006.
35. Pekka Havisto, 'Introduction', *Afghanistan: Post Conflict Environmental Assessment*, UNEP, 2003.
36. *Op cit*, n.32.
37. Ibid, p.11.
38. The first State of Environment (SOE) Report for Afghanistan, produced by the National Environmental Protection Agency (NEPA) with assistance from the United Nations Environment Programme (UNEP), point out that both surface and groundwater resources have been severely affected by the drought, as well as by uncoordinated and unmanaged extraction. It has been pointed out that in many cases, deep wells have been drilled without considering the long-term impacts on regional groundwater resources, including traditional *karez* systems (underground water canals). Water resources across the country are also threatened by contamination from waste dumps, chemicals and open sewers.

5

Securing Afghanistan's Natural Resources as a Reconstruction Agenda

> "The environment and natural resources are crucial in consolidating peace within and between war-torn societies [...] Lasting peace in Darfur will depend in part on resolving the underlying competition for water and fertile land. And there can be no durable peace in Afghanistan if the natural resources that sustain livelihoods and ecosystems are destroyed. The United Nations attaches great importance to ensuring that action on the environment is part of our approach to peace. Protecting the environment can help countries create employment opportunities, promote development and avoid a relapse into armed conflict".
>
> *UN Secretary-General's message on the International Day for Preventing the Exploitation of the Environment in War and Armed Conflict, New York, November 6, 2008.*

Natural resources are more often than not, the cause of conflict in a fledging conflict-prone state. As a result, resource management or the failure of it, may lead to outbreak of violence because of the attempts to control natural resources or grievances caused by inequitable wealth sharing or environmental degradation. Besides, it may be used for funding and sustaining the conflict and insurgencies. Afghanistan is generally perceived in terms of its deteriorating security and resurging insurgency. But beyond the rhetoric of insurgency and terrorism, or interconnected with it, are concerns affecting millions of Afghans threatened by resource deprivation. They are the ones who live on the threshold and for them water and environmental security are core concerns and insecurities, such as, these clearly fall into the category of human security. In the case of Afghanistan, with nearly a quarter of a century of conflict, a civil strife shattering 60 per cent of the country's infrastructure, a devastating drought, widespread food insecurity and degraded natural resource base, the post-2001 government in the country with agendas, such as, security, good governance, and self-sustainability as a top priority[1] faces an enormous challenge in terms of securing the country's natural resources as a reconstruction agenda. Within a framework of Natural security intertwined with human security, the paper argues that effective natural resource management and recovery is clearly an essential part of Afghanistan's secure future. The paper also argues in favour of a holistic approach for water management.

Securing "Natural Security" of the People

In the 21st century, the security of nations will increasingly depend on the security of its natural resources, or "natural security" as the modern global economy depends on access to energy, minerals, potable water, and arable land to meet the rising expectations of a growing world population, and that access is by no means assured.[2] At the same time, increasing consumption of these resources has consequences, such as, climate change and biodiversity loss, which will challenge the security of the nations all over the world. Natural security ultimately means sufficient, reliable, affordable, and sustainable supplies of natural resources for the economy of a nation and therefore its citizens. It is being argued that energy and climate change challenges are linked to other natural resource challenges, most notably non-fuel mineral supplies, water, land use/food supply, and biodiversity.[3] At the same time, there are ways in which conservation, water rights negotiations, and other environmental strategies can complement and enhance national security strategies, and ways in which national security strategies are unlikely to succeed without addressing such concerns. For example, peace in Afghanistan will be contingent on economic, civic, and political development as much as military successes and even President Obama has been harping on this point time and again. A 2003

UNEP report found, however, that most of Afghanistan's natural resources are severely degraded and that any recovery would depend on restoration of these resources.[4] This understanding fits into the category of the wide human security discourse which has prompted the broadening of the narrow agenda of security studies to include issues that threaten individual well-being within and outside the scope of the state and regardless of the occurrence of large-scale, armed conflict (which, nonetheless, comprises a major threat to multiple dimensions of human security).[5] Human security moves away from a traditional state-centric perspective to concentrate on the needs of the individual.[6] According to former United Nations Secretary-General Kofi Annan, human security can no longer be understood in purely military terms. Rather, it must encompass economic development, social justice, environmental protection, democratisation, disarmament, and respect for human rights and the rule of law.[7] Therefore, in todays' world, security should be conceptualised holistically embracing all these elements of socio-economic development. Moreover, the concept of human security places development concerns on the security agenda and can help to provide protection for citizens in states where institutions remain underdeveloped, therefore very much applicable to the case of Afghanistan.

Co-relation Between Natural Resource Management and Conflict

Natural resources and the environment can contribute to peacebuilding through economic development, employment generation, and sustainable livelihoods. Co-operation over the management of natural resources and the environment provides new opportunities for peacebuilding that should also be pursued. Failure to manage natural resources could also lead to the outbreak of violence and its sustainment. Because of all these factors, a new challenge for the United Nations has been to provide support to weak States—especially, but not limited to, those recovering from war—in the management of their natural resources to avoid future conflicts.[8] UN Secretary Generals like Kofi Annan and Ban Ki-Moon have time and again emphasised the importance of resources management and conflict prevention "In a series of reports on conflict prevention, Secretary-General Kofi Annan, pointed to the threats emanating from environmental degradation and resource scarcity. Ban Ki-Moon has emphasised that environmental degradation has the potential to destabilise already conflict-prone regions, especially when compounded by inequitable access or politicisation of access to scarce resources".[9]

Research by Paul Collier and Anke Hoeffler at the World Bank[10] suggests that countries whose wealth is largely dependent on the exportation of primary commodities—a category that includes both agricultural produce and natural resources—are highly prone to civil violence. In explaining the correlation between primary commodities and conflict, Collier and Hoeffler argue that conflict may be explained either by greed or by grievances, such as feelings of ethnic or political marginalisation. They conclude (in large part based on the correlation between primary commodities and conflict) that to understand the causes of contemporary civil wars we should forget about political and cultural arguments and focus instead on the greed of rebels and especially on their trade in natural resources.[11]

It is being argued that natural resource management or the failure of it, may lead to outbreak of violence because there are attempts to control natural resources or grievances caused by inequitable wealth sharing or environmental degradation. Countries that depend on the export of a narrow set of primary commodities may also be more vulnerable to conflict. Besides, it may be used for financing and sustaining the conflict. In the event of a conflict extractive "high-value" resources may be exploited to finance armed forces, or become strategic considerations in gaining territory. In such cases, the duration of conflict is extended by the availability of new sources of financing, or complicated by efforts to gain control over resource-rich areas. It could also undermine peacemaking in case individuals or splinter groups that could lose access to the revenues generated by resource exploitation if peace were to prevail. Once a peace agreement is in place, the exploitation of natural resources can also threaten political reintegration and reconciliation by providing economic incentives that reinforce political and social divisions.[12]

In the Rio Declaration, it has been pinpointed that warfare is inherently destructive of sustainable development. States shall therefore need to respect international law providing protection for the environment in times of armed conflict and co-operate in its further development, as necessary. Peace, development, and environmental protection are interdependent and indivisible and accordingly states need to resolve all their environmental disputes peacefully and by appropriate means in accordance with the Charter of the United Nations.[13] Though amicable resolution of all environmental disputes may be a huge challenge, yet it is prudent of national leaders to work with neighbours in that direction.

Environmental Situation in Afghanistan

Environmental damage in Afghanistan has been quite substantial, more so because of prolonged warfare. Attempts have been made to assess the scale of destruction following the convening of the *Loya Jirga* in 2002. A mandate for environmental management was included in the new transitional governmental structure. For the first time in the history of the country, a ministerial–level body was established to support conservation of the environment and sustainable development of Afghanistan's natural resources which has evolved into a National Environmental Protection Agency (NEPA). One of the first tasks was to identify the most pressing environmental needs. In co-operation with the United Nations Environment Programme (UNEP), NEPA embarked on post-conflict environmental assessment during late 2002.[14] Together with Afghan authorities, local communities, and international and national experts, UNEP and NEPA carried out a series of assessment missions in 35 rural locations and 38 urban sites. This work culminated in 2003 with the publication of UNEP's Post-Conflict Environmental Assessment of Afghanistan.

The protracted conflict that has beleaguered Afghanistan and its people for nearly 30 years has damaged not only the country's society and institutions, but also its environment.[15] The report showed how the long-term consequences of war and overexploitation of Afghanistan's once rich natural resources has created serious environmental threats. The main impacts are the depletion and overuse of important resources (forests, biodiversity, water), which exacerbates the stressful socio-economic conditions and the impact of natural hazards; reduced access to natural resources; erosion of the rule of law; collapse of traditional governance systems and processes; pollution with toxic rocket fuel, spilled oil and land mines, making essential land, and pastures unsafe to use.[16] Moreover surface and groundwater scarcity and contamination, massive and ongoing deforestation, desertification of important wetlands, soil erosion, air pollution, and depleted wildlife populations are some challenges. In addition, the prolonged lack of water and the rapid disappearance of half of the country's forest and woodland cover turned thousands of people into environmental refugees. This has led to increased population pressure on over-burdened urban areas and could generate new small-scale conflicts over access to scarce resources. National capacity to address these problems is severely limited as a result of the collapse of local and national forms of governance and resource management.[17] In fact, the most serious issue in Afghanistan is the long-term environmental degradation caused, in part, by a complete collapse of local and national forms of governance.[18]

Environmental degradation has a large scale impact on the population. Almost 80 per cent of the country's population (19 million people) live in rural areas. That portion of the population relies heavily on productive natural resources, which makes it extremely vulnerable to the impacts of local and global phenomena (such as, droughts, natural disasters, climate change, and desertification) and the degradation of natural resources through erosion and pollution of soil and water. The influx of returning refugees, sheer population growth, and the creation of new environmental refugees and internally displaced persons—as a result of droughts, natural disasters, climate change, and desertification– exert additional stress on natural resources. Afghanistan's fast growing urban centres are not free from the impact of environment. Populations in the urban pockets consume increasing amounts of agricultural goods and energy. Due to over-population in many urban areas and the high concentration of pollution sources, such as, cars and industries, the residents suffer from severe air pollution, poorly organised collection and disposal of waste, lack of sanitation and access to safe drinking water. There is also a shortage of green open spaces.[19]

The rich mineral resources of Afghanistan (gas, coal, copper, gold, rare metals), currently unexploited, could be the focus of major investment and development once stability and investment conditions improve. However, this could also bring adverse environmental and social impacts, if such projects are not designed and implemented within a proper, modern regulatory framework.

Ecosystems

Rich and healthy ecosystems are fundamental for securing the livelihoods of the majority of Afghanistan's population. Rangelands, forests and biodiversity products are nature's key constituents and are rightly considered "the wealth of the poor" in Afghanistan because rural people living close to them depend on natural and agricultural ecosystems to provide tangible goods and services[20]: crops, fruit, grazing, timber, hunting, medicine and also erosion control, pollination and water drainage stability. It is understood that alpine pastures, cedar forests, unspoilt wilderness and rare animals have huge tourist potential once Afghanistan becomes politically stable and peaceful. A combination of various driving forces, such as war and lack of control coupled with a series of natural disasters, population growth, and increasing demand for natural resources at home and abroad led to significant depletion of resources, leaving them fragmented and reducing productivity.

The vast areas of the country contaminated with landmines and depleted forests, especially in the north and east, are the direct results of the war and conflict-related damage to the environment. At present the rangelands of Afghanistan occupy about 30 million hectares, representing roughly 45 per cent of the country's territory. However, large areas which are considered 'barren land' or 'waste land' are also used for grazing, particularly in winter. The total grazeable area is therefore much larger, estimated at 70–85 per cent of the total land area, providing habitat and forage for nearly 35 million livestock as well as numerous wild animals. Indirectly rangelands have significant export potential and generate income for the rural population via livestock subproducts carpets and rugs, wool, and medicinal plants (Ferrula, Bunicum, Rosa, etc). Regrettably the country's many rangelands are in poor condition, with overgrazing a common problem, while competition between farmers for the use of scarce productive rangelands is increasing.

In the mountains overgrazing is the main factor in increased soil erosion and forest degradation, hampering forest regeneration. During the last few decades, the number of livestock, in particular sheep and camels, has substantially decreased. But degraded rangelands remain the fact of everyday life. Changes in vegetation and its productivity (as well as changes in climatic patterns such as rain, snow, and the length of the vegetative season) have forced the farmers to shift grazing from traditional to higher ranges. This in turn increases pressure on the alpine ecosystems, where vast areas of vegetation—formerly highly productive grasslands—have been converted into grazing-resistant cushion shrub lands. Rangelands are essential for Kuchi pastoralists[21] (estimated to comprise 20 per cent of the rural population) and for a large part of the settled population who derive their income from rearing animals and employment in the livestock industry. Over the last 30 years livestock populations in Afghanistan have fluctuated from between about four million cattle and more than 30 million sheep and goats to the lowest levels recorded in the country's recent history (end of the drought) with 3.7 million cattle and approximately 16 million sheep and goats.

Illegal logging has shrunk Afghanistan's forest cover by 50 per cent.[22] It is the main factor in the decline and disappearance of forests. It is indeed alarming that if deforestation continues at its present rate, all forest will have disappeared in three decades A few centuries ago deciduous and evergreen forests covered five per cent of Afghanistan's current land area, including one million hectares of oak and two million hectares of pine and cedar growing mostly in the eastern part of the country.

Open woodland dominated by pistachios, almonds, and junipers occupied a third of the land area. Today most of the original forests have gone. By the middle of the 20th century, the total forest cover of Afghanistan was estimated at 3.1–3.4 million hectares. Forest now occupies less than 1.0–1.3 million hectares (2 per cent of county's total area), with just 0.5 million hectares of forests with 10 per cent crown density, including 0.05 million hectares with 50 per cent crown density. The forest area declined at the rate of three per cent a year from 2000 to 2005 (equal to annual removal and conversion of 30 000 hectares of forestland).

Many forests have disappeared over the last three decades of conflict and as a result of indiscriminate logging. The largest areas of forest are located in the eastern provinces of Nuristan, Kunar, and Nangarhar. Even in Khost 65 per cent of the forests have been destroyed.[23] Remote sensing (satellite image analysis) of these provinces in 1978 and 2002 revealed that forest cover there has been reduced by more than 50 per cent. Several factors are driving the rapid decline and degradation of forests. One of them is demand for timber for trading in Afghanistan and abroad, especially neighbouring Pakistan. Recently (in 1992–2002, including the Taliban's use of the forest trade as a source of revenue), massive logging and smuggling significantly contributed to forest reduction (50–200 timber truckloads a day or 150,000–500,000 cubic metres of wood annually) in the eastern provinces of Afghanistan. Local communities have lost control over the resources on which they depend for their survival, and forest resources are now largely used for immediate profit by organised crime syndicates and traders. War has also inflicted damage on forest ecosystems.

During the 1980s many pistachio trees were uprooted or depleted by Soviet military forces, while intense fighting led to an increase in the risk of forest fires. Other causes of the current deforestation include non-sustainable practices such as tree felling for energy/fuelwood[24] and construction (including increasing urbanisation needs); poor forest management; feeble incentives for reforestation; lack of community involvement and awareness; and agricultural and urban encroachments on forest land. The loss of forest cover does not only have environmental impacts, but also leads to economic losses.

In the 1970s Badghis and Takhar provinces of northern Afghanistan were covered with productive pistachio forests and earned substantial revenue from their nuts. These forests almost totally disappeared in just three decades and with them the associated revenue and ecological benefits. It is difficult to calculate the indirect economic losses from the reduction in key forest functions—such as, erosion and flood control, soil fertility, and biodiversity benefits—but clearly these costs are high. Finally, since the productivity of the country's rangelands and forests is declining, people have been forced to move from rural to urban areas in search of alternative livelihoods, increasing the growth of urbanisation.

With increased international military presence and government control in Kunar Province, as well as local infrastructure development and tighter control over timber-smuggling, the rate of deforestation seems to have declined in recent years. But in view of the shortage of impartial information sources and inadequate research, there is no way of checking this at present. Nor is it clear whether this promising trend will continue, in view of the economic value of forest products being very high. In some of Afghanistan's northern provinces a very encouraging trend towards in reforestation has also been observed.

Much as for the rangelands and forests, a great deal of Afghanistan's wildlife heritage is under threat.[25] The important feature of biodiversity is its high dynamism, and cross-border and seasonal migration, which helps to maintain animal populations in adequate numbers. The Wakhan Corridor is one of the few intact high mountain ecosystems, home to populations of endangered snow leopards and other mammals, including Marco Polo sheep. However, hunting is occurring in many regions of the country, either for sport or food, or to supply fur for sale to foreigners in Kabul. The legal status of protected areas is currently in question, pending approval of protected areas regulations under the Environment Law. Even though the protected areas regulations and management plans are currently under development, effective field-level management to protect and conserve their ecological integrity and wildlife is limited, pending finalisation of the plans and regulations (with the notable exception of the proposed Band-e Amir national park). Against this background, the proactive efforts of NEPA and the Ministry of Agriculture, Irrigation and Livestock (MAIL) to collaborate with neighbouring states to promote conservation of cross-border ecosystems are gaining momentum.[26]

Afghanistan's wildlife and biodiversity could be a critical component for future tourist revenue so protection of these resources should be attempted. Dasht-e Nawar and Ab-e Estada are important potential protected areas, especially as habitats and staging posts for waterfowl and migratory birds. However, due to their location and the associated security concerns, access to the sites is limited which has in turn delayed the implementation of any effective management regimes.. Unfortunately many varieties of cultivated species were lost during the period of conflict and the seed collections of many wild ancestors, that might have been resistant to pests and drought extremes, were destroyed.

Natural Disasters and Climate Change

Every year natural disasters damage the economy, hamper reconstruction and development, and claim human lives. According to the Afghanistan Information Management Service, the country's "high level of poverty, lack of livelihood and income generating opportunities, chronic health problems and poor state of infrastructure, all add to the burden of natural disasters on the people of Afghanistan".

Poverty and social and economic pressures, such as, migration, unemployment and land tenure practices have made Afghans more vulnerable by forcing them to live in disaster-prone locations, often on unsafe land and in unsafe shelters or low-cost dwellings, there being no other land available. Since the country is located in a zone of high-seismic activity, earthquakes are common. In 1998, alone they claimed more than 9,000 lives. Flooding and mudslides are real dangers in the mountains and valleys, particularly in spring and summer when snow starts melting or glacier lakes suddenly burst causing destructive flash floods. Prolonged drought and dust storms can also wreak extensive damage, with nationwide impacts. Severe drought may result in up to

10,000 casualties per year. Extreme winter conditions bring high losses in agriculture and infrastructure. These factors add to the burden of environmental degradation and place stress on ecosystems. Uncoordinated management of water resources and irrigation schemes during droughts could cause inter-communal and even inter-state disputes. Drought and mismanagement of ground water have caused the water table to drop almost all over the country, including the capital—Kabul city. In January–February 2008, parts of Afghanistan were facing their harshest winter in 25–50 years, and more than 1,200 people died, according to Afghanistan's National Disaster Management Authority (ANDMA).

Destruction of natural resources and/or rapid urban growth, in particular when accompanied by the influx of poor migrants from rural areas, are the main factors aggravating vulnerability to hazards in many parts of the world, and the same applies to Afghanistan. The accelerated, and often uncontrolled, growth of cities has contributed to the ecological transformation of their immediate surroundings. It is essential to mention global climate change and its impact on the environment. Ecosystem services, soil water content, and conditions and rangelands are most affected by climatic hazards and changes. The effects on food crops and livestock are similarly high. Irrigated agriculture, livestock herders, and dry land farmers are considered the most susceptible to the impacts of weather hazards and climatic changes. Climate change might worsen Afghanistan's predicament and it is crucial to make plans to adapt to these changes and also reduce greenhouse gas emissions in the country. Under Afghanistan's National Adaptation Plan of Action (NAPA) for Climate Change project, it was decided that the priority for facilitating adaptation to climate change was improved water management and efficiency of use, and land and water management at the watershed level. Other priorities include agro-meteorological observations, horticulture and agro-forestry, adaptive rangeland management, and terracing and erosion control.

Land Use, Agriculture, and Soil

Due to its socio-economic and geographical circumstances, Afghanistan has been severely affected by land degradation for decades. This in turn is a contributing factor to increased ecological migration and further stress on the ecosystem. Broad indicators show that the cost of desertification to Afghanistan is colossal and constantly increasing. Soil fertility is being degraded by poor agricultural practices; grazing patterns have changed as conflict, land claims and drought have affected traditional grazing patterns; and irrigation systems are being affected by silting and flooding. As in other developing countries, there are many direct and underlying reasons for land degradation, complicated by inadequate national policy, infrastructure, resources, and governance, as well as the sense of insecurity that characterises periods of war and conflict.

A critical component of economic growth and human development is the agricultural sector. Hence, sustaining livelihoods in Afghanistan is primarily governed by appropriate environmentally sound management of land resources. However, with its current status and yield capacities, the agricultural sector has now become somewhat inefficient, and poses increasing pressure on natural resources.

Afghanistan happens to be one of the most heavily mined countries in the world where landmines have been planted indiscriminately contaminating grazing lands, agricultural fields, and irrigation systems. Land mines and unexploded ordnance (UXO) still litter vast areas of the country, making some agricultural land unsafe for public use.[27] Landmines kill or maim an estimated 10 to 12 people every day in Afghanistan. At one point the area contaminated by landmines in Afghanistan covered almost 780 square kilometres (making Afghanistan one of the most heavily mined countries in the world). So far more than 400,000 landmines have been destroyed, but a significant portion of the contaminated land has yet to be cleared (on average, 15–30 sq km of land is cleared annually).

Afghanistan is not agriculturally self-sufficient and must rely on food aid. In the light of the rising population and the possibility of severe droughts, impacting on the nation's agricultural productivity, land is of paramount importance. Against this background, barren land (deserts, cliffs, etc.) occupies a third of the total land area, whereas the amount of agricultural land under cultivation and pasture has dropped in the last two or three decades either through abandonment (due to lack of water availability and damage to irrigation systems) or degradation (due to soil erosion, salinisation, reduced soil fertility). Arable land per capita stood at 0.55 hectares in 1980, and only 0.25 hectares in 2007. The succession of dry years in 1999–2004 and the severe drought of 1999-2001 substantially reduced the cultivated area and also put great pressure on grazing land and the Kuchi nomadic people. The shortcomings of agriculture resulted in mass migration of population to urban centres. Agricultural production in Afghanistan is limited by very high dependence on water from melting snow and ice and rainfall. As a result, crop harvests vary dramatically from year to year depending on the weather.

Human Development and Water Security

> Water is essential to a long and healthy life. It is also critical for education. Proximity to clean water means that children do not have to travel long distances to collect water and, thus, risk losing out on an education because they are too tired in the classroom. Water is also necessary for a decent standard of living because a healthy agricultural sector depends on the regular supply of water.
>
> *Afghanistan's Human Development Report, 2011*

Talking from a Human Security Perspective, "water is a source of life, livelihoods, and prosperity". A sufficient supply of water for life requires providing access to enough safe water to meet basic needs and household needs and ensure basic survival. Water for life is increasingly recognised as a fundamental right and as instrumental in attaining health security.[28]

It is often argued that shortage of water often leads to conflict. Access to water, while often viewed as a development issue, is increasingly recognised as a security concern.[29] Marsden and Arnold-Forster has argued that, as with any commodity in short supply, water scarcity invites competition among groups that may result in conflict on multiple levels, from the interpersonal to the international. Water may not be the primary cause of conflict, but there is no denying that strong links exists between water scarcity and conflict. As described by Ismail Serageldin, "if the wars of this century were fought over oil, the wars of the next century will be fought over water".[30]

The two critical human development challenges facing Afghanistan are securing access to water for all—regardless of gender, ethnicity, and socioeconomic status and providing protection against water-related shocks. A household that is deprived of water is deprived of human development potential. Indicators suggest that Afghanistan is not a water-scarce country and in theory, it is endowed with sufficient water to meet domestic, agricultural, industrial, and environmental needs. Afghanistan possesses an estimated overall surface water availability of 2,775 cubic metres per capita per year. Experts consider 1,700 cubic metres per capita per year sufficient to satisfy the water demand of a given population for domestic, food production, industrial, energy, and environment.

Resource availability in itself is not the only solution. It remains burdened by constraints that limit the capacity to make full use of the potentially available resources. The relatively significant amounts of water available in the country hide important variations within and across river and sub-river basins. The distribution of the available water does not always correspond with the location of the irrigable land and the settled populations. For example, while the Panj-Amu river basin holds almost 40 per cent of the country's available water resources, at more than 7,400 cubic metres per capita per day, it only accounts for 13 per cent of the irrigated land.

Irrigation is not available to most agricultural lands. The Northern river basin holds 20 per cent of all irrigated land but receives only 3 per cent of the country's total water resources flow within the basin's hydrological borders. Irrigation reaches only an estimated 1.8 million hectares of land, only 60 per cent of the levels of the mid-1970s. Population growth, economic development, and improved standards of living will be the main drivers of water scarcity in coming decades. As economies grow, the demand for water for domestic uses, agriculture and industry will increase. It is projected that, in Afghanistan by 2025, the amount of water available per capita will have declined by approximately 36 per cent relative to 2004.

As pointed out in the chapter on urban vulnerabilities we have seen how urbanisation will also result in more demand, which, in the case of Kabul, is already causing grave concern. Projections for the capital city indicate that, by 2050, six times more water will be required. The prospect of water scarcity in most river basins of Afghanistan raises serious human development issues. First, food security and food self-sufficiency are threatened. Feeding the population and limiting the country's dependence on commercial food imports are becoming more challenging. Since 2001, more people have been able to access clean water in rural and urban areas through government and donor-driven projects. The share of households that now enjoy access to municipal water is growing in the cities of Herat (85 per cent), Kabul (35 per cent) and Kunduz (50 per cent). The construction of an estimated 100,000 new water points is another sign of progress.

Most of Afghanistan's neighbours depend on surface resources originating from within Afghanistan. Afghanistan only has a river water treaty with Iran on the Helmand River.[31] The country's water resources must be shared with other riparian nations and proper frameworks established. Because Afghanistan is planning to develop domestic water resources, it must address these trans-boundary water management issues so as to reap the human development benefits. There is a strong incentive to develop local water management infrastructure, including through large-scale infrastructure projects, but Afghanistan must also engage in dialogue with riparian countries.

As pointed out earlier, unsafe water and poor sanitation is the cause of various water-borne diseases and deaths. Only 27 per cent of the population has access to an improved water source, the lowest share in the world. Sanitation is in a dismal state as the share of the population with access to improved sanitation facilities is 5 per cent nationwide and only 1 per cent in rural areas, making Afghanistan the worst place in the world for sanitation. Apprehensions are rife that at the current rate of progress, Afghanistan will not meet the Millennium Development Goal for water until 2042, 22 years after the target. However, a recent World Bank Report has shown that twenty fragile states have made progress on the Millennium Development Goals among which Afghanistan have met the target on improved access to water.[32]

Poor water quality and sanitation has a tremendous impact on Afghan children who bear disproportionate cost of such inadequacies. The under-five mortality rate is around 161 per 1,000 live births. Of these deaths, 23 per cent are directly attributable to contaminated water and poor sanitation. Thus, every hour, six children die because of the effects of diarrhoea. Repeated bouts increase the likelihood of persistent diarrhoea, which is associated with malnutrition. About 54 per cent of children aged 6–59 months are stunted (low height for age), and over 67 per cent are underweight.

Uneven distribution is visible in the way water is divided among the provinces and this undermines the universality principles of water access. Water supply and sanitation coverage differs significantly from province to province. Only 27 per cent of the population has access to an improved water source. The share of the population with access to improved sanitation facilities is even lower, at five per cent nationwide and only one per cent in rural areas ranging from only six per cent in Helmand Province to 56 per cent in Kabul Province, where water authorities are focussing on the rehabilitation of water systems. Geographical barriers explain the rates of poor coverage in some provinces.

The urban-rural divide is very prominent and a significant urban-rural divide characterises the disparities in access to improved water sources. Nationally, 27 per cent of Afghans enjoy access to improved water sources, but the share falls to 20 per cent in rural areas, where 75 per cent of the population resides. Poor sanitation and lack of access to safe drinking water are common in such areas. Conflicts over water access are one aspect of the daily routine of collecting water, which causes mental stress and can affect the well-being of entire households. One of the most daunting challenge facing people living in illegal settlements and settlements for internally displaced persons is the state of sanitation.

Observations

Human security is often neglected as debates on hard security issues in Afghanistan gain precedence in public discourse. But since the link between conflict and scare resources has been established, there is no scope to neglect the ever-increasing importance of natural resources in conflict management. There is an urgent need to develop adequate legal instruments such as laws, regulations, policies, and procedures to regulate and address the problems of biodiversity conservation. Afghanistan's participation in regional and global water partnerships will be soon a pre-requisite for the future use of international waters. Afghanistan needs to develop an appropriate information base covering the quantity and quality of its water resources, a comprehensive assessment of current and future water needs and availability, implementation of modern Integrated Water Resources Management (IWRM) principles and the establishment of functional river basin management institutions to help to respond effectively to the needs of users and the environment. Community-based natural resource management approaches to rangelands and forests could be a useful way to conserve natural resources. Timber moratorium should be issued by the central government to reduce illegal logging and re-forestation and tree-planting activities should be encouraged especially in areas where communities are using forest range and other biological resources sustainably. Without public awareness the environment cannot be protected. Therefore, there is an urgent need to strengthen public awareness to reduce vulnerability, need to implement climate change adaptation projects and capacity–building programmes to address local and national needs on integrated disaster risk management as many impacts could be reduced or even avoided through effective environmental management, conservation, and early warning. All these could be done in co-operation with neighbours through the exchange of data and expertise, and building of professional and inter-sectoral relations through a regional co-operative regime.

NOTES

1. Afghanistan's Environmental Recovery: A Post-conflict Plan for People and their Natural Resources, UNEP, http://postconflict.unep.ch
2. Burke, Sharon, *Natural Security*, Working Paper, Center for a New American Security, June 2009, p.9.
3. Ibid, p.5.
4. Silja Halle (ed.), *From Conflict to Peacebuilding: The Role of Natural Resources and the Environment*, United Nations Environment Programme, February 2009.
5. Sultan Barakat, *The Forgotten Front: Water Security and the Crisis in Sanitation: Vulnerability, Water and Human Security*, Background Paper to the Afghan Human Development Report 2011 CPHD, p.3.
6. Tadjbakhsh, Shahrbanou and Chenoy, Anuradha M., *Human Security: Concepts and implications*. Abingdon, Oxford: Routledge, 2007.
7. Kofi Annan, 'Towards a Culture of Peace: Letters to Future Generations', 2005, http://www.unesco.org/opi1/lettres/TextAnglais/AnnanE.html
8. UN Secretary-General's High-level Panel on Threats, Challenges and Change, *A more secure world: our shared responsibility: Report of the High-level Panel on Threats, Challenges and Change* (A/59/565). United Nations General Assembly, New York, 2004.
9. Ban, K., Secretary-General's statement at open Security Council debate on Energy, Security and Climate, New York, 17 April, 2007.
10. Paul Collier and Anke Hoeffler, "Economic causes of civil conflict and their implications for policy", Chester A. Crocker, *et al.* (ed.) *Managing Global Chaos*, United States Institute of Peace, Washington, DC, 2000.
11. Macartan Humphreys, "Natural Resources, Conflict, and Conflict Resolution: Uncovering the Mechanisms", *The Journal of Conflict Resolution*, Vol. 49, No. 4, *Paradigm in Distress? Primary Commodities and Civil War*, Aug., 2005, pp. 508-537.
12. United Nations Environment Programme, *From Conflict to Peacebuilding: The Role of Natural Resources and the Environment*, 2009, p. 8.
13. UN General Assembly, *Report of the United Nations Conference on Environment and Development*, Annex 1, Principles 24, 25, 26, United Nations General Assembly. Rio de Janeiro, 1992.
14. Afghanistan's National Environmental Protection Agency was established in 2005. In the same year, Afghanistan's first Environmental Law was drafted and

signed by President Hamid Karzai. It then went though amendments by the National Assembly and the final version was finally promulgated in early 2007. The law defines the agency's function as well as its powers. NEPA serves as Afghanistan's environmental policy-making and regulatory institution. It's role is to regulate, co-ordinate, monitor and enforce environmental laws. The agency is expected to play a major role in environmental protection, as well as to be the central point in dealing with the management of Afghanistan's environment so that it benefits all the citizens of Afghanistan.

15. UNEP and NEPA, *Afghanistan's Environment 2008*, 2008.
16. Ibid, p. 5.
17. Afghanistan's Environmental Recovery: A Post-conflict Plan for People and their Natural Resources, UNEP, August 2006.
18. Pekka Havisto, 'Introduction', *Afghanistan: Post Conflict Environmental Assessment*, UNEP, 2003.
19. *Op cit*, n 13, p.5.
20. To demonstrate the economic value of these natural resources, it is worth noting that three decades ago Karakul fur, wool, cotton, fruit, grapes, raisins, nuts and forest products represented 80 per cent of Afghan exports. Today, more than half a million farmers are involved in horticultural production with a total export value of 127 million US dollars. In comparison opium cultivation has a value of one to three billion US dollars at farm gate prices (50 per cent of GDP) and involves an estimated three million people.
21. Kuchis are Afghan Pastun nomads from the Ghilzai confederacy leading a pastoral nomadic lifestyle.
22. Glenn Hurowitz, "Illegal logging funding Taliban attacks on US troops", www.grist.org/article/illegal-logging....
23. Hedayatullah Khostai, "Khost forests shrink, thanks to illegal logging", *Pajhwok Afghan News*, 8 December, 2011.
24. Afghanistan-SACEP (South Asia Co-operative Environment Programme). www.sacep.org/html/mem_afghanistan
25. Flamingos have not bred successfully in Afghanistan for about eight years; Siberian cranes have not been observed for 20 years. Several mammalian species—such as the Caspian tiger (Panthera tigris virgata) or cheetah (Acinonyx jubatus ventucus)—are on the verge of global extinction and have not been seen in Afghanistan for decades. Others—such as markhor (Capra falconeri)—are considered endemic and live only in Afghanistan and adjacent territories.
26. There is an on-going initiative to establish a transboundary protected area in the Wakhan Corridor in the Pamir-Karakorum mountains (meeting point of Afghanistan, Tajikistan, Pakistan, and China), linking prospective protected areas of Afghanistan with corresponding areas in neighbouring countries. The Government of Afghanistan intends to nominate Bande-Amir, in the centre of Afghanistan—comprising six azure lakes and travertine dams—for World Heritage Site status.
27. "Landmine Use in Afghanistan", Human Rights Watch Backgrounder, October 2001. Landmine Monitor Report, 2001.

28. *Op cit*, n.5.
29. Ibid, p.5.
30. *Frontline*, 1999.
31. Margaret J. Vick, "Sharing Central Asia's Waters: The case of Afghanistan", International Water Law Project, January 19,2013. www.internationalwaterlaw.org/.../sharing-central-asias-waters-the-case-
32. "Twenty Fragile States Make Progress on Millennium Development Goals", World Bank Report, May 2013, www.reliefweb.int/.../afghanistan/twenty-fragile-states-make-progress-millenni...

6

Reconstructing Alternative Security within a South Asian NTS Framework

Whether the concept of human security is relevant for post-colonial regions like South Asia where states are still struggling with post-industrial political-institutional issues of nation-state formation is a matter of debate and discussion. The post-Cold War concerns with human security are not part of the pre-dominantly realist official discourse of security in this region. The reciprocal nuclear tests of India and Pakistan in 1998 have given a renewed legitimacy to realist notions of security. As discussed in the first chapter, scholars of international politics have attached priority to state (territorial) security and universalised the notion that the states are engaged in a constant competition of 'rationalisation' of security.[1] Circumstantial evidence of this can be found during the first half of the twentieth century which witnessed fierce interstate competition for territorial aggrandisement and the resultant two World Wars. Drawing from the philosophical writings of Thomas Hobbes and Machiavelli, the writings of E.H. Carr and Hans J. Morgenthau created a tradition that defined international politics, like any other politics, as a struggle for power.[2] States, according to the realist tradition, in order to remain secure have to acquire Power.[3] Thus, accumulation of power is prescribed as the prime activity of the states as it serves the most fundamental national interest, i.e., security defined in terms of territorial integrity. In continuation of the realist tradition, Kenneth N. Waltz, identified the anarchic condition and the uneven distribution of power among the members of the international system as structural compulsions for states to accumulate power to ensure their survival (sanctity of the territory).[4]

The Cold War defined international system that emerged after the end of World War II, closely approximated Realism's description and following its prescriptions states were engaged in an arms race that knew no limits. Mutual Assured Destruction (MAD) was invented as the most suitable method for ensuring security of the state and was used as the rationale for vertical and horizontal proliferation of arms. Scholars like Waltz and Mearsheimer advocated that the arms race would ensure peace and stability in the international system. Waltz advocated that the Cold War period would be the longest peaceful period in the world. The credit for this long peace is attributed to the bi-polar nature of the international system and the presence of nuclear weapons.[5] The numerous regional wars fought in various parts of the world and the millions deaths therein were termed as wars at the periphery without having any impact on the core of international system. Viewing international politics as a struggle for power and analysing security as a derivative to power has resulted in a 'Security Dilemma',[6] "a structural notion in which the self-help attempts of states to look after their security needs tend automatically to lead to rising insecurity for others as each interprets its own measures as defensive, and the measures of others as potentially threatening".[7]

In the South Asian region, while groups demanding a more people-centred conception of security have challenged this view of security, the debate on human security has remained at the level of rhetoric and has not fed into policy-making in the region. The discussion on the current security situation in South Asia gives us an idea about how perilous the security environment is. Now if one delves into the causes of this condition it would be noticed that South Asian States have religiously followed a notion of security that is not endogenous to the region. States in South Asia got entangled in an 'insecurity complex'[8] *vis-à-vis* each other which led to three principal negative manifestations according to B.K. Mishra.[9] According to him these negative manifestations are mutual hostility, emphasis on relative gains rather than absolute gains and the drawback to identify the actual threats which he calls the blurring of the vision of the reality.

He argues that South Asia is characterised by the persistence of mutual hostility between its members, primarily between India and

Pakistan. The military preparedness by both India and Pakistan is a product of the attitude of mutual hostility that is premised on the "enemy image" of the other and the threat perception that emanates from such an image of the other.[10] Both India and Pakistan suffer from the inherited notion that the ultimate objective of the other is to inflict harm thus prudence demands a deterrence posturing which creates a chain reaction of similar perception at the other end. This mutual perceptual hostility is also manifested in their non-military behaviour towards each other. One could logically argue that India being the major power in the region, may not consider other members of the region as threats but the same cannot be said of other states and particularly about Pakistan. Attempts to destabilise India from within with active help to groups that are challenging the unity of India has been a consistent policy of Pakistan from the day of its formation. Not only Pakistan, other smaller members of the region also nourish similar attitude towards India. Countries like Bangladesh have also at times got convinced about utility of being hostile to India and acted in manners that works in cross purpose to the peace and stability of the region. Sheltering Indian insurgents and playing to the designs of anti-India forces within the region and outside has been considered a justified policy.[11] Nepal feels India to be looming too large over herself and considers this as an existential threat to her image as an independent nation.[12] Sri Lanka remains apprehensive of India treating it as a security backyard. It is believed that Sri Lanka is willingly walking into the networks that are not totally benign to India. This mutual hostility between India and the other members of the region is more clearly visible in their multilateral engagements where the calculation of relative gains scuttles any meaningful co-operation.

Our theoretical understanding says that countries considering each other as rivals will not come together face to face at such smaller arrangements. If they consider each other as competitors, then they come together but remain worried about each other's (relative) gains rather than their own absolute gains. If they consider each other as friends then they wholeheartedly co-operate. Thus, sates remain worried about relative gains *vis-à-vis* others in any arrangement only when the trust level is low. Failure of South Asian Association for Regional Co-operation (SAARC) in gaining momentum explains the lack of mutual trust among the members. There have been various explanations to the failure of SAARC but the moot factor is the relative gains calculation by the members over the absolute gains that can be obtained by each of the member of the group. Explaining initial reluctance of Pakistan towards the formation of SAARC, Muhammad Jamshed Iqbal writes, "Pakistan assumed that it might be an Indian strategy to organise the other South Asian countries against Pakistan and ensure a regional market for Indian products, thereby consolidating and further strengthening India's economic dominance in the region".[13] Similar worries by other members of SAARC have prevented any substantial co-operation under SAARC. Bangladesh had also denied India transit facility for importing gas from Myanmar and this can be explained only in terms of possible relative gain of India *vis-à-vis* the other members of the region. Despite having the compulsion to pool economic resources to stimulate growth, the concerns of relative gains prevents any convergence from emerging among the countries of South Asia.

Under the realist notion of the international system and the definition of security, the vision of the reality is blurred. Threats created perceptually dominate the thinking of the actors in the region and thus prevents them from identifying the actual threats that can be termed existential to the state system in the region.

The strategies of the human security approach differ essentially from the realist military centred approach to security. Realist strategies are invariably premised on the threat and use of military power. On the other hand, the human security approach prescribes a co-operative global approach towards conflict resolution with inbuilt guarantees for freedom of expression, representation, and action for all as the preferred approach to security. The military centred approach to conflict resolution itself is identified as a threat to human security. A discussion on various basic human indices and the problems each member of the South Asian community faces would make it clear that the real security threat is not what the states do perceive *vis-à-vis* one another, rather the security threats are very much within the states. The region represents almost 23 per cent of the world population, but share only 2.5 per cent of world gross national income (1,339 billion US $ in 2007).[14] Average per capita income at US$ 880 is only 11 per cent of the world average of US $ 7,995.[15]

Some general human development statistics are shown in the table below.

Table 3: South Asia (General Statistics)

	2007	2008
Population, total (millions)	1,522.66	1,545.06
Population Growth	1.5	1.5
GNI per capita, PPP (US $)	2,535	2,697
PEOPLE		
Life expectancy at birth (years)	64	64
Fertility Rate, total (births per woman)	2.9	2.9
Mortality rate, under 5 (per 1000)	79	76
Malnutrition prevalance, weight for age (% of children under 5)	—	41
Ratio of girls to boys in primary and secondary education (%)	91	—
ENVIRONMENT		
Agricultural land (% of land area)	54.9	—
Energy Use (kg of oil equivalent per capita)	484	—
Electric power consumption (Kwh per capita)	482	—

Source: World Bank.

A comparative study of some of the human development indices of South Asian countries *vis-à-vis* their developed counterparts in Asia or the west give an idea about the difference between the regions. The birth rates, for example are much higher than their counterparts in the west.

Table 4: Birth Rate, Crude (Per 1,000 People) in South Asian Countries[16]

Country Name	*2007*	*2008*
Afghanistan	47	47
Bangladesh	22	21
Bhutan	22	21
India	23	23
Maldives	19	19
Nepal	26	25
Pakistan	30	30
Sri Lanka	19	19

In comparison the birthrates in the developed countries of the west and Asia are lower.

Table 5: Birth Rates in Some of the Countries in the West and Asia

Country Name	*2007*	*2008*
Australia	14	14
Canada	11	11
China	12	12
Japan	8.63	8.70
USA	14	14
UK	13	13

Sources: (1) United Nations Population Division. 2009. World Population Prospects: The 2008 Revision. New York, United Nations, Department of Economic and Social Affairs (advanced Excel tables), (2) Census reports and other statistical publications from national statistical offices, (3) Eurostat: Demographic Statistics, (4) Secretariat of the Pacific Community: Statistics and Demography Programme, and (5) U.S. Census Bureau: International Database.

Table 6: Death Rate, Crude (Per 1,000 People) in South Asia [17]

Country Name	*2007*	*2008*
Afghanistan	20	20
Bangladesh	6.71	6.59
Bhutan	7.21	7.12
India	7.40	7.40
Maldives	4.62	4.57
Nepal	6.55	6.41
Pakistan	7.03	6.92
Sri Lanka	5.80	5.80

Sources: (1) United Nations Population Division. 2009. World Population Prospects: The 2008 Revision. New York, United Nations, Department of Economic and Social Affairs (advanced Excel tables), (2) Census reports and other statistical publications from national statistical offices, (3) Eurostat: Demographic Statistics, (4) Secretariat of the Pacific Community: Statistics and Demography Programme, and (5) U.S. Census Bureau: International Database.

Life expectancy at birth indicates the number of years a newborn infant would live if prevailing patterns of mortality at the time of its birth were to stay the same throughout its life. Life expectancy at birth in particularly low in conflict-prone Afghanistan and on an average the rate is lower for south Asian countries than their counterparts in the west.

Table 7: Life Expectancy at Birth in South Asia

Country Name	*2007*	*2008*
Afghanistan	44	44
Bangladesh	66	66
Bhutan	66	66
India	63	64
Maldives	71	72
Nepal	66	67
Pakistan	66	67
Sri Lanka	74	74

Sources: Male and female life expectancy source: (1) United Nations Population Division. 2009. World Population Prospects: The 2008 Revision. New York, United Nations, Department of Economic and Social Affairs (advanced Excel tables), (2) Census reports and other statistical publications from national statistical offices, (3) Eurostat: Demographic Statistics, (4) Secretariat of the Pacific Community: Statistics and Demography Programme, and (5) U.S. Census Bureau: International Database.

Table 8: Life Expectancy at Birth for other Countries

Country Name	*2007*	*2008*
Australia	81	81
Canada	81	81
China	73	73
Japan	83	83
USA	78	78
UK	80	80

Apart from these factors, majority of States in the region have failed to evolve into stable and successful political units. The countries are chronically threatened by intra-state tensions arising from various forces (ranging from identity based variables to political dissidence, dynamics of democracy) that exploit governments' inadequacies resulting in a perpetual pressure on political 'order'. Countries like Pakistan and Bangladesh adequately fit into the term 'Garrison States'[18] for they have dwindled between pseudo-democracies to military-authoritarian systems. Relatively, participatory democracies have done no better; Sri Lanka and India and the newly included Afghanistan present a rather confusing picture of their performances. These countries are plagued by dissension of various hues and magnitudes, thus forcing one to question the nature of their democratic polity. It would be better to club Bhutan, Nepal, and Maldives as countries bearing political legacies marked by pre-dominant leadership thus making political alternatives almost non-viable.[19] Political instability has evolved as a serious concern as all these countries struggle towards what Huntington would describe as 'democratic consolidation'.[20] Much of the democratic picture is distorted by the increasing allegations of human rights violations as states have increasingly concentrated on their 'police' role. Moreover, all the nations also face the pernicious evils—endemic corruption, social exclusion and inefficient civil services—that plague them uniformly.[21]

Collectively, South Asia also is seen as a region of non-performing democracies struggling to improve their unsatisfactory economic conditions. As post-colonial units, the countries opted for a basic state structure in close resemblance to democratic welfarism. Their failure to attain the minimum requirements of limiting (thus controlling) population, raising the rate of literacy and securing employment makes every governmental effort at enhancing the economic profile of the country simply self-defeating. Contemporary projections of the World Bank for 2025 put India's population at 1.3 billion, Pakistan's at 244 million, Bangladesh's at 180 million, Nepal's at 38 million and Sri Lanka's at 24 million.[22] Such tremendous population pressure is feared to undermine economic growth and progress. South Asia has a large population living in poverty and misery. At the turn of the 21st Century, World Bank showed that South Asia was one of those regions where the number of people earning less than $1 a day had risen over 500 million.[23] The failure of the respective South Asian governments to deliver the basic benefits of economic growth has raised the issue of deprivation that can be qualified through the various socio-economic issues that constitute the non-conventional aspect of national security—gender issues, health problems, education, problem of child labour to name only a few.

South Asia is fast emerging as an area with lukewarm gender sensitivity which finds expression in female infanticide, female malnutrition, denial of basic healthcare, and education to the girl child and increasing rate of violence against women. A recent study on education and girl child in South Asia, gives a very detailed picture of the kind deprivation and victimisation they face. The factors that are responsible are not only of social or religious character but are also found in extreme economic conditions of abject poverty and political situations like wars and conflicts.[24] Human trafficking and flesh trade in South Asia are almost beyond control and are related to a wide array of factors staring from mainly—social traditional role demarcation[25] to situations related to the problems of Internally Displaced Persons (IDP), refugees and migrants. Often forced prostitution is accompanied by kidnapping and violence. However, violence against women is an act occurring at random. A presentation on the various aspects of such violence relates to a plethora of acts ranging from child infanticide to forced prostitution, marital rapes, honour killings, acts of *Sati*, declining state of women's health, particularly, vulnerability to the dreaded HIV and denial of medical attention.[26]

Table 9 throws light on education and political participation of women in the different South Asian countries.

It is needless to say that there is a non-dissociable relation between population explosion, health hazards and a host of other problems. A large section of the South Asian population comprises of children and women who are victims of various health problems. It is reflective of the failure of the governments to achieve the much required population control. However, what is of serious concern to the South Asian countries are the rising threats of epidemic health hazards ranging from post natural disaster epidemics to tuberculosis and HIV/AIDS. A World Bank Report adequately analyses the fallout of health problems, particularly epidemic attacks that are certainly applicable to South Asia, "In many developing countries, injuries, HIV/AIDS, and TB could shave several points off the GDP growth rate by winnowing the number of prime age adults. Together with increased outlays on those suffering from chronic psychiatric ailments, these diseases could also substantially raise expenditures on health care". The states are further challenged by the inability to control the movement of infected persons across the region as IDPs and illegal migrants.

The success of a democratic welfare polity depends much on the responsible role of the society and the government as well. Education is therefore an indispensable ingredient in the making of a conscious and capable society that is able to contribute to the positive functioning

Table 9: Education and Political Participation of Women

Country	*Adult Literacy Rates (%) (ages 15 and older) 2004*		*Literate Women as Per cent of Literate Men*	*Girls Share of Primary Enrollment*	*Girls Share of Secondary Enrollment*	*Women's Share of Tertiary Education*	*% of Parliamentary seats in Single or Lower Chamber Occupied by Women*
	Men	*Women*					
1	14	15	16	17	18	19	20
Afghanistan	43	13	36	29	16	20	27
Bangladesh	54	41	60	50	51	32	15
Bhutan	-	-	-	47	51	34	3
India	73	48	67.7	47	43	38	8
Maldives	96	96	98.3	48	52	70	12
Nepal	63	35	60.1	46	45	28	17
Pakistan	64	35	53.1	41	41	43	21
Sri Lanka	92	89	96.1	49	49	-	5

Sources: Columns 14, 15, 16 – Human Development Report 2007/2008.
For Afghanistan – Human Development Report, 2006.

of the kind of socio-political system that we see in South Asia. Unfortunately, the region has a rather sad record of successful literacy. It is interesting to learn that the children who have been enrolled in some kind of school is above 80 per cent for most of South Asia. However, it is disheartening to learn that the fraction of children who are able to continue up to fifth grade (completing primary education) is rather low.[27] In fact, in India, the percentage of children that continue with their education is less than 60 per cent. Pakistan is known as a nation of dropouts and the literacy rate is less than 50 per cent.[28] Other nations are not doing much better. Poor and inadequate education leads to further social complications like stagnation in economic performance, unemployment, social disharmony, rise in socio-economic crimes, and the overall failure of a democratic system to achieve stability and progress. Moreover, young generations without proper education fall prey to cheap unskilled labour making the issue of child and forced labour a serious issue all over South Asia. Around the turn of the century a report by the World Bank Group sees that even after a conservative estimate, some 20-30 million child labour forces live in the five large South Asian countries. The picture is likely to look bleaker as in 2000 it was reported that for the year 2000, the ILO estimated 601,000 economically active children in Afghanistan, 269,000 girls and 332,000 boys between the ages of 10-14, representing 24.2 per cent of this age group.[29] Forced child labour is also associated with other kinds of insecurity problems such as forced recruitment in terrorist outfits. In Afghanistan, children were pulled out of school to join various armed groups[30] and in Sri Lanka, LTTE is known for its recruitment of children as fighters.[31] Therefore, states are feared to face the challenge of dissident movements so long as the non-state forces take advantage of the uneducated younger generation of South Asia.

Environmental issues are gaining increased attention as they have begun to challenge the concept of good governance. In South Asia, the issue of environmental problems must be seen in close association with the concept of development which is fundamental to the success of democratic welfarism in South Asian systems. However, the delicate balance between environmental securities and the need for economic development has been seriously disturbed by the chronic problem of poverty.[32] Therefore, the idea of sustainable development can deliver desired goods when poverty is a lesser challenge. As long as poverty dominates the development trajectory, threats of resource depletion increase, and so do conflicts over them. Over exploitation of resources will exacerbate the pauperisation of those denied of resources. Therefore, there continues to be a relentless process of bickering and conflicts (more often than not accompanied by violence) over land masses, forest areas, and water bodies. Poverty and environmental degradation appears not only to be mutually reinforcing, but also creating a vicious circle which has engulfed a large section of the masses of South Asia. The challenge of environmental insecurity for the states of the region is not likely to be quelled in the near future because of the institutional drawbacks within the region.

With the pre-occupation of this notion of nation building one major aspect of the same was neglected or at least not handled carefully. That is the 'political accommodation' of various identities that populate most of the South Asian states. Except Maldives and Bhutan all South Asian states are multi-ethnic, multi-cultural, multi-religious, and even multi-linguistic. These identities command the primordial loyalties. "People are not willing to give up their petty loyalties and nor are they ready to accept and accommodate other faiths".[33] The persistence of these primordial identities and their manifestations in the form of demands of 'proto-nationality'[34] or assertions of sub-national identities can be ascribed to the failure of South Asian states to deliver up to the expectations of their citizens resulting in a sense of economic deprivation of different communities. The absence of a well articulated national identity for the sub-groups of these multi-group societies, and the growing economic disparity among communities have created a fertile ground for the rise of sub-national identities within each of the South Asian states.

Almost all the states of South Asia face threats from assertions of sub-national identities having regional consequences. India, being a vast country of more than 1 billion, houses all the major religions of the world and contains within its boundary numerous ethnic communities. Since independence, it has witnessed sub-national identity problems of various natures. Without listing all of them only the case of its north-east region may suffice to substantiate the arguments. At least "30 armed resurgent groups operate in this region of India with demands varying from secession to autonomy and right of self-determination".[35] Pakistan faces similar problems in Baluchistan, Paktunistan, Sindh, and the erstwhile East Pakistan (now the sovereign state of Bangladesh). "The regional assertion based on the ethnic identities came to the fore in more pronounced ways in the 1990s. Ethnic disaffection was simmering in Baluchistan and North West Frontier Province (NWFP) since the 1970s. Similarly, the Mohajirs of Pakistan were emerging as an important ethnic group with the growth of Muhajir Qaumi Movement (MQM) since the 1980s as a major force in Urban centres in Sindh, especially in Karachi and the twin city of Hyderabad. The Sindhi assertion has long been there since 1950s".[36] Though Bangladesh remains largely free from ethnic violence, increasing use of its territory by religious extremists, pan-Islamist terrorist outfits, and insurgents operating in India's Northeast, constitute serious internal security threats for Bangladesh. The violent movement in the Chittagong Hills Tracts (CHT), brought to an end through an Accord in 1997, still remains a matter of concern. The assertion of Tamil identity in Sri Lanka is a well-documented fact. These identities transcend the political boundaries and form nexus with similar forces in the region and pose serious existential challenges to the South Asian states. Identifying this nexus among the militant groups P. Sahadevan writes:

> Most of the militant groups in India's northeast have forged operational co-ordination or strategic alliances against the Central government in their separate fight for their cause. A military nexus between Khalistan and Kashmir militants seemed to have existed during the Punjab crisis. While waging a war against the Sri Lankan Army and the Indian Peacekeeping Force (IPKF) in Sri Lanka, the Liberation Tigers of Tamil Eelam (LTTE) had allegedly cultivated or developed military network with a number of militant groups in India. At the height of the movement for Baluchistan there was a convergence of Baluch and Pakhtun forces against the Pakistani government. Later, in 1986, the Sindhis joined them to form a common political front. The Chakma rebels of the Chittagong Hill Tracts (CHT) of Bangladesh maintained military contacts with the insurgents in India's northeast.[37]

The dimensions of the non-conventional security issues further reiterate the common observation that "the extent of human deprivation of the masses of South Asia is colossal".[38] A volley of statistics can be hurled at the respective states to prove the extent of their failure to provide the basics of decent livelihood—being looked into as the lack of 'good governance'. The allegation of poor governance clubbed with that of multifaceted deprivation is stronger because the region is one of the most militarised zones of the world. Most of the countries have elaborate defence budgets. There is also a need to understand that the severity of deprivation has nourished the ground for anti-state activities well galvanised by primordial and other cultural ties. The states of the region only face the symptomatic challenges of what lie beneath such primordial claims. As the parameters of non-conventional challenges to security continue to expand, South Asian states are destined to be engulfed with the very realistic challenge of maintaining cohesion and order within their countries. In the case of South Asia, conventional and non-conventional security challenges seem to be mutually reloaded. If the South Asian states "focused primarily on military solutions to the problems of national security, the non-military tasks are likely to grow ever more difficult to accomplish and dangerous to neglect".[39] South Asian states can be best described as frogs floating on water that is being gently boiled without realising that the slowly increasing heat of the water is threatening their existence.[40]

Observations

Contemporary Afghanistan is a complex environment characterised by powerful and competing agendas. While there have been development successes, most notably in health and education, the optimism that flourished in the few years after 2001 has much diminished. While there have been successes on several fronts, there is no room for complacency. The country's newly-established democratic process has already been undermined by widespread vote rigging, and conflict is causing increasing numbers of civilian and military deaths each year. Afghanistan remains one of the poorest countries in the world, one that will be dependent on international aid for years to come. An autonomous and modernising Afghan state requires governance systems that are effective and accountable. While there has been heavy investment in building a strong centralised state, this has not been complemented by commensurate attention to local government at the provincial and district level. As a result of this neglect the separation of powers between the executive, legislature, and judiciary is not clear at a local level; local governance policy is too complex and confused, legislation on local representative bodies fails to devolve power or responsibility in any meaningful way; donor policies have contributed to the lack of co-ordination of government structures.[41] Co-ordination among government structures remains imperative for promotion of human security as a state policy.

The complexity of pursuing human security objectives through military means is clearly evident upon an examination of the international effort in Afghanistan. The practice, so far, in Afghanistan have not been consistent with the stated valuation of human security and the protection of Afghan civilians. The failure to protect human security is twofold: first, international forces have inadequately addressed the threat posed to civilians by the Taliban insurgency and associated terrorist groups. Second, the tactics employed by international military forces have failed to adequately discriminate between civilians and combatants and have directly resulted in increasing numbers of civilian casualties. These failings indicate that there is sufficient violation of the emergent international doctrine of human security, and serious questions to the validity of official claims that the international communities are protecting the human security of civilians in Afghanistan. Moreover, it is argued that the effective application of the principles of human security to the conduct of counterinsurgency (COIN) by international military forces would greatly improve the likelihood of success in the long-term Afghan state-building project.

Afghanistan's human security threat constitute a larger regional threat because it can be argued that lack of human security remains one of the major causes of regional threats like insurgency, terrorism, arms trafficking, drugs trafficking which have trans-national connotation. In order to address these interconnected problems, states need to co-operate in a regime to tackle the issue. Regional institutions should be developed within regional organisations like the SAARC. After decades of instability, Afghanistan faces new challenges, yet has an opportunity to realise its potential as a "land bridge" between Central Asia, South Asia and the West Asian region. At the 14th South Asian Association for Regional Co-operation (SAARC) summit, President of Afghanistan H.E. Mr Hamid Karzai asserted that "Afghanistan's political and economic isolation must never be repeated. Instead, enhanced economic co-operation must be pursued for the sake of regional economic and political stability". Regional organisations should build the capacity of institutions to deal with the human security threats because the ability of humanitarian disaster, instability, and poverty to create displacement and migration, promote illicit trans-border economies and provide support for terrorist networks, have revealed that all countries and regions are radically interdependent and interconnected.

Human security provides the conceptual bridge capable of linking military tactics with the broader strategic objectives being pursued by the international community in Afghanistan. Application of the principles of human security is a means by which the deficiencies of past military practice may be redressed, and which will likely result in greater success for both the state-building and counterinsurgency aspects of the Afghan mission. An international military operation grounded on human-centric principles, primarily preservation of the lives of Afghan civilians, is more likely to realise success in its ultimate goal of winning the support of the Afghan people and reducing their co-operation with and toleration of the Taliban-led insurgency. While effective counterinsurgency and human security are not synonymous, they are synchronous, meaning that the successful application of one is likely to result in advancements towards or satisfaction of the other. As described by recent changes to American counterinsurgency doctrine: "the cornerstone of any COIN effort is establishing security for the civilian populace. Without a secure environment, no permanent reforms can be implemented and disorder spreads". Strategies in any sector that improve human security will contribute towards the efficacy of counterinsurgency, and effective COIN will result in improved human security for the Afghan people. When combined, the application of human security principles to the execution of counterinsurgency will result in the most likely satisfaction of the objectives of both.

Developing a Human Security Paradigm

While there is broad agreement on what constitutes threats to human security, effective strategies to achieve this goal can be devised only by factoring in the socio-political context of the problems and conflicts. For this, a more focussed and yet dynamic definition of human security that lends itself to reinterpretation within specific political, economic, and cultural contexts is needed. Kanti Bajpai proposes a 'Human Security Audit' to measure the *"direct and indirect threats* to individual bodily safety and *freedom the capacity to deal with threats*, namely, the fostering of norms, institutions, and democratisation/representativeness in decision-making structures".[42] This index suggested by Kanti Bajpai, with qualitative and quantitative inputs is a step towards greater clarity in conceptualising human security. This application of this index along the same lines as the Human Development Index and the Humane Governance Index formulated by Mabbub-ul-Haq, enables an identification of problem areas for each country and consequently is a valuable tool in addressing problems of human security.[43] While King and Murray provide a fair list of issues to be addressed under the agenda of human security, Bajpai provides a useful tool to implement the agenda of human security. A human security audit would not only help identifying all the issues that are perceived to be threats by the population but also would provide flexibility to accommodate emerging human security issues and to eliminate the addressed issues.

The most interesting aspect of human security is the argument that security has to be analysed from the perspective of individual as an entity. There are differences in determining the core values of human security but it is not that important so far as the idea is concerned. The analytical core of human security is its emphasis on the individuals. The idea of human security becomes clear when the objective of human security is taken into account. It tries to eliminate conditions that give rise to conflict and insecurity. Secondly, it tries to change aims, identities, and aspirations. Thirdly, it ensures livelihoods opportunities for individuals. Given these core concepts of human security its plausibility of being applied to the security scenario of South Asia is evident. The problems of food security, health security, community security, personal security, all have a dimension that can be effectively dealt with only through a combination of social reform and state action.

Insecurity in the South Asian region not only has military connotation but also has economic and socio-political connotations. The core of the insecurity situation in the region is related to the sense of relative deprivation *vis-à-vis* the idea of "Nation". The violent manifestations in the form of insurgency and terrorism are most often related to real and at times imaginary deprivations. The state centric approach adopted by the South Asian nation-states has failed to assure the people of the region of the intent of the nation states to assimilate the people of the region in the national mainstreams. The available alternative approach that can be used to address the security concerns of the South Asian region is regional integration but the two pre-conditions essential for regional integration, i.e., (a) Matured nationalism, and (b) Parity in Economic standards is lacking in this region. Regional associations like SAARC have not been successful in fashioning co-operative relations between South Asian countries as the strategies for conflict resolution have been premised on the use of force.

Therefore, a new approach must be developed on the basis of reconstructed idea of security that addresses the issue of 'sense of relative deprivation' and the issue of non-functionality of the nation-states of the region. To succeed in implementing the human security agenda South Asian states must functionally disinvest themselves. They should create institutions involving stakeholders in various issues related to the human security needs of the general population of the region. Some scholars doubt the validity of human security approach precisely on the ground that the list under human security is unending and thus unusable. But a list of human security issues can be prepared that would narrow human security to workable levels. The *Human Development Report* of 1994 itself identifies seven dimensions of human security: personal, environmental, economic, political, community, health, and food security. Scholars like Gary King and Christopher Murray advance the idea of preventing the population from slipping into the condition of generalised poverty.[44] Further, they identify five indicators to measure human security for the individual and the group and those are: poverty, health, education, political freedom, and democracy.[45]

In South Asia, the issues of territorial sovereignty still prevail. The post-colonial processes of nation-building are still in progress in this region and the resultant friction of identities has revealed itself in territorial disputes between India and her neighbours. Further, while the end of the Cold War mitigated the threat of nuclear war between the superpowers, the possibility of nuclear conflict exists in South Asia making the conflict prone situation more dangerous. These territorial disputes pose a tangible threat to state security and the violent strategies adopted by states to solve these disputes seriously endanger human security. The latter problem, however, cannot be addressed in isolation of the threats to state security. In this case, then human security is entwined with state security and each becomes an aspect of the other.

In the context of South Asia, the real and perceived victims can be made part of the process of addressing their grievances. Every issue identified through periodic human security audit must be addressed through an institution created specifically for that purpose. Such institutions would be known as 'functional institutions'[46] involving not only government but also non-government stakeholders, such as, representatives of the states, technocrats, and civil society representatives. This will address the prime problem of erasing the idea that the nation-states are not functioning, and most importantly the sense of relative deprivation could be arrested from getting manifested in more and more ways. Real participation in the process of amelioration of grievances would reduce the incentive to participate in activities that impedes the development of the region. The institutions created on specific issues will be secular (not based on primordial identities) and temporary thus would never jeopardise the legitimacy of the state. Further, accountable functioning of the functional institutions would add strength to the nation-states' ability to deliver and would thus facilitate the integration of various primordial identities into the national mainstreams of the nation states they are part of. However, the SAARC can be useful in formulating strategies based upon the human security approach wherein the security of one state is not the cause of insecurity for its neighbour.

The solution for the problem of the region, if any, lie in greater democratisation of conflict resolution mechanisms between states. A broader political process that gives representation to people directly affected by territorial conflicts and working on human security components into conflict prevention and conflict resolution strategies is required. The objective should be the gradual upgradation of non-violent strategies of conflict resolution to form the core of foreign policies in this region. An incremental approach with state and non-state actors playing reciprocally strengthening roles, rather than a polarised approach stressing only one aspect of the problem, is more likely to succeed in South Asia.

NOTES

1. Rationalisation implies that states try to ensure perpetual security.
2. Hans J. Maorgenthau, *Politics Among Nations: A struggle for Power and Peace*, 3rd edn., Knopf, New York, 1965, p. 28. Also see, E.H. Carr, *The Twenty Years Crisis 1919-1939: An Introduction to the Study of International Relations*, Macmillan, London, 1966.
3. Binoda Kumar Mishra, "Constructing South Asian Security: Breaking Away From the (In)Security Complex", Paula Banerjee and Amrita Dey (eds.), Security Dilemmas of South and South-East Asia, Frontpage, Kolkata, 2012, pp.31-57.
4. For a detailed discussion on Kenneth N. Waltz's neo-realist approach, see Kenneth N. Waltz, *Theory of International Politics*, Addison-Wesley, Reading, Mass., 1979.
5. Kenneth N. Waltz, "The Emerging Structure of International Politics", in Michael E. Brown, Sean M. Lynn-Jones, and Steven E. Miller (eds.), *The Perils of Anarchy: Contemporary Realism and International Security*, The MIT Press, Cambridge, Massachusetts, London, 1995, p. 42. For a complete discussion on Waltz's argument on the utility of Nuclear Weapons for ensuring international peace, see Kenneth N. Waltz, "The Spread of Nuclear: The More May Be Better", *Adelphi Paper*, No. 171, International Institute for Strategic Studies,

London, 1981. For Mearsheimer's argument on Bi-Polarity and International Stability, See John J. Mearsheimer, "Back to the Future: Instability in Europe After the Cold War", *International Security*, Vol. 15, No. 1, Summer 1990, pp.5-56.

6. John H. Herz introduced the term 'Security Dilemma' in the early 1950s. For more, see John H. Herz, "Idealist Internationalism and the Security Dilemma", *World Politics*, Vol. 2, 1950, pp. 157-80; John H. Herz, *Political Realism and Political Idealism*, University of Chicago Press, Chicago, 1951.
7. Barry Buzan, *People, States, and Fear: The National Security Problem in International Relations*, Wheatheaf Books Ltd., Sussex, 1983, p. 3.
8. See, Waheguru Pal Singh Sidhu and Jing-dong Yuan, *China and India: Cooperation or Conflict?,*: India Research Press, New Delhi, pp. 45-78
9. Binoda Kumar Mishra, "Constructing South Asian Security: Breaking Away From the (In)security Complex". Paper presented at a Two-day International Seminar on The Current Security Scenario in South and Southeast Asia, 25-26 March 2008, University of Calcutta.
10. Moonis Ahmar, "South Asian Security in the New Millennium", in Rajesh M. Basrur, *Security in the New Millennium: Views from South Asia*, India Research Press, New Delhi, 2001, p. 204.
11. The degree and extent of such policies by Bangladesh varies from regime to regime. But an anti-India posturing is considered expedient for the promotion of national interest.
12. Recent demand by the Nepal political elite to do away with the Indo-Nepal Friendship treaty of 1950 points to this attitude. Jehan Perera argues that "India tends to demand a high price in terms of exclusive relations" with its smaller neighbours. For details, see Jehan Perera, "Indo-Sri Lanka Relations: Recent Trends", in Deve Raj Dahal and Nischal Nath Pandey (eds.) *Comprehensive in South Asia*, Manohar Publications, New Delhi for Friedrich Ebert Stiftung, Kathmandu and Institute of Foreign Affairs, Kathmandu, 2006, p. 107.
13. Muhammad Jamshed Iqbal, "SAARC: Origin, Growth, Potential and Achievements", *Pakistan Journal of History & Culture*, Vol. 27, No. 2, 2006, p. 132. Available at, http://www.nihcr.edu.pk.
14. Dr. Muhammad Aslam Khan, "SAARC: Achievements and limitations", *South Asian News Agency*, www.sananews.com.pk.
15. Ibid.
16. Crude birth rate indicates the number of live births occurring during the year, per 1,000 population estimated at midyear. Subtracting the crude death rate from the crude birth rate provides the rate of natural increase, which is equal to the rate of population change in the absence of migration, http://data.worldbank.org/indicator/SP.DYN.CBRT.IN (accessed on 12.4.2010).
17. Crude death rate indicates the number of deaths occurring during the year, per 1,000 population estimated at midyear. Subtracting the crude death rate from the crude birth rate provides the rate of natural increase, which is equal to the rate of population change in the absence of migration, http://data.worldbank.org/indicator/SP.DYN.CDRT.IN (accessed on 12.3.2010).
18. The term has been used by Monica Bhanot for Pakistan, however the influence

of the army in Bangladesh politics is no lesser and therefore the term may also be applied, for Bangladesh. See Monica Bhanot, *op. cit.* no. 8.

19. Nepal has recently turned democratic again but far short of achieving political stability.
20. Huntington has discussed elaborately on the conditions for democratic transitions and consolidation in third world countries; he also sees the difficulties in achieving democratic consolidation. For a in depth idea see, Samuel P. Huntington, *The Third Wave: Democratization in the Late Twentieth Century* (Norman: University of Oklahama, 1991).
21. See "Overview" in *Human Development in South Asia 1999, The Crisis of Governance,* (for The Mahbub ul Haq Human Development Centre, New York: Oxford University Press, 1999), p. 3.
22. Monica Bhanot, *op. cit.* no. 9.
23. See "Figure 11" in "Entering the 21st Century", *World Development Report 1999/2000,* (New York: Oxford University Press, 2000), p. 25.
24. Alexandra Mathieu, "Reaching the Girls in South Asia: Differentiated Needs and Responses in Emergencies", *Report by the United Nations Children's Emergency Fund and United Nations Girls' Education Initiative,* March 2006, http://www.ungei.org/resources/files/unicef_Reachinggirlsinsouthasia.pdf.
25. For example, in Nepal, the Badi tribe carries the tradition of their women providing entertainment to the feudal lords. In India there is the notorious practice of Devdasis and Deukis related to temple sex not to forget the tradition of 'Baiji Kothas' who entertained the rich and the powerful.
26. Radhika Coomaraswamy, "The Various Contours of Violence Against Women in South Asia", *Paper presented at the Fifth South Asia Ministerial Conference Celebrating Beijing Plus Ten,* organized by Government of Pakistan and UNIFEM South Asian Regional Office, Islamabad, Pakistan, 3-5 May 2005.
27. "Education in South Asia", report by *The South Asian,* September 26, 2004, http://www.thesouthasian.org/archives/2004/education_in_south_asia.html.
28. "Pakistan is a Nation of Dropouts", report by *One World South Asia,* October 7, 2006, http://southasia.oneworld.net/article/view/134044/1/.
29. "Afghanistan in Reports on the worst form of Child Labour" *The Global March Against Child Labour,* http://www.globalmarch.org/resourcecentre/world/afganistan.pdf.
30. Ibid. To learn more on Child recruitments in Afghanistan see, "Afghanistan: Children Devasted by War, Afghanistan's Lost Generation", *Report by Amnesty International,* November 1, 1999, http://web.amnesty.org/library/Index/engASA110131999.
31. For details on the process of recruitment of children to the LTTE see, "Living in Fear: Child Soldiers and the Tamil Tigers in Sri Lanka", *Report by the Human Rights Watch,* Vol. 13(C), November 2004, http://hrw.org/reports/2004/srilanka1104/2.htm.
32. For a good overview on this aspect of poverty's role in exacerbating environmental complications, see, Adil Najam, "The Human Dimensions of Environmental Insecurity: Some Insights From South Asia", http://wwics.si.edu/topics/pubs/najam.pdf.

33. Mini Pathak, "Problems of Nation-Building and Inter-State Relations in South Asia", in Gopal Singh and Ramesh Chauhan (eds.), *South Asia Today*, Anamika Publishers, New Delhi 2005, p.137.
34. Proto-Nationality refers to Replication of the concept of the nation-state.
35. Wasbir Hussain, "India's North-East: The Problem—Part 1", *Manipur Online*, May 9, 2006, http://www.manipuronline.com/North-East/May2006/NEtheproblem09_1.htm.
36. Sudhir K. Singh, "Ethnicity and Regional Aspirations in Pakistan", *J&K Insights*, http://www.jammu-kashmir.com/insights/insight20020101d.html.
37. P. Sahadevan, *op. cit.* no. 1.
38. Bhanot, *op. cit.* no. 2, p.3.
39. Richard Ullman, "Redefining Security", *International Security*, Vol. 8, No.1, 1983, p. 153.
40. Robert Ornstein and Paul Ehrlich originally used this analogy to criticise the realists for overemphasizing the short term territorial security needs and ignore other non-conventional domestic security threats. See, Robert Ornstein and Paul Ehrlich, *New World, New Mind* (London: Methun, 1989) p. 74, Cited in Ken Booth, "Security in Anarchy: Utopian Realism in Theory and Practice", *International Affairs*, Vol. 67, No. 3, 1991, p. 538.
41. Douglas Saltmarshe and Abhilash Medhi, *Local Governance in Afghanistan:A View from the Ground*, AREU Synthesis chapter, AREU, Kabul, June 2011.
42. For details on Human Security Audit, see Kanti P. Bajpai, "Human Security: Concept and Measurement", *Kroc Institute Occasional Paper*, No 19:OP:1, August 2000. Available at, http://www.nd.edu/?krocinst/ocpapers/po_19_1.pdf
43. Sonika Gupta, " Dilimiting Human Security", ISYP Conference, on "Advancing Human Security", Halifax, Nova Scotia, July 15-17, 2003.
44. The concept of 'generalised poverty' include not only income but also the deprivation of any basic capabilities. For details, see Gary King and Christopher J. L. Murray, "Rethinking Human Security", *Political Science Quarterly*, Vol. 116, No. 4, 2001-02, pp. 585-610.
45. Gary King and Christopher Murray, ibid. p. 598.
46. The idea of functional institutions has been advocated by scholars like David Mitrany, Ernst B. Haas, B. Rosamond. To some extend Robert O. Keohane and Stanley Hoffman have also contributed to this literature. Ernst B. Haas, *The Uniting of Europe; Political, Social, and Economic Forces, 1950-1957*, Stanford: Stanford University Press, 1958, Haas, *Beyond the Nation-State: Functionalism and International Organization*, Stanford: Stanford University Press, 1964. David Mitrany, *The Progress of International Government*, New Haven: Yale University Press, 1933. Mitrany, "The Prospect of European Integration: Federal or Functional", *Journal of Common Market Studies*, 1965. Mitrany, *A Working Peace System*, Chicago: Quadrangle Books, 1966. Mitrany *The Functional Theory of Politics*, New York: St. Martin's Press, 1976. B. Rosamond, *Theories of European integration*, Macmillan, New York : St. Martin's Press, Basingstoke, 2000. R. O. Keohane, and S. Hoffmann The New European Community: Decision-making and Institutional Change. Boulder, Colorado: Westview Press, 1991. Inis L. Claude Jr., *Swords into Plowshares*, New York: Random House, 1964.

APPENDICES

APPENDIX 1

National Environmental Protection Agency Strategy for Afghanistan National Development Strategy

(WITH FOCUS ON PRIORITIZATION)

MINISTRY OFFICIAL	Sulaiman Shah Sallari
RESPONSIBLE AND DESIGNATION	Acting Executive Deputy Director
DATE OF SUBMISSION	March 15, 2007

SECTION ONE: OVERALL SECTOR GOALS AND RESULTS

1.1 Goals

To protect the environmental integrity of Afghanistan and support sustainable development of its natural resources through the provision of effective environmental policies, regulatory frameworks and management services that are also in line with the Afghanistan MDGs.

1.2 Expected Results (specific achievements with a five year perspective)

A. Priority Expected Results

1. By 2012, establishment and implementation of legal and regulatory frameworks and management services for "brown" issues, including the protection of air quality, water quality, waste management, and pollution control.
2. By 2012, establishment and implementation of legal and regulatory frameworks and management services for "green" issues, including natural resource management.
3. NEPA is capable of taking the lead in environmental management through the enhancement of its professional capacity.
4. Regular dissemination of a public environmental awareness campaign and provision of environmental information to other Government authorities.

5. Achievement of Afghanistan's MDGs related to the environment.

B. Other Expected Results

1. Improved coordination with line ministries and other government departments.
2. Support to Government and other stakeholders through the integration of environmental issues into development policies, benchmarks and government programmes.
3. Participatory processes and public awareness contribute to compliance and enforcement.

SECTION TWO: CONTEXTUAL ANALYSIS

2.1 Analysis of the Current State of the Sector

Approximately 80% of the population of Afghanistan directly relies on the natural resource base of the country to meet its daily needs. In 2003, the UNEP post-conflict environmental assessment in Afghanistan found that many livelihoods are under threat by the alarming degree of environmental degradation caused by a combination of conflict, poverty, population growth and survival tactics. Already, the lack of basic natural resources, such as clean water or trees, has lead to the collapse of many rural livelihoods, turning many people into environmental refugees and increasing population pressures in urban centres. The decline in the country's natural resource based has increased vulnerability to natural disasters and food shortages, thereby further increasing poverty and decreasing opportunities for sustainable livelihoods. Human health is also directly threatened by pollution hotspots and inadequate waste management and sanitation practices. Key aspects of Afghanistan's current state of the environment include the following:

Urban Environment. In the urban environment, human health is being placed at risk by poor solid and liquid waste management practices and a lack of uncontaminated drinking water and sanitation infrastructure. Adequate landfills do not exist in any towns and cities, and no measures are being taken in relation to existing dumpsites to prevent groundwater contamination or reduce toxic emissions arising from the burning of solid waste. Furthermore, many polluting industrial activities are being undertaken without regard for environmental protection or the health of workers.

Surface and Groundwater. Water is the key to the health and well-being of the Afghan people. Approximately 75-80% of the population requires consistent access to water to maintain agricultural production. The damage to the water resources of the country is immense. Drought and uncoordinated and unmanaged extraction of both ground and surface water resources has severely depleted the available water resource base resulting in a water quantity crisis. Similarly, water quality is threatened by contamination from waste dumps, chemicals and open sewers. Due to mismanagement of surface water, many of Afghanistan's wetlands are completely dry and no longer support wildlife populations or provide agricultural inputs.

Forests and Rangelands. The forests and woodlands of Afghanistan provide key resources for the livelihoods of the Afghan population. Timber products such as fuelwood for cooking and construction materials for shelter are extremely important for overall survival. Non-timber forest products, such as nuts, leaves, mushrooms, and forest-related flora and fauna, are also important for the food security of people. In addition, forests prevent land from eroding, and maintain an ecological balance in ecosystems and water catchment areas. Illegal harvesting is depleting forests and woodland resources rapidly, and widespread (over-grazing is preventing regeneration. Satellite analyses conducted by UNEP in 2002 revealed that conifer forests in the provinces of Nangarhar, Kunar and Nuristan have been reduced by an average of 50 percent since 1978. The loss of forests and vegetation, excessive grazing and dry land cultivation expose soil to serious erosion. As such the productivity of the land base is declining, driving people from rural to urban areas in search of food and employment.

Soils. The soils of Afghanistan are one of the most important foundations for the Afghan economy. They are the basis for agriculture and animal husbandry, and at the same time support the growth of natural vegetation. However, due to decades of overuse and poor management, many of the soils are slowly eroding and land productivity is being reduced. Some of the degradation is so severe that recovery cannot take place without human intervention. One of the most threatening impacts arising from loss of soil and vegetation is desertification and increased flood risk.

Air. Dust and vehicle emissions (exacerbated as a result of the use of lowgrade hydrocarbons) in Afghanistan's urban areas are the main factors adversely affecting air quality. Current assessments of vehicle density in the country amount to 500 000 cars, 30 000 buses and 50 000 trucks – figures that are growing rapidly. During late autumn and winter, air quality is worsened by domestic emissions arising from increased use of ovens, stoves and open fires. Electricity shortages and a lack of fuelwood mean that households resort on occasions to burning packaging materials, often resulting in the release of toxic emissions.

Wildlife and Biodiversity. Afghanistan's wildlife heritage is also under threat. Flamingos have not bred successfully in Afghanistan for four years, and the last Siberian crane was seen in 1986. While the Wakhan Corridor contains healthy populations of endangered snow leopards and other mammals, including Marco Polo sheep, active hunting is occurring in many regions of the country, either for sport, for food, or in order to supply furs for sale to foreigners in Kabul. The legal status of all protected areas is currently in question. The protected areas regulations and management plans are currently under development, but no management is taking place to protect and conserve their ecological integrity and wildlife until the regulations and management plans are finalized. Furthermore, less than one percent of the land base is contained within protected areas – none of which cover the dwindling conifer forests of the east. As Afghanistan's wildlife and biodiversity could be a critically important component for future tourism revenue, attention should be given towards protecting these resources before the opportunity is missed forever.

If the current environmental problems in Afghanistan are not addressed, the following impacts can be expected.

- Existing chemical contamination of air, soil and water resources at pollution hotspots will threaten human health and undermine workforce stability and economic productivity.
- Vulnerability to natural disasters and food shortages will increase, which will hinder development efforts and compound humanitarian crises.
- Unequal distribution of water resources could lead to severe water scarcity in some regions, threatening human livelihoods, creating environmental refugees, compounding adverse humanitarian conditions and increasing regional tensions.
- The adverse environmental impacts of reconstruction and development projects will create a large set of new environmental

problems and impacts to livelihoods if not regulated and mitigated. Addressing these problems will have significant long-term financial implications for the government of Afghanistan.

- Unsustainable use of water resources could threaten agricultural production and food security, as well as wetland ecology and biodiversity.
- Mismanagement of municipal, industrial and military wastes could lead to further contamination of air, soil, and water resources (with adverse impacts on human health and well-being, as well as the environment) and to the creation of new pollution hotspots.
- Continued deforestation combined with livestock grazing and water scarcity will lead to increased soil erosion, desertification and reduced fertility and ecosystem services.
- Continued loss of vegetation and green cover and mismanagement of soil will lead to floods, mudslides, deterioration of groundwater quality, and rapid run off of water during the wet season.
- Continued declines in biodiversity and increased listing of endangered species due to habitat loss and the lack of an effective protected areas system.
- Environmental refugees could be created due to land degradation and resource scarcity.
- Environmental investments may be conducted in an overlapping and non-coordinated way leading to inefficiency, redundancy and non-optimal use of limited resources.
- Citizens of Afghanistan will lack basic environmental information on the key problems faced by the country, and on the location of pollution hotspots.
- Donors, UN agencies and the international community will lack information on the key environmental investment needs for 2007 and beyond.

If environmental issues are not mainstreamed into the reconstruction agenda and national budget, the basic prerequisites for sustainable development will not be met.

The recent establishment of an environmental function within the centralized government system reflects Afghanistan's development priorities. Still a nascent function, environment has changed organizational location and structure since its inception. In 2002, the new function was first housed in the Ministry of Irrigation, Water Resources and Environment (MIWRE) as the Department of Environment. In January 2005, the Department of Environment was separated from MIWRE and was subsequently declared an independent Department of Environment. In May 2005 the environmental function was given the status of an independent National Environmental Protection Agency (NEPA).

2.2 Analysis of Key Strategic Elements and Processes in Past Programming that Contributed to Success

The environmental challenge for post-conflict countries involves rehabilitation of both physical degradation and the associated collapse of national and sub-national governance. To this end the focus of NEPA and the environment sector has been strengthening of environmental management capacity through: national environmental coordination; public administration reform and human resources development; environmental impact assessment; environmental legislation, regulations and standards; sub national environmental affairs and community-based natural resource management; monitoring, information and analyses; environmental policy development and planning; environmental communications, outreach and education; and multilateral agreements and regional cooperation.

2.3 Analysis of Constraints, Restraints and Assumptions

A. Regulatory and Governance Environment

The integrated nature of environmental concepts necessitates a similar system for environmental management. While NEPA is the lead government authority in regard to environmental management, other institutions are also involved. The development of environmental management in Afghanistan is co-occurring with the establishment of the overall system of governance, thus inter- and intragovernmental relationships necessary for the implementation of and compliance with relevant laws and regulations are untested. For example, land ownership disputes may affect implementation and enforcement of natural resource laws, regulations and associated government projects. The combination of the disruption of Afghanistan's system of governance and destruction of its natural resources prompted the promulgation of an Environment Law, published in the Official Gazette in January 2006, as the first legal instrument related to the country's environment. The Environment Law is based on international standards that recognize the current state of Afghanistan's environment while laying a framework for the progress of governance leading to effective environmental management. NEPA is currently developing sets of regulations under the Environment Law addressing the following sectoral areas: environmental impact assessment (EIA); integrated pollution control (IPC); protected areas management; ozone depleting substances; and compliance and enforcement.

With respect to multilateral environmental agreements and regional cooperation, Afghanistan has primarily concentrated on "green" transboundary issues concerning protection and preservation with NEPA and the Ministry of Agriculture and Irrigation dividing duties as the respective focal points. Afghanistan has signed but not ratified the Basel Convention regarding transboundary movement and disposal of hazardous waste, and is in the process of acceding to the Convention on Migratory Species (CMS) and the Ramsar Convention on Wetlands. The Ministry of Agriculture and Irrigation is the focal point for the UN Convention on Biological Diversity (UNCBD), the UN Convention to Combat Desertification (UNCCD) and the Convention on International Trade of Endangered Species (CITES).

Afghanistan has also ratified the ozone treaties, the Vienna Convention and the Montreal Protocol, and the UN Framework Convention on Climate Change (UNFCCC) with NEPA as the focal point.

B. Capacity Analysis

NEPA's capacity to implement its mandate remains relatively limited but the impending completion of the Policy, Reform and Restructuring (PRR) process will provide a stable organizational structure with staff hired under appropriate Terms of Reference following a transparent recruitment process.

The organizational transition of the environment function since 2002 has precluded the consistent development of technical and managerial skills within both NEPA and other governmental authorities involved in environmental management. Similarly, there has been little opportunity in Afghanistan's recent history to develop a functioning education and administrative system to support environmental management.

Donor attention has primarily focused on project implementation rather than integration with the government. Coordination between environmental actors and stakeholders in Afghanistan has occurred since 2002 but complimentarity and understanding of respective programmatic and budgetary needs and priorities remains sporadic. Without effective coordination, respective responsibilities and rights under the Environment Law as well as subsequent laws and regulations will restrict the government's capacity for environmental management.

C. Security Situation

The security situation may pose significant constraints on field mobility of NEPA staff and on the level of cooperation between the national, provincial and district levels of government. NEPA staff operating in southern and eastern provinces will most likely continue to experience limited mobility. However, as a regulatory and coordinating body rather than an implementing body, NEPA's primary interaction with stakeholders will be as a coordinator thereby limiting its actual field exposure.

SECTION THREE: STRATEGY

Overall Strategy for Achieving Expected Results

The initiation of the I-ANDS has provided a framework for NEPA's strategy for achieving the expected interim results for environmental management. Above all, NEPA's coordination function will ensure that environmental issues are integrated into the I-ANDS and, thus, environmental priority needs are included in Afghanistan's continued development. The growing demand from the Afghan public, international community and Government of Afghanistan for environmental information and leadership indicates that NEPA's mandate is timely and crucial.

NEPA's priority results are designed to position the environment as a key feature to Afghanistan's economic and social development. As the lead for environmental management, NEPA requires a functioning institutional structure with staff qualified to perform the necessary technical, administrative and coordination duties.

Thus the most effective strategy option for NEPA focuses on strengthening its coordination and technical capability to provide Government and other stakeholders with the tools to understand how environment is integrated into policies and activities for Afghanistan's development.

Poverty reduction: The degradation of Afghanistan's environment and natural resource base, on which its population is so heavily dependent to satisfy its livelihood needs, has led to lingering poverty and health issues. Effective environmental management will revive livelihood options based on natural resources and reduce environmental health risks that undermine workforce stability and economic productivity.

Economic growth: Afghanistan's population is largely dependent upon the country's environment and natural resources for its economic and social well-being. Improving environmental management and halting and ultimately reversing degradation to ecosystems and the natural resource base is therefore vital for the long-term economic empowerment and well-being of the Afghan people.

Productivity increase: Afghanistan's economy is currently limited to production from only a few sectors, contrary to the past where natural resources assumed a large percentage of the GNP. Strengthened environmental management will contribute to improved local production and national production as well as a healthier workforce.

Cost efficiency and cost effectiveness: The cost of Afghanistan's environmental degradation is apparent. The Environment Law and the development of associated regulations and standards will establish the Government's goals and applicable standards for environmental quality and use of resources. This system is designed to protect Afghanistan's environment while allowing for sustainable productive use. In addition, an informed and educated public will contribute to reduction in activities harmful to the environment.

Longer term sustainability: Ultimately, protecting the environment and ensuring sustainable use of natural resources (including forests and rangelands, in respect of which many local level conflicts arise) will contribute to a more secure and stable situation in Afghanistan – the basic prerequisite for sustainable long-term economic growth and social prosperity.

Potentials of external and government financing: Both external and government acknowledgement of environment as a priority to Afghanistan's development is increasing. Improved environmental management will demonstrate NEPA's ability to carry out its mandate and help the Government and external donors coordinate to determine effective and appropriate financing.

Cross-cutting issues: While environment itself is a cross-cutting issue, it features importantly in other cross-cutting issues. **Gender equity:** Female candidates recruited in previous training opportunities offered by UNEP to NEPA; gender sensitivity training was offered to numerous NEPA officials; color printed books on women and the environment have been distributed to stakeholders; women's role in environmental protection is an important aspect of public awareness; gender equity is reflected in the Environment Law. NEPA will ensure that recommendations and guidelines as outlined in the National Action Plan for the Women of Afghanistan are appropriately considered in its own workplans. **Counter Narcotics:** NEPA will eventually have the ability to monitor the toxicity of substances used in eradication campaigns. The rehabilitation of natural resources and restoration of associated livelihoods will gradually provide an incentive for poppy-growers to return to a more sustainable form of livelihood. **Regional Cooperation:** Regional cooperation on shared environmental resources is recognized as a fundamental principle in the Environment Law. NEPA is cooperating with Pakistan and Iran on ozone and wetland-related treaties. **Anti Corruption:** Appropriate checks and balances in regard to decision-making have been incorporated into the Environmental Law to deter corruption. The PRR is almost complete for both NEPA headquarters and provincial hub offices following a transparent recruitment process. NEPA will ensure that recommendations and guidelines as outlined in a National Anti-Corruption Strategy are appropriately considered in its own work plans.

SECTION FOUR: PROGRAMMING

NEPA's programming for 1386 builds upon the coordination and technical capacity building efforts initiated over the past 1.5 years with external support. The programming is categorized into the following areas that will still require significant external support:

Training and Capacity Building

- On-going professional development for NEPA staff in Kabul central and regional offices

Legal and Regulatory Frameworks

- Development of "brown" regulations and management services for the protection of air quality, water quality, waste management and pollution control
- Development of "green" regulations and management services for natural resource management

Public Information and Awareness

- Development of a National Environmental Awareness Campaign through TV and radio in rural and urban areas
- Environmental education curriculum development for primary and secondary levels with

Ministry of Education

- Development of environmental education courses with Kabul University
- Information dissemination channels established with other government authorities

Environmental Information and Policy

- Development of a national environmental data collection framework
- Biennial production of the State of the Environment report
- Development of a National Environmental Policy

Training and Capacity Building: This program and associated activities are the foundation for NEPA's strategy. NEPA staff have benefited from various training opportunities provided by partner institutions such as UNEP, ADB and ACC/UNOPS. In order to provide accurate information and effective dissemination, NEPA will initiate a comprehensive and on-going training and capacity building program with donor and implementing partners, in a phased approach, to develop and reinforce staff skills.

Legal and Regulatory Frameworks: With the promulgation of the Environment Law and recent publication of the Environmental Impact Assessment (EIA) policy and regulations, and with further regulatory instruments and a national environmental policy in the pipeline, NEPA is poised to begin educating institutions about the components of these legal instruments and their overall application, to develop the processes and systems required for implementation, and, ultimately, to begin adequately enforcing the framework. These activities are central to attainment of the environment benchmark in the I-ANDS. NEPA will begin working with relevant government authorities to develop air quality, water quality, waste management and pollution control regulations following international standards for such "brown" environmental issues. The establishment of these regulations will help mainstream the government of Afghanistan's standards for environmental quality. Similarly, further "green" or environmental protection regulations will establish the government's standards for its natural resources including forests and areas of environmental significance such as national parks.

Public Information and Awareness: Public participation is a key feature of the Environment Law and the EIA regulations, and will similarly become a component of further environmental laws and regulations. As a coordinating body, NEPA's role includes helping to inform stakeholders, including the Afghan public, of their rights under the legal and regulatory framework. Thus, NEPA will initiate a public awareness campaign in both urban and rural areas via TV and radio to disseminate messages about Afghanistan's environment and the government's decisions regarding its use and protection. NEPA will also work with the Ministry of Education and Kabul University to develop environmental materials to teach Afghan students about the relevance and importance of the environment to their daily lives and to begin building a cohort of Afghan professionals with the knowledge and ability to further environmental management in Afghanistan. Finally, NEPA will prioritize the establishment of environmental focal points in key government authorities, such as the Ministry of Agriculture, Irrigation and Livestock, the Ministry of Public Health, the Ministry of Education and municipalities to provide timely and relevant environmental information.

Environmental Information and Policy: Sound environment policy decision-making and a reliable policy analysis process depends on quality scientific information collected from reliable environmental monitoring systems. Capacity building in the area of environmental information analysis and the scientific base for policy formulation is the key towards the sustainable use of environment resources and sustainable development of the country. The absence of environmental policies and environmental monitoring will affect the development of the environment sector unless a comprehensive program is established. With stakeholder consultation, NEPA will develop and issue a National Environmental Policy, establish a regular environmental monitoring system and associated database and produce a biennial State of the Environment report to document changes in Afghanistan's environment.

SECTION FIVE: ROLE ANALYSIS

NEPA's designation as the lead agency for environmental management confers a broad coordination mandate with many partners. As a cross-cutting issue, environment is included in many of the benchmarks of the Afghanistan Compact, thus NEPA is responsible for advising the CGs and Technical Working Groups on mainstreaming environmental issues into their respective activities and those of the associated stakeholders. The Environment Law, and the subsequent development of regulations, standards and policies for the components in the Law, will articulate the rights and responsibilities of all stakeholders impacted by these legal instruments. The legal framework for Afghanistan's environmental management is nascent, but the Government recognizes that communities, particularly rural communities, have a role in the management of Afghanistan's natural resources. Therefore stipulations for community management, including rights and responsibilities for both communities and Government, are integral. Similarly, the poor and vulnerable groups whose subsistence relies on natural resources or whose health and well-being is affected by environmental conditions will feature within the rights and responsibilities for stakeholders.

NEPA's current partners include the United Nations Environment Programme, Asian Development Bank and Wildlife Conservation Society. NEPA needs significant external assistance to develop the internal capacity to conduct its mandate, thus the next 5 years comprising this Strategy are crucial for NEPA to garner the assistance necessary to develop into a self-functioning institution.

SECTION SIX: PRIORITIZATION OF PROJECTS (PROGRAM BUDGET BASED ON 5 YEARS)

Priority 1 Group (list projects in order of priority)	*Budget*	*Priority 2 Group (list projects in order of priority)*	*Budget*	*Priority 3 Group (list projects in order of priority)*	*Budget*	*Priority 4 Group (list projects in order of priority)*	*Budget*
Training and Capacity Building/Strategic planning and administrative training for Kabul central and regional staff	500,000	Programme/project 1 –		Programme/project 1 –		Programme/project 1 –	
Legal and Regulatory Framework Development/ Stakeholder consultation and outreach activities	500,000	Programme/Project 2 –		Programme/Project 2 –		Programme/Project 2 –	
Public Environmental Awareness campaign and environmental education curriculum	500,000	Programme/Project 3 –		Programme/Project 3 –		Programme/Project 3 –	
Development of informational materials for environmental focal points and other stakeholders	250,000	Programme/Project 4 –		Programme/Project 4 –		Programme/Project 4 –	
Environmental Information and Policy	500,000	Programme/Project 5 –		Programme/Project 5 –		Programme/Project 5 –	

SECTION SEVEN : MONITORING AND EVALUATION

Strategic Goal—To protect the environmental integrity of Afghanistan and support sustainable development of its natural resources

Objectives	*Expected Results*	*Indicators Risk*	*Program*
1) Deliver internal training and capacity building to NEPA staff to strengthen their technical, coordination and outreach skills; 2) Regulatory frameworks and management services established for the protection of air quality, water quality, waste management, pollution control and natural resource management; 3) Public information and awareness campaign and development of environmental education curriculum for primary, secondary and tertiary levels; 4) Environmental Information and Policy.	**Impact** 1) Environmental awareness and regulatory information accessible to the public, government and other stakeholders; 2) NEPA technical, coordination and outreach capabilities further developed; 3) Economic and business development based on the environment sector is supported	1) % NEPA staff trained in outreach, coordination and technical skills; 2) Increase in coordination meetings led by NEPA; 3) Number of environmental information materials distributed by NEPA; 4) Increase in coordination meetings led by NEPA; 5) National urban air quality, and water quality, waste management, pollution control and natural resource management standards established and approved; 6) % of population with access to public awareness programs and education; 7) Environmental information and monitoring system established;	
Project 1 – Technical, administrative/managerial and strategic planning training for Kabul central and regional office staff.	**Outcome 1 –** 1) NEPA staff trained in technical aspects related to their respective job duties; 2) Creation of strategic plan with associated coordination and annual work plans for the Kabul central and regional offices; 3) NEPA assumes more direct coordination role for environmental management stakeholders regarding laws, regulations, environmental information.	1) Increase in technical assistance to public, government, international and national institutions and other 2) Number of work plans created in association to the strategic plan; 3) Outputs based on adherence to work plans; 4) NEAC and CEC meetings held regularly; 5) Increased environmental mainstreaming related to the benchmarks provided through the ECCTG	

Project 2 – Legal and regulatory framework development	**Outcome 2 –** 1) NEPA conducts public and institutional consultation and outreach regarding the purpose and function of the Environment Law and associated regulations; 2) NEPA begins working with relevant institutions to ensure compliance with and enforcement of the Environment Law; 3) Issuance of water quality, air quality, waste management, pollution control regulations and management services; 4) Issuance of natural resource management regulations and management services.	1) Number of public consultations and outreach programs held; 2) Number of outreach and training programs held for institutional stakeholders; 3) Number of training sessions conducted for NEPA staff; 4) Number of EIA permits and pollution control licenses granted by NEPA in total; 5) Number of permits, licenses granted by NEPA or enforcement penalties issued related to water quality, air quality and waste management; 6) Issuance of protected areas regulations; 7) Effective cooperation between different parts and levels of government established.
Project 3 – Develop and disseminate a public environmental awareness campaign	**Outcome 3 –** 1) A TV/radio program about the relevance of Afghanistan's environment to daily lives and well-being broadcast in urban and rural areas; 2) Primary and secondary school environmental curriculum developed with the Ministry of Education; 3) Environmental curriculum developed with Kabul University	1) Number of TV/radio stations broadcasting the awareness campaign; 2) % of population with access to the awareness program; 3) % of primary and secondary school students receiving environmental education as part of their curriculum; 4) Number of Kabul University students enrolled in environmental education course as part of their degree.
Project 4 – Establishment of environmental monitoring and information system.	**Outcome 4 –** 1) A framework for collecting and analyzing environmental data is established; 2) Quality environmental information is used to make environmental decisions.	1) Environmental database created to store and analyse environmental data; 2) Development of a National Environmental Policy; 3) Afghanistan State of the Environment report produced and distributed.

APPENDIX 2

United Nations Security Council

Distr.: General

10 October 2013

Resolution 2120 (2013)

Adopted by the Security Council at its 7041st meeting, on 10 October 2013

The Security Council,

Reaffirming its previous resolutions on Afghanistan, in particular its resolutions 1386 (2001), 1510 (2003), 2011 (2011), 2041 (2012), 2069 (2012) and 2096 (2013),

Reaffirming also its resolutions 1267 (1999), 1368 (2001), 1373 (2001), 1822 (2008), 1904 (2009), 1988 (2011), 1989 (2011), 2082 (2012) and 2083 (2012), and *reiterating* its support for international efforts to root out terrorism in accordance with the Charter of the United Nations,

Recalling its resolutions 1265 (1999), 1296 (2000), 1674 (2006), 1738 (2006) and 1894 (2009) on the protection of civilians in armed conflict, its resolutions 1325 (2000), 1820 (2008), 1888 (2009), 1889 (2009), 1960 (2010) and 2106 (2013) on women and peace and security, and its resolutions 1612 (2005), 1882 (2009),1998 (2011) and 2068 (2012) on children and armed conflict, *noting as well* the reports of the Secretary-General on sexual violence in conflict (S/2013/149) and children and armed conflict (S/2013/245) and the conclusions of its Working Group on Children and Armed Conflict (S/AC.51/2011/3),

Reaffirming its strong commitment to the sovereignty, independence, territorial integrity and national unity of Afghanistan,

Recognizing that the responsibility for providing security and law and order throughout the country resides with the Afghan Authorities, *stressing* the role of the International Security Assistance Force (ISAF) in assisting the Afghan Government to improve the security situation and build its own security capabilities, and *welcoming* the cooperation of the Afghan Government with ISAF,

Underlining the pivotal importance of strengthening Afghan ownership and leadership, consistent with the Kabul Process, in all fields of governance,

Welcoming the conclusions of the International Conference on Afghanistan in Bonn (S/2011/762) which declared that the Process of Transition, to be completed by the end of 2014, should be followed by a Transformation Decade (2015-2024) in which Afghanistan consolidates its sovereignty through strengthening a fully functioning, sustainable state in the service of its people, and *welcoming further* the strategic consensus between the Government of Afghanistan and the International Community on a renewed and enduring partnership for this Transformation Decade based on firm mutual commitments, and *welcoming* the conclusions of the Tokyo Conference on Afghanistan (S/2012/532) and the adoption of the Tokyo Mutual Accountability Framework to support the sustainable economic growth and development of Afghanistan, in which the Afghan Government and the International Community reaffirmed their mutual commitments, as well as the outcome of the Tokyo Mutual Accountability Framework Senior Officials Meeting held in Kabul on 3 July 2013,

Recognizing once again the interconnected nature of the challenges in Afghanistan, *reaffirming* that sustainable progress on security, governance, human rights, rule of law and development as well as the cross-cutting issues of counternarcotics, anti-corruption and accountability are mutually reinforcing and that governance and development programmes prioritized for implementation in transition should be consistent with the goals set forth in the Tokyo Declaration and the National Priority Programmes and *welcoming* the continuing efforts of the Afghan Government and the international community to address these challenges through a comprehensive approach,

Stressing in this context the need for further efforts by the Afghan Government to fight corruption, promote transparency and increase its accountability, in line with the Afghan Government's commitment to strengthen measures to combat corruption as reinforced in the Tokyo Conference Conclusions and the Tokyo Mutual Accountability Framework,

Welcoming the long-term commitments taken by Afghanistan's international partners, including NATO, the European Union (EU), neighbouring states and regional partners to continue supporting

Afghanistan beyond transition, including during the Transformation Decade, *welcoming also* the process by which Afghanistan and its regional and international partners are entering into long-term strategic partnership and other agreements, aimed at achieving a peaceful, stable and prosperous Afghanistan, and *stressing* the importance of their complementary nature, including with future bilateral partnerships decided by the Government of Afghanistan,

Underlining the significance of the agreement reached between the Government of Afghanistan and countries contributing to ISAF, at the North Atlantic Treaty Organization (NATO) Summit in Lisbon, to gradually transfer full security responsibility in Afghanistan to the Government of Afghanistan countrywide by the end of 2014, *welcoming* continued progress towards the completion of the security transition, notably the 18 June 2013 milestone when all areas of Afghanistan entered the transition process and Afghan forces assumed the lead for security nationwide, *underlining* ISAF's continuing role, in support of the Government of Afghanistan, in promoting a responsible transition and the importance of the enhancement of the capabilities of the Afghan National Security Forces (ANSF),

Acknowledging the progress made and the challenges remaining in security sector reform and governance, *welcoming* the continued commitment of international partners, including NATO and the European Union, to helping the ANSF and the Afghan security sector, *welcoming* support and assistance extended to the Afghan National Police by the NATO Training Mission in Afghanistan, the European Union police mission (EUPOL Afghanistan), and the European Gendarmerie Force (EGF) and, in the context of transition, *welcoming* the increased capacities and capabilities of the ANSF, *stressing* the need for Afghanistan together with international donors to further strengthen the Afghan National Army and the Afghan National Police, *urging,* inter alia, continued professional training measures to ensure Afghan capability to assume, in a sustainable manner, increasing responsibilities and leadership of security operations and maintaining public order, law enforcement, the security of Afghanistan's borders, the preservation of the constitutional rights of Afghan citizens, and the protection of the rights of Afghan women and girls as well as to increase its efforts in disbandment of illegal armed groups and counter narcotics, as outlined most recently in the Chicago Summit Joint Declaration and the Tokyo Declaration,

Welcoming the Chicago Summit Joint Declaration on Afghanistan which stresses the long-term commitment, beyond 2014, to lasting peace, security and stability in Afghanistan, *noting* the responsibility of the Government of Afghanistan to sustain a sufficient and capable ANSF supported by the international community, *welcoming*, in this context, the decision of the international community, taken at the International Conference on Afghanistan in Bonn on 5 December 2011, to support the training, equipping, financing and capability development of the ANSF beyond the end of the transition period, *welcoming* as reaffirmed in the Chicago Summit Joint Declaration the financial sustainment of the ANSF with a clear view to the assumption, no later than 2024, of full financial responsibility for its own security forces by the Government of Afghanistan, *welcoming* the decision of the Government of Afghanistan and NATO for NATO to work towards continuing to train, advise and assist the ANSF post-2014, and *noting* that any new mission should have a sound legal basis, as stated in paragraph 14 of the Chicago Summit Joint Declaration on Afghanistan,

Welcoming the commitment of Afghanistan and its regional partners, with the support of the international community, to strengthen regional security and cooperation for a secure and stable Afghanistan, *welcoming* regional initiatives on Afghanistan such as the Heart of Asia Process on Regional Security and Cooperation for a Secure and Stable Afghanistan, the Regional Economic Cooperation Conference on Afghanistan (RECCA) initiative as well as initiatives such as those being implemented in the framework of the South Asian Association for Regional Cooperation (SAARC), the Shanghai Cooperation Organization (SCO), the Collective Security Treaty Organization (CSTO), the EU, the Organization for Security and Cooperation in Europe (OSCE) and other relevant initiatives aimed at increased regional economic cooperation with Afghanistan such as enhanced trade, infrastructural connectivity and strengthened local and regional networks of transportation along historical trade routes, energy supply, integrated border management, *welcoming* the outcome of the "Istanbul Conference for Afghanistan: Security and Cooperation in the Heart of Asia" of 2 November 2011 and the follow-up "Heart of Asia-Ministerial conference Kabul" on 14 June 2012, and the Heart of Asia Ministerial Conference in Almaty on 26 April 2013, at which implementation plans of all confidence-building measures in the areas of disaster management, counter-terrorism, counter-narcotics, regional infrastructure, trade, commerce and investment opportunities and education were adopted, and the Senior Officials Meeting in New York on 23 September 2013, and *looking forward* to the Fourth Heart of Asia Ministerial Conference in Tianjin, China, in 2014, *noting* that the Heart of Asia process is intended to complement and cooperate with, and not substitute for, existing efforts of regional organizations, particularly where they relate to Afghanistan,

Recognizing the importance of the contribution of neighbouring and regional partners as well as regional organizations including the EU, OSCE, SCO, CSTO and SAARC to the stabilization of Afghanistan, *stressing* the crucial importance of advancing regional cooperation as an effective means to promote security, governance and development in Afghanistan, *welcoming* and supporting increased regional efforts towards the continued implementation of previous declarations of good-neighbourly relations,

Stressing the central and impartial role that the United Nations continues to play in promoting peace and stability in Afghanistan by leading the efforts of the international community, noting, in this context, the role of the United Nations Assistance Mission in Afghanistan (UNAMA) as transition moves forward, *stressing* the need for coordination and mutual support between ISAF and UNAMA, *taking due account* of their respective designated responsibilities and the evolving nature and adjusted size of the international community's presence,

Expressing its serious concern about the security situation in Afghanistan, in particular the ongoing violent and terrorist activities by the Taliban, Al-Qaida and other violent and extremist groups, illegal armed groups and criminals, including those involved in the production, trafficking or trade of illicit drugs, as described in the reports of the Secretary-General since the adoption of UNSCR 2011 (2011), and the strong links between terrorism activities and illicit drugs, resulting in threats to the local population, including children, as well as to the national security forces and international military and civilian personnel,

Welcoming the efforts of the Government of Afghanistan to update and improve the National Drug Control Strategy, with a particular emphasis on a partnership approach to ensure joint, effective implementation and coordination, *encouraging* ISAF to further, effectively support, within its designated responsibilities, Afghan-led sustained efforts, including efforts by the ANSF, to address drug production and trafficking, in cooperation with relevant international and regional actors, *recognizing* the threat posed by illicit drug production, trade and trafficking to international peace and stability in different regions of the world, and the important role played by the United Nations Office on Drugs and Crime (UNODC) in this regard, and *remaining concerned* at the serious harm that opium cultivation, production and trafficking and consumption continue to cause to the security, development and governance of Afghanistan as well as to the region and beyond, and *commending* the Paris Pact Initiative as one of the most important frameworks in the fight against opiates originating in Afghanistan,

Expressing also its concern over the harmful consequences of violent and terrorist activities by the Taliban, Al-Qaida and other violent and extremist groups and illegal armed groups on the capacity of the Afghan Government to guarantee the rule of law, to provide security and basic services to the Afghan people, and to ensure the full enjoyment of their human rights and fundamental freedoms, *Reiterating* its support for the continuing endeavours by the Afghan Government, with the assistance of the international community, including ISAF and the Operation Enduring Freedom (OEF) coalition, to further improve the security situation and to continue to address the threat posed by the Taliban, Al-Qaida and other violent and extremist groups and illegal armed groups, and *stressing* in this context the need for sustained international efforts, including those of ISAF and the OEF coalition,

Condemning in the strongest terms all attacks, including improvised explosive device (IED) attacks, suicide attacks, assassinations and abductions, indiscriminate targeting of civilians, attacks against humanitarian workers and targeting of Afghan and international forces and their deleterious effect on the stabilization, reconstruction and development efforts in Afghanistan, and *condemning further* the use by the Taliban, Al-Qaida and other violent and extremist groups and illegal armed groups of civilians as human shields,

Welcoming the Afghan Government's achievements in banning ammonium nitrate fertilizer, and urging continued action to implement regulations for the control of all explosive materials and precursor chemicals, thereby reducing the ability of insurgents to use them for improvised explosive devices, and calling upon the international community to support the Afghan Government's efforts in this regard,

Recognizing the continuing threats posed by the Taliban, Al-Qaida and other violent and extremist groups and illegal armed groups as well as the challenges related to the efforts to address such threats, and *recognizing* the role of measures introduced by the Security Council in resolutions 1267 (1999), 1988 (2011), 1989 (2011), 2082 (2012) and 2083 (2012) in combating these threats and supporting the Afghan-led peace and reconciliation process,

Expressing its serious concern with the high number of civilian casualties in Afghanistan, in particular women and children, the increasingly large majority of which are caused by Taliban, Al-Qaida and other violent and extremist groups and illegal armed groups, *condemning* in the strongest terms the high number of attacks targeting schools, including their burning and forced closure, their use by armed groups, and the intimidation, abduction and killing of education personnel, particularly those attacks targeting girls' education by armed groups including the Taliban and *welcoming*, in this context, the listing of the Taliban in the annex of the report of the Secretary-General on children and armed conflict (S/2013/245) pursuant to Security Council resolution 1998 (2011), *condemning also* the increased targeted killing of women and girls, in particular high level female officials, reaffirming that all parties to armed conflict must take all feasible steps to ensure the protection of affected civilians, especially women, children and displaced persons, including from sexual violence and all other forms of gender based violence, *calling* for all parties to comply with their obligations under international humanitarian and human rights law and for all appropriate measures to be taken to ensure the protection of civilians, and *recognizing* the importance of the ongoing monitoring and reporting to the United Nations Security Council, including by ISAF, of the situation of civilians and in particular civilian casualties, and noting in this regard the work of the ISAF Civilian Casualties Mitigation Team,

Recalling that women play a vital role in the peace process, as recognized in Security Council resolution 1325 (2000) and related resolutions, *welcoming* the commitment by the Government of Afghanistan to develop and implement Afghanistan's Security Council Resolution 1325 (2000) National Action Plan and to identify further opportunities to support the participation of women in the Afghan led peace and reconciliation process, the presentation by the Government of Afghanistan of its first progress report on the implementation of the

Convention on the Elimination of All Forms of Discrimination against Women, and efforts to continue to accelerate full implementation of the National Action Plan for Women in Afghanistan, to integrate its benchmarks into the National Priority Programmes and to develop a strategy to implement fully the Elimination of Violence Against Women law,

Taking note of the further progress made by ISAF and other international forces in minimizing the civilian casualties, as recognized in the 2013 midyear report by UNAMA on the protection of civilians in armed conflict, *urging* ISAF and other international forces to continue to undertake enhanced efforts to prevent civilian casualties, including the increased focus on protecting the Afghan population as a central element of the mission, and noting the importance of conducting continuous reviews of tactics and procedures and after-action reviews and investigations in cooperation with the Afghan Government in cases where civilian casualties have occurred and when the Afghan Government finds these joint investigations appropriate, as well as continuing cooperation with the ANSF towards the further institutionalization of protection of civilians, especially women and girls,

Expressing its strong concern about recruitment and use of children by Taliban forces in Afghanistan as well as the killing and maiming of children as a result of the conflict, and attacks on schools and hospitals in contravention of applicable international law, *supporting* the decree by the Minister of the Interior reaffirming the government's commitment to preventing violations of the rights of the child dated 6 July 2011, *welcoming* the progress made on the implementation of the Action Plan, and its annex, on Children Associated with the ANSF, signed in January 2011, in particular the establishment of the Afghan Inter-Ministerial Steering Committee on Children and Armed Conflict, the appointment of a focal point on child protection, and the endorsement by the Afghan Government of a road map to accelerate compliance with the Action Plan, *calling* for the full implementation of the provisions of the plan, in close cooperation with UNAMA, *recognizing* in this regard NATO's high-level commitments on children and armed conflict and NATO's positive response to the request by the Special Representative for Children and Armed conflict to assist in the full implementation of the Action Plan and its annex, and *encouraging* ISAF to assist the Afghan Government with its full implementation,

Stressing in this context the importance of further progress by the Afghan Government in ending impunity and strengthening judicial institutions, in the reconstruction and reform of the prison sector, and the rule of law and respect for human rights within Afghanistan, including for women and girls, and in particular women's rights under the Constitution to fully participate in the political, economic and social spheres of Afghan life, and *welcoming*, in this regard, the National Police Plan and the objectives set therein for increased training in human rights, including gender issues, and increased recruitment of women, as well as continuing ISAF support for the ANSF towards increased recruitment, training and retention of women,

Reiterating its call on all Afghan parties and groups to engage constructively in peaceful political dialogue as within the framework of the Afghan Constitution and to work together with international donors for the socioeconomic development of the country and to avoid resorting to violence including through the use of illegal armed groups, *supporting* the aims of the High Peace Council, and *recognizing* the importance of regional support for advancing the Afghan-led and Afghan-owned peace and reconciliation process,

Reiterating its firm commitment to support the Government of Afghanistan in its efforts to advance the peace and reconciliation process, in line with the Kabul Communiqué and the Bonn Conference Conclusions, and within the framework of the Afghan Constitution and application of the procedures introduced by the Security Council in its resolutions 1988 (2011) and 2082 (2012), as well as other relevant resolutions of the Council,

Welcoming the continuing efforts of the Afghan Government to advance the peace and reconciliation process, including by the High Peace Council and the implementation of the Afghanistan Peace and Reconciliation Programme, to promote an inclusive, Afghan-led dialogue on reconciliation and political participation as laid forth in the 20 July 2010 Kabul Conference Communiqué on dialogue for all those who renounce violence, have no links to international terrorist organizations, including Al-Qaida, respect the constitution, including its human rights provisions, notably the rights of women, and are willing to join in building a peaceful Afghanistan, and as further elaborated in the principles and outcomes of the 5 December 2011 Bonn Conference Conclusions supported by the Government of Afghanistan and the international community, with full respect for the implementation of measures and application of the procedures introduced by the Security Council in its resolutions 1267 (1999), 1988 (2011) and 2082 (2012) as well as other relevant resolutions of the Council, *calling on* all relevant states to remain engaged in the peace process, and *recognizing* the impact terrorist attacks have on the Afghan people and risk having on future prospects for a peace settlement,

Recognizing that an increased number of the Taliban have reconciled with the Government of Afghanistan, have rejected the terrorist ideology of Al-Qaida and its followers, and support a peaceful resolution to the continuing conflict in Afghanistan, *recognizing also* that notwithstanding the evolution of the situation in Afghanistan and progress in reconciliation, security remains a serious challenge in Afghanistan and the region,

Recognizing also the increased number of reintegrees that have joined the Afghanistan Peace and Reintegration Programme (APRP), and *encouraging* further efforts to address remaining operational challenges, including through an appropriate vetting mechanism, and *further encouraging* the international community to support this Afghan-led effort,

Recalling the Government of Afghanistan's commitments, most recently at the Tokyo Conference, to strengthen and improve Afghanistan's electoral process, including long-term electoral reform, in order to ensure that future elections will be transparent, credible, inclusive and democratic, *welcoming*, in this regard, the adoption of a legal framework to govern elections, the appointment of new members and the election of new Chairpersons for the Independent Election Commission and the Independent Electoral Complaints Commission, and *reaffirming* that Afghanistan's peaceful future lies in the building of a stable, secure, economically sustainable state, free of terrorism and narcotics and based on the rule of law, strengthened democratic institutions, respect for the separation of powers, reinforced constitutional checks and balances, good economic governance, including in the fight against corruption and the guarantee of citizens' rights,

Welcoming the efforts of the international community carried out to strengthen the coherence of military and civilian actions, including those within the framework of ISAF,

Welcoming also the continued coordination between ISAF and the OEF coalition, and in-theatre cooperation established between ISAF and the EU presence in Afghanistan,

Expressing its appreciation for the leadership provided by NATO and for the contributions of many nations to ISAF and to the OEF coalition, which operates within the framework of the counter-terrorism operations in Afghanistan and in accordance with the applicable rules of international law,

Determining that the situation in Afghanistan still constitutes a threat to international peace and security,

Determined to ensure the full implementation of the mandate of ISAF, in coordination with the Afghan Government,

Acting for these reasons under Chapter VII of the Charter of the United Nations,

1. *Decides* to extend the authorization of the International Security Assistance Force (ISAF), as defined in resolution 1386 (2001) and 1510 (2003), until 31 December 2014;
2. *Authorizes* the Member States participating in ISAF to take all necessary measures to fulfil its mandate;
3. *Recognizes* the need for ISAF to meet all its operational requirements, welcomes the agreement between the Government of Afghanistan and countries contributing to ISAF to transfer full security responsibility in Afghanistan to the Afghan Government country-wide by the end of 2014 and the ongoing implementation of the transition process since July 2011, and *calls upon* Member States to contribute personnel, equipment and other resources to ISAF and to continue to pursue their efforts to support security, stability and transition in Afghanistan;
4. *Welcomes* the strong commitment of the Government of Afghanistan to further develop, with the support of ISAF nations, an ANSF which is governed by the Afghan Constitution and is capable of providing peace, security and stability to all Afghans operating under effective civilian leadership and in accordance with the rule of law, and respecting and promoting human rights, including the rights of women, and capable of contributing to the region's security through the stabilization of the situation in Afghanistan;

5. *Welcomes* the commitment by NATO and the Afghan Government to further develop the NATO-Afghanistan Enduring Partnership signed at Lisbon in 2010 in all its dimensions, up to 2014 and beyond, and in particular the intention expressed therein to provide, within the framework of the Enduring Partnership, sustained practical support aimed at improving and sustaining Afghanistan's capacity and capability to tackle continued threats to its security, stability and integrity, and to contribute to the region's security through the stabilization of the situation in Afghanistan;
6. *Stresses* the importance of continued cooperation to develop ANSF capabilities including, in a comprehensive framework, the functionality, professionalism and accountability of the Afghan security sector, *encourages* ISAF and other partners to sustain their efforts, as resources permit, to train, mentor and empower the Afghan National Security Forces, in order to accelerate progress towards the goal of self-sufficient, sustainable, accountable and ethnically balanced Afghan security forces providing security and ensuring the rule of law throughout the country, *welcomes* the increasing leadership role played by the Afghan Authorities in security responsibilities throughout the country, and *welcomes* the substantial progress made in the expansion and capability of the Afghan National Army and the Afghan National Police and *stresses* the importance of supporting the further professionalization of these institutions;
7. *Calls upon* ISAF and the NATO Senior Civilian Representative to continue to work in close consultation with the Afghan Government and the Special Representative of the United Nations Secretary-General in accordance with Security Council resolution 2096 (2013) as well as with the OEF coalition in the implementation of the ISAF mandate;
8. *Requests* the leadership of ISAF to keep the Security Council regularly informed, through the United Nations Secretary-General, on the implementation of its mandate, including through the timely provision of quarterly reports, and its final report in December 2014 should be a comprehensive one;
9. *Decides* to remain actively seized of this matter.

APPENDIX 3

Statistics

Under Nourished (FAO Definition) by World Region in Millions

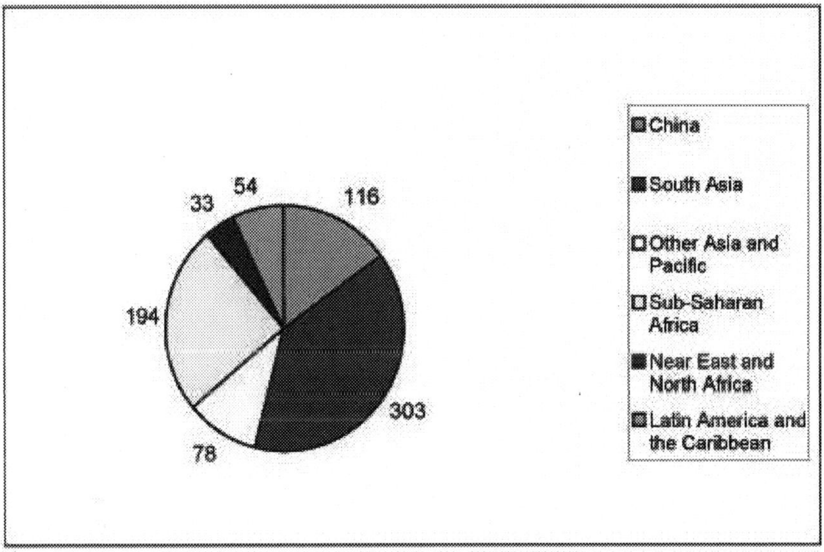

Source: The State of Food Insecurity in the World, FAO, 2001.

Resources for Education: 6.1% of Government Spending Goes to Education

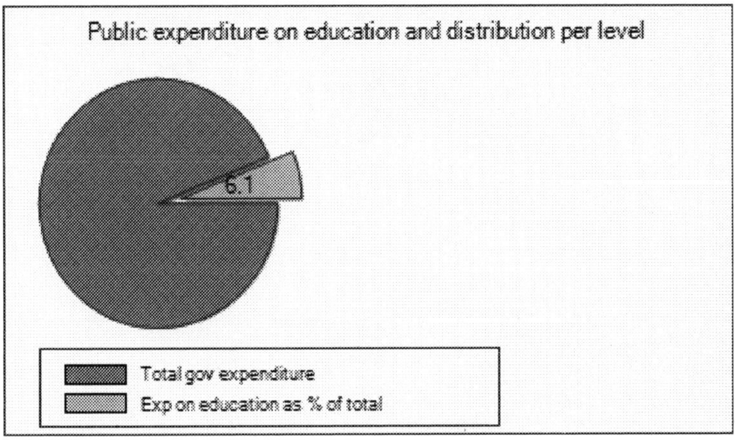

Source: UNESCO Institute for Statistics.

Figure:Female Literacy Rates, by Province

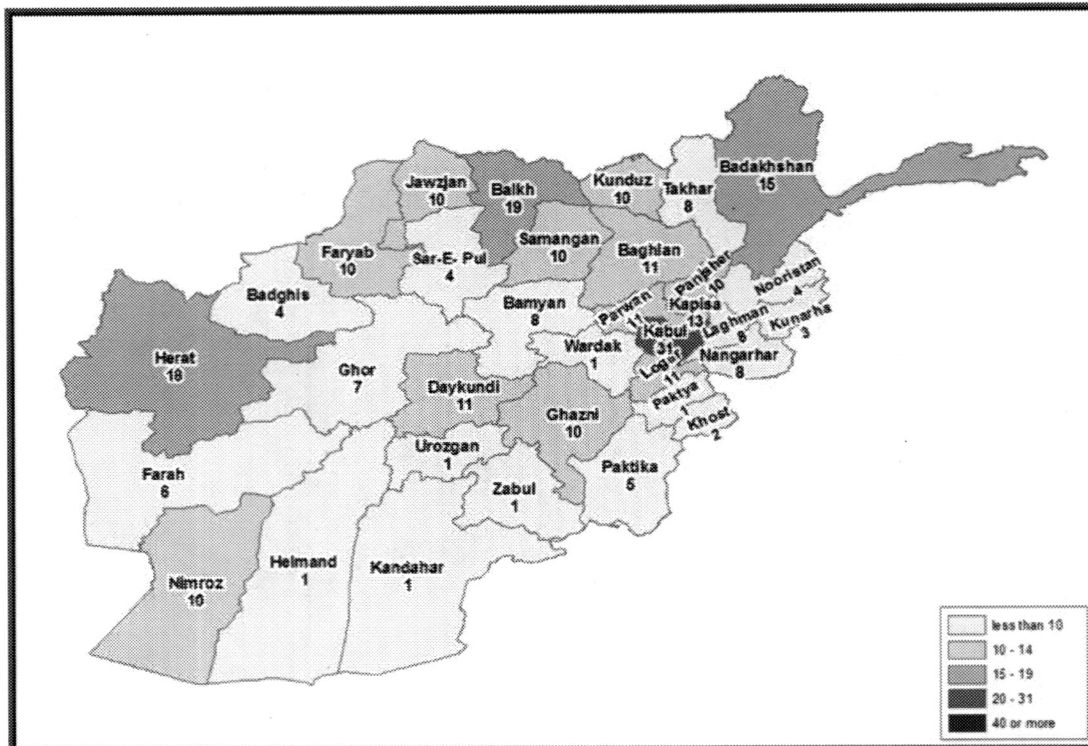

Source: National Risk and Vulnerability Assessment 2007/08(NRVA): A Profile of Afghanistan.

Figure 2: Male Literacy Rates, by Province

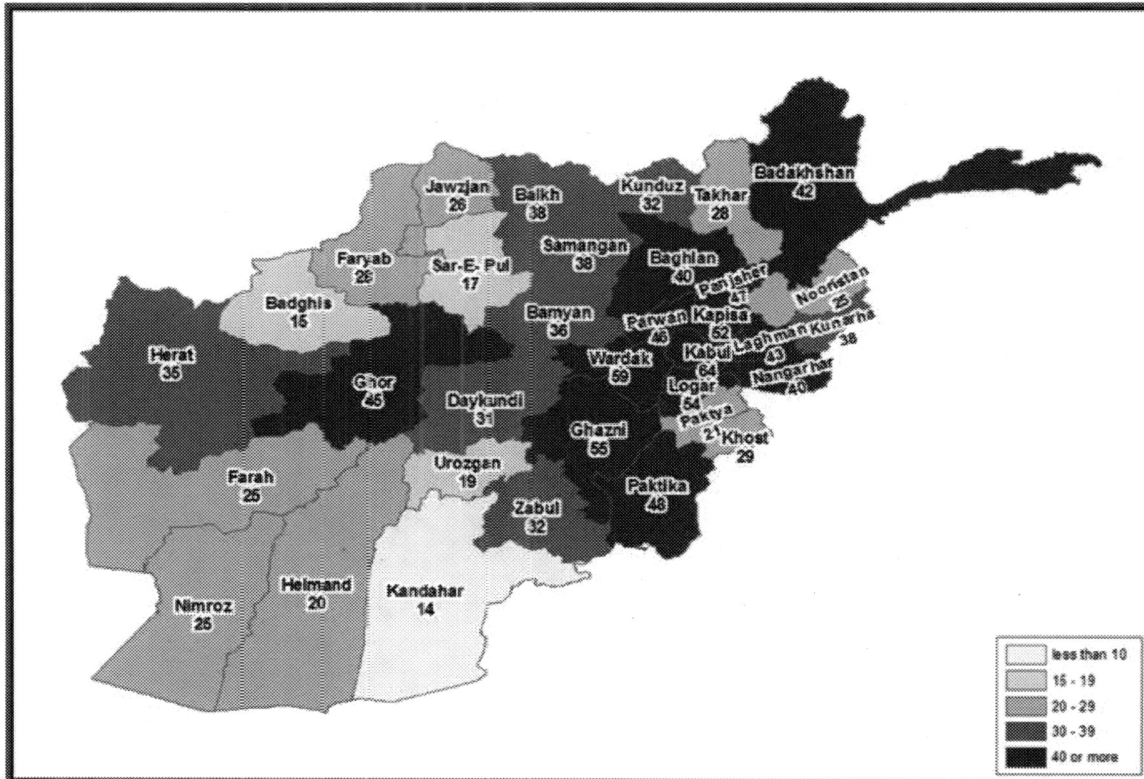

Source: NRVA 2007/08: A Profile of Afghanistan.

Figure 3: Share of the Total Population with Access to Safe Drinking Water

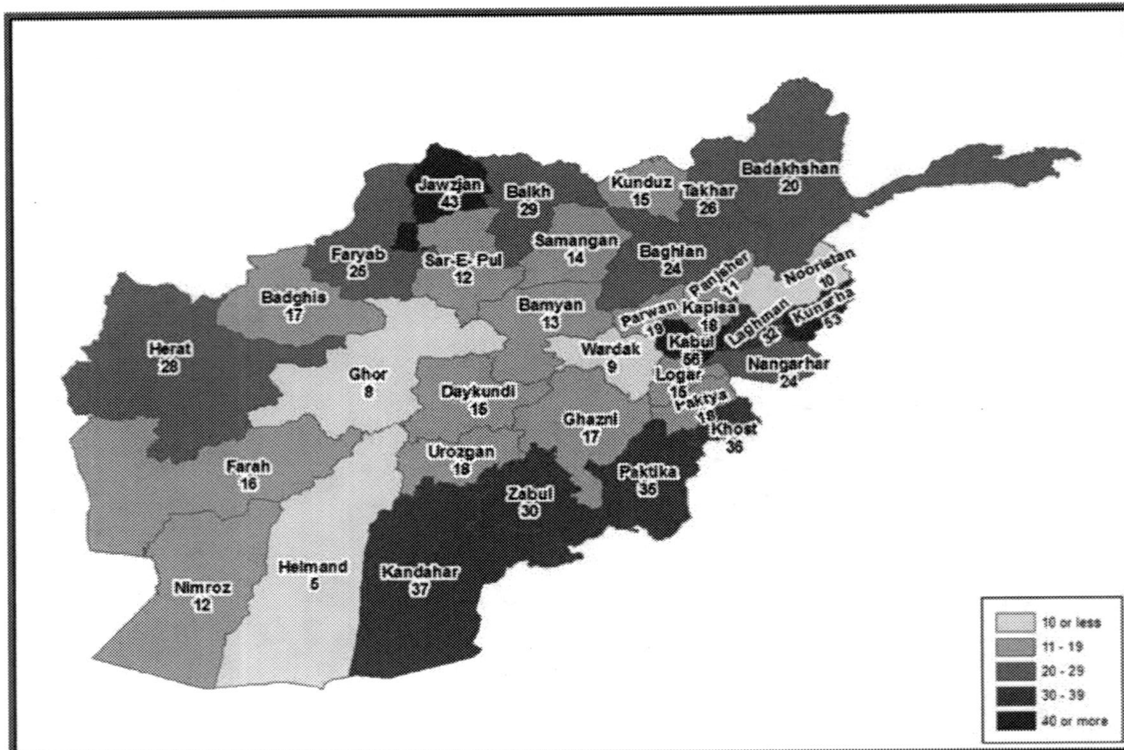

Source: NRVA 2007/08: A Profile of Afghanistan.

Figure 4: Percentage of Children Aged 12-23 Months with Full Immunization

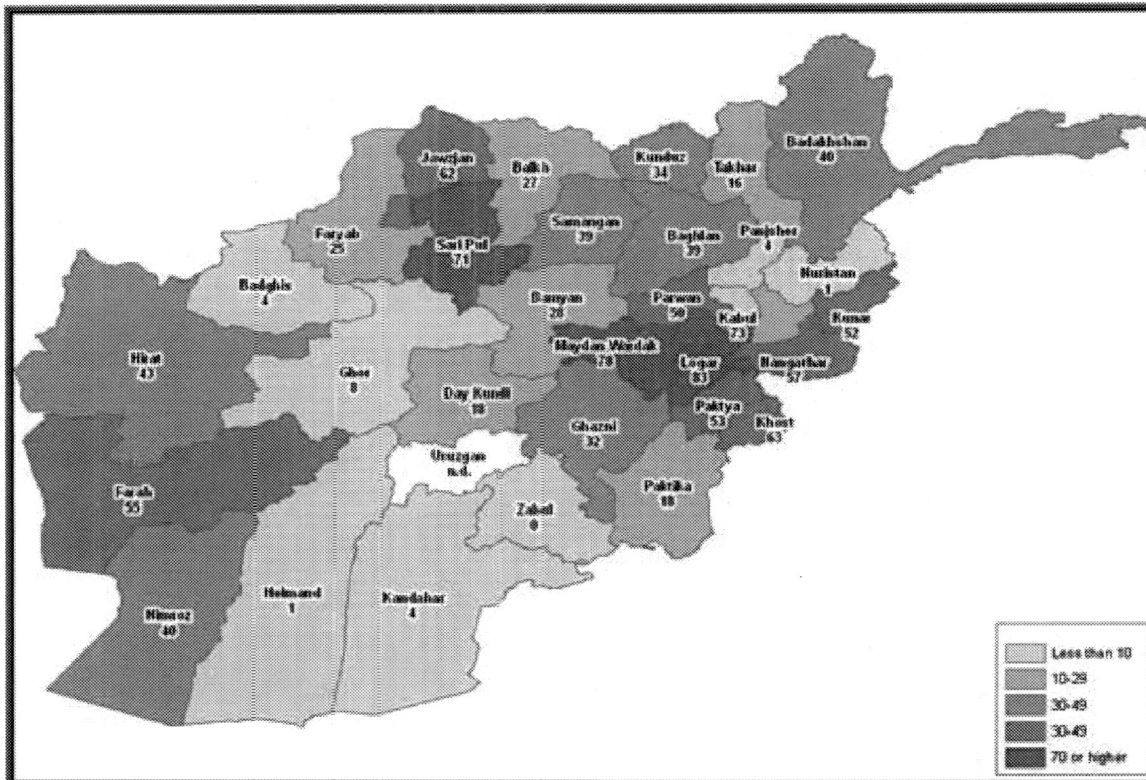

NRVA 2007/08: A Profile of Afghanistan.

Key Indicators for Asia and the Pacific 2013
Afghanistan

Item	1995	1996	1997	1998	1999	2000	2001	2002	2003	2004	2005	2006	2007	2008	2009	2010	2011	2012
POPULATION[a]																		
Total population *million; as of May*	19.4	19.8	20.2	20.6	21.1	21.5	21.9	22.3	22.8	23.2	23.7	24.2	24.5	25.0	25.5	26.0	26.5	27.0
Population density *persons per square kilometer*	30	30	31	31	32	33	33	34	35	36	36	37	38	38	39	40	41	41
Population *annual change, percent*	1.9	1.9	1.9	1.9	1.9	1.9	1.9	1.9	1.9	2.0	1.9	2.0	2.0	2.0	2.0	1.9	1.9	1.9
Urban population *percent of total population*	18.1	18.4	18.8	19.2	19.4	19.8	20.1	20.6	20.7	20.1	20.2	20.2	21.1	21.3	21.6	21.9	22.2	22.6
LABOR FORCE[b] *thousand*	...	...	...	...	...	...	7560	7707	7857	8231	...	...	...	...	...	...	...	...
Employed	...	...	...	...	...	...	7305	7447	7592	7954	...	...	...	...	...	...	...	...
Agriculture	...	...	...	...	...	...	5083	5181	5282	5534	...	...	...	...	...	...	...	...
Industry	...	...	...	...	...	...	452	461	470	492	...	...	...	...	...	...	...	...
Services	...	...	...	...	...	...	1105	1126	1148	1203	...	...	...	...	...	...	...	...
Others	...	...	...	...	...	...	666	679	692	725	...	...	...	...	...	...	...	...
Unemployed and unclassified	...	...	...	...	...	...	255	260	265	277	...	...	...	...	...	...	...	...
Unemployment rate *percent*	...	...	...	...	...	...	3.4	3.4	3.4	3.4	...	...	...	...	...	...	...	...
Labor force *annual change, percent*	...	...	...	...	...	...	...	1.9	1.9	4.8	...	...	...	...	...	...	...	...
NATIONAL ACCOUNTS *million Afghanis; fiscal year beginning 21 March*																		
At Current Prices																		
GDP by industrial origin at current market prices	...	...	...	...	...	...	...	202531	240671	267311	327745	375152	518611	541112	632715	746856	903990 *	...
Agriculture	...	...	...	...	...	...	...	87425	98805	88955	112194	122511	174343	150133	196843	207301	241743 *	...
Mining	...	...	...	...	...	...	...	264	290	638	880	1224	2213	2481	2921	4473	10396 *	...
Manufacturing	...	...	...	...	...	...	...	34288	37462	43484	51150	57030	86148	91879	80437	90943	117171 *	...
Electricity, gas, and water	...	...	...	...	...	...	...	121	280	312	461	562	630	527	630	640	605 *	...
Construction	...	...	...	...	...	...	...	8700	12240	20714	30135	39371	41500	43741	49954	57552	65199 *	...
Trade[c]	...	...	...	...	...	...	...	20350	22681	24709	28786	32010	44850	48097	49812	59679	71687 *	...
Transport and communications	...	...	...	...	...	...	...	20274	31032	37443	37888	47466	71926	91481	116364	145913	174419 *	...
Finance[d]	...	...	...	...	...	...	...	1289	2398	3365	4460	5688	7249	9222	12504	16259	18670 *	...
Public administration	...	...	...	...	...	...	...	10000	11257	14487	25469	29674	46920	57137	58449	84473	111704 *	...
Others	...	...	...	...	...	...	...	17250	18857	25857	26877	28053	29638	32084	43019	52326	59919 *	...

Item	1995	1996	1997	1998	1999	2000	2001	2002	2003	2004	2005	2006	2007	2008	2009	2010	2011	2012
Taxes less subsidies on production and imports	...	...	...	...	..	...	...	2570	5369	7347	9446	11563	13194	14330	21782	27300	32477 *	...
Structure of Output *percent of GDP at current factor cost*																		
Agriculture	...	...	...	...	...	...	...	43.7	42.0	34.2	35.2	33.7	34.5	28.5	32.2	28.8	27.7	...
Industry	...	...	...	...	...	...	...	21.7	21.4	25.1	26.0	27.0	25.8	26.3	21.9	21.3	22.2	...
Services	...	...	...	...	...	...	...	34.6	36.6	40.7	38.8	39.3	39.7	45.2	45.9	49.8	50.1	...
Expenditure on GDP at current market prices	...	...	...	...	...	...	...	202531	240671	267311	327746	375152	518611	541113	632717	746855	903990	...
Private consumption	...	...	...	...	...	...	...	225164	304573	322140	379330	410643	566336	612492	623348	727199	820217	...
Government consumption	...	...	...	...	...	...	...	15514	21972	26701	32882	40346	53600	54633	71800	104639	149385	...
Gross fixed capital formation	...	...	...	...	...	...	...	22875	28243	47474	71475	91913	97418	97969	110052	130424	143043	...
Increase in stocks	...	...	...	...	...	...	...	...	...	...	...	...	...	...	...	...	...	...
Exports of goods and services	...	...	...	...	...	...	...	60068	97871	82525	85319	93257	87408	93417	90464	73164	76431	...
Less: Imports of goods and services	...	...	...	...	...	...	...	121090	211988	211529	241260	261007	286151	250549	259560	328043	314643	...
Statistical discrepancy	...	...	...	...	..	...	...	...	...	...	...	...	...	-66849	-3387	39472	29557	...
Structure of Demand *percent of GDP at current market prices*																		
Private consumption	...	...	...	...	...	...	...	111.2	126.6	120.5	115.7	109.5	109.2	113.2	98.5	97.4	90.7	...
Government consumption	...	...	...	...	...	...	...	7.7	9.1	10.0	10.0	10.8	10.3	10.1	11.3	14.0	16.5	...
Gross domestic capital formatione	...	...	...	...	...	...	...	11.3	11.7	17.8	21.8	24.5	18.8	18.1	17.4	17.5	15.8	...
Exports of goods and services	...	...	...	...	...	...	...	29.7	40.7	30.9	26.0	24.9	16.9	17.3	14.3	9.8	8.5	...
Imports of goods and services	...	...	...	...	...	...	...	59.8	88.1	79.1	73.6	69.6	55.2	46.3	41.0	43.9	34.8	...
Statistical discrepancy	...	...	...	...	...	...	...	...	...	...	...	...	...	-12.4	-0.5	5.3	3.3	...
At Constant Prices																		
GDP by industrial origin at 2002 market prices	...	...	...	...	...	...	...	202530	219195	224329	246541	269127	312437	319729	374800	386931	423652 *	...
Agriculture	...	...	...	...	...	...	...	87425	90398	77323	86777	93430	113199	99945	123252	101045	105499 *	...
Mining	...	...	...	...	...	...	...	264	256	493	580	695	1214	1247	1412	2018	3834 *	...
Manufacturing	...	...	...	...	...	...	...	34288	35559	37035	38250	39472	41263	42231	44468	46175	47585 *	...
Electricity, gas, and water	...	...	...	...	...	...	...	121	173	163	195	197	215	178	201	201	182 *	...
Construction	...	...	...	...	...	...	...	8700	11842	18495	24460	31798	34978	38474	41065	44216	50091 *	...
Trade [c]	...	...	...	...	...	...	...	20353	19553	19385	20183	20574	23533	24064	26101	27485	30464 *	...
Transport and communications	...	...	...	...	...	...	...	20274	28758	31664	29602	34600	46645	56859	67100	82601	90939 *	...
Finance [d]	...	...	...	...	...	...	...	1289	2068	2641	3129	3658	3807	4617	6555	7492	7938 *	...

Item	1995	1996	1997	1998	1999	2000	2001	2002	2003	2004	2005	2006	2007	2008	2009	2010	2011	2012
Public administration	...	...	...	...	...	...	...	10000	9704	11366	17857	19073	24619	28587	30626	38904	47470 *	...
Others	...	...	...	...	...	...	...	17249	16256	19999	18885	18198	16041	16357	22607	24221	25849 *	...
Taxes less subsidies on production and imports	...	...	...	...	...	...	...	2570	4628	5764	6623	7432	6923	7170	11413	12573	13801 *	...
Growth of Output *annual change, percent*																		
GDP	...	...	...	...	...	...	...	...	8.2	2.3	9.9	9.2	16.1	2.3	17.2	3.2	9.5 *	...
Agriculture	...	...	...	...	...	...	...	...	3.4	-14.5	12.2	7.7	21.2	-11.7	23.3	-18.0	4.4 *	...
Industry	...	...	...	...	...	...	...	...	10.3	17.5	13.0	13.7	7.6	5.7	6.1	6.3	9.8 *	...
Services	...	...	...	...	...	...	...	...	10.4	11.4	5.4	7.2	19.3	13.8	17.2	18.1	12.2 *	...
Investment Financing at Current Prices																		
Gross domestic capital formation [e]	...	...	...	...	...	...	...	22875	28243	47474	71475	91913	97418	97969	110052	130424	143043 *	...
Gross domestic saving	...	...	...	...	...	...	...	-38147	-85874	-81530	-84467	-75837	-101325	-126013	-62433	-84979	-65612 *	...
Savings and Investment *percent of GDP at current market prices*																		
Gross domestic saving	...	...	...	...	...	...	...	-18.8	-35.7	-30.5	-25.8	-20.2	-19.5	-23.3	-9.9	-11.4	-7.3 *	...
Gross domestic capital formation [e]	...	...	...	...	...	...	...	11.3	11.7	17.8	21.8	24.5	18.8	18.1	17.4	17.5	15.8 *	...
At Current Market Prices *Afghanis*																		
Per capita GDP	...	...	...	...	...	...	...	9269	10818	11512	13884	16932	20625	21644	24812	28725	34113 *	...
PRODUCTION INDEXES *period averages*																		
Agriculture *2004–2006 = 100*	82.9	89.2	96.4	103.0	102.4	85.9	78.5	95.2	98.3	96.4	107.1	96.5	106.5	98.7	114.6	113.4	109.1 *	...
ENERGY *annual values*																		
Coal *thousand metric tons*																		
Production	5	3	2	2	...	...	...	21	35	34	33	35	247	347	500	725	1480	...
Consumption	5	3	2	2	...	...	...	21	35	34	33	35	247	347	500	725	1480	...
Electricity *million kilowatt-hours*																		
Production	179	222	...	465	454	697	676	557	827	781	907	917	1007	827	937	936	621	...
Consumption	...	...	...	...	...	...	444	301	741	623	691	684	715	839	1313	1467	1700	...
PRICE INDEXES *March 2004 = 100; period averages*																		
Consumer (national)	...	...	...	...	...	...	...	...	...	100.0	111.9	122.0	127.4	156.1	163.7	156.4	177.8	192.7
Food	...	...	...	...	...	...	...	...	...	100.0	109.1	117.5	124.5	164.2	171.3	155.7	177.4	191.2
Nonfood	...	...	...	...	...	...	...	...	...	100.0	116.3	129.1	132.1	143.2	151.7	157.5	178.5	195.1
Consumer (Kabul)	...	...	...	...	...	...	...	...	...	100.0	114.9	125.8	131.8	159.1	164.3	155.8	181.7	202.2
Food	...	...	...	...	...	...	...	...	...	100.0	111.6	118.5	126.0	164.5	165.9	149.1	176.4	193.1
Nonfood	...	...	...	...	...	...	...	...	...	100.0	120.2	137.5	140.9	150.6	161.7	166.6	190.2	216.6

Item	1995	1996	1997	1998	1999	2000	2001	2002	2003	2004	2005	2006	2007	2008	2009	2010	2011	2012
Implicit GDP deflator *2002 = 100*	...	...	...	...	...	...	...	100.0	109.8	119.2	132.9	139.4	166.0	169.2	168.8	193.0*	213.4	...
***Price Indexes** annual change, percent*																		
Consumer price index (national)	...	...	...	...	...	...	...	...	...	...	11.9	9.0	4.4	22.5	4.9	-4.5	13.7	8.4
Food price index (national)	...	...	...	...	...	...	...	...	...	...	9.1	7.7	6.0	31.9	4.3	-9.1	13.9	7.8
Nonfood price index (national)	...	...	...	...	...	...	...	...	...	...	16.3	11.0	2.3	8.4	5.9	3.8	13.3	9.3
Implicit GDP deflator	...	...	...	...	...	...	...	...	9.8	8.5	11.6	4.9	19.1	2.0	-0.3	14.3	10.5	...
MONEY AND BANKING *million Afghanis; as of end of period*																		
Money supply (M1)	...	...	...	...	...	...	...	22164	29116	38953	55663	89252	114895	158376	212648	261215	297865	319164
Currency in circulation	...	...	...	...	...	...	...	20080	26914	37116	42515	49566	57501	73842	92545	126300	141326	142761
Demand deposits (excluding government deposits)	...	...	...	...	...	...	...	2083	2202	1836	13148	39686	57395	84534	120103	134915	156540	176403
Quasi-money	...	...	...	...	...	...	...	177	265	1669	3074	2066	4740	4151	13707	17429	20506	19675
Money supply (M2)	...	...	...	...	...	...	...	22341	29380	40622	58737	91317	119635	162527	226355	278644	318371	338840
Foreign assets (net)	...	...	...	...	...	...	...	...	...	62838	90133	108946	160996	181909	220638	273946	338705	425376
Domestic credit	...	...	...	...	...	...	...	14951	-19819	-4869	-13421	-11559	6799	20367	33223	35457	-20306	-44492
Claims on government sector (net) [f]	...	...	...	...	...	...	...	14951	-19819	-4869	-21314	-37252	-32101	-29941	-35876	-48157	-62132	-86566
Claims on private sector	...	...	...	...	...	...	...	...	...	...	...	21529	38391	49842	69652	83114	42276	43024
Claims on other financial institutions	...	...	...	...	...	...	...	...	...	...	7893	4164	509	466	-553	500	-450	-950
Other items	...	...	...	...	...	...	...	...	...	-19017	-17975	20712	2173	8008	18445	-36346	57654	41641
***Money supply (M2)** annual change, percent*	...	...	...	...	...	...	...	...	31.5	38.3	44.6	55.5	31.0	35.9	39.3	23.1	14.3	6.4
***M2** percent of GDP at current market prices*	...	...	...	...	...	...	...	11.0	12.2	15.2	17.9	24.3	23.1	30.0	35.8	37.3	35.2	...
Deposit Money Banks [g]																		
Demand deposits	...	...	...	...	...	...	...	170	2721	7974	13043	22308	34692	61240	83361	107579	121964	139934
Savings deposits	...	...	...	...	...	...	...	133	322	1007	2651	9557	19960	27333	38031	39284	46887	6832
Time deposits	...	...	...	...	...	...	...	...	...	114	531	1168	3891	4689	9609	9673	11574	45478
GOVERNMENT FINANCE *million Afghanis; fiscal year beginning 21 March*																		
Central Government																		
Total revenue and grants	...	...	...	...	...	...	...	14104	20203	29434	39362	50200	56990	137975	131843	156626	215363	...
Total revenue	...	...	...	...	...	...	...	5864	10168	12689	22586	30994	33662	41426	52473	80474	93663	...
Current revenue	...	...	...	...	...	...	...	5864	10168	12689	22586	30994	33662	41426	52473	80474	93663	...
Taxes	...	...	...	...	...	...	...	...	...	...	12501	12326	12182	41426	40191	68974	78766	...
Nontaxes	...	...	...	...	...	...	...	...	...	...	10085	18667	21480	–	12282	11500	14897	...
Capital receipts	...	...	...	...	...	...	...	...	...	...	...	...	...	...	...	...	...	...

Item	1995	1996	1997	1998	1999	2000	2001	2002	2003	2004	2005	2006	2007	2008	2009	2010	2011	2012
Grants	...	...	...	...	...	...	...	8240	10035	16745	16776	19206	23328	96550	79370	76151	121700	...
Total expenditure and net lending	...	...	...	...	...	...	...	16634	31187	43719	54016	79341	98844	114436	131304	153867	199181	...
Total expenditure	...	...	...	...	...	...	...	15514	31187	43719	54016	79341	98844	114436	131304	153867	199181	...
Current expenditure	...	...	...	...	...	...	...	...	...	...	22362	38180	48117	45336	43991	110485	149385	...
Capital expenditure	...	...	...	...	...	...	...	...	...	...	31654	41161	50727	69100	87313	43381	49796	...
Net lending	...	...	...	...	...	...	...	1120	...	...	...	...	...	...	...	...	...	...
Current surplus/deficit	...	...	...	...	...	...	...	5864	10168	12689	224	-7186	-14455	-3911	8482	-30011	-55722	...
Capital account surplus/deficit	...	...	...	...	...	...	...	...	...	...	-31654	-41161	-50727	-69100	-87313	-43381	-49796	...
Overall budgetary surplus/deficit	...	...	...	...	...	...	...	-2530	-10984	-14285	-14654	-29141	-41854	23539	539	2759	16182	...
Government Finance *percent of GDP at current market prices*																		
Total revenue	...	...	...	...	...	...	...	2.9	4.2	4.7	6.9	8.3	6.5	7.7	8.3	10.8	10.4	...
Taxes	...	...	...	...	...	...	...	...	...	...	3.8	3.3	2.3	7.7	6.4	9.2	8.7	...
Total expenditure	...	...	...	...	...	...	...	7.7	13.0	16.4	16.5	21.1	19.1	21.1	20.8	20.6	22.0	...
Overall budgetary surplus/deficit	...	...	...	...	...	...	...	-1.2	-4.6	-5.3	-4.5	-7.8	-8.1	4.4	0.1	0.4	1.8	...
EXTERNAL TRADE *million US Dollars; calendar year*																		
Exports, fob	166	128	144	159	166	137	68	100	144	305	384	416	454	545	403	388	376	414
Imports, cif	387	661	604	462	1012	1176	1696	2452	2101	2177	2470	2744	3022	3020	3336	5154	6388	8932
Trade balance	-221	-533	-460	-303	-846	-1039	-1628	-2352	-1957	-1872	-2086	-2328	-2568	-2475	-2933	-4766	-6012	-8518
External Trade *annual change, percent*																		
Exports	58.2	-22.8	12.6	10.3	4.4	-17.4	-50.5	47.1	44.0	111.8	25.9	8.3	9.1	20.0	-26.1	-3.7	-3.1	10.1
Imports	-1.0	70.8	-8.6	-23.5	119.1	16.2	44.2	44.6	-14.3	3.6	13.5	11.1	10.1	-0.1	10.5	54.5	23.9	39.8
Direction of Trade *million US Dollars; calendar year*																		
Exports, total	166.0	128.0	144.7	151.2	122.8	142.2	84.2	88.0	208.5	182.6	236.1	230.6	340.6	478.5	445.7	499.9	465.3	536.3
1. Pakistan	14.0	25.5	29.8	25.4	36.0	35.5	23.7	27.8	28.3	44.6	48.4	59.8	74.2	84.7	108.5	137.8	154.3	177.5
2. India	7.0	3.9	3.1	21.6	20.8	22.9	18.1	16.6	31.8	39.4	50.5	36.8	82.3	118.7	109.7	131.4	109.0	133.5
3. United States	5.3	16.0	10.2	16.0	8.4	2.6	0.6	4.3	57.2	22.9	61.5	41.6	69.8	79.0	113.0	79.3	18.7	31.2
4. Tajikistan, Rep. of	0.0	2.1	0.7	0.4	0.1	0.1	0.1	0.3	1.5	3.6	3.1	5.9	24.6	61.0	40.2	36.2	40.6	46.7
5. Russian Federation	12.1	7.2	7.5	6.5	5.8	4.9	2.5	4.4	5.9	3.7	3.5	10.5	8.1	13.5	13.1	17.7	25.5	10.2
6. Germany	8	9	9	7	6	5	6.6	5.0	4.5	10.3	3.7	2.8	5.7	3.2	4.9	26.7	12.8	16.2
7. Iran	–	–	–	–	–	–	0.7	0.1	0.9	3.6	5.5	6.4	8.4	11.2	9.2	11.7	13.5	15.5
8. United Arab Emirates	–	3.6	2.7	3.6	3.6	–	–	–	3.0	3.9	5.0	6.1	7.9	10.0	9.4	10.8	12.4	14.3
9. Netherlands	0.2	0.2	0.0	0.0	0.0	2.6	0.0	0.1	0.0	0.2	0.1	0.2	0.2	33.0	1.6	1.2	2.3	4.1
10. Finland	1.5	0.5	4.4	5.3	5.4	8.8	6.3	6.0	6.3	5.0	9.7	12.2	9.7	10.5	4.7	7.0	9.0	11.6

Item	1995	1996	1997	1998	1999	2000	2001	2002	2003	2004	2005	2006	2007	2008	2009	2010	2011	2012
Imports, total	387.4	660.8	604.3	462.5	490.3	620.8	556.1	1034.7	1609.8	1963.4	3063.7	3854.0	4918.5	6103.2	6888.7	8421.5	10398.4	9457.2
1. United States	4.4	18.5	12.5	7.6	19.8	12.2	6.6	87.9	66.7	173.4	287.5	459.3	537.6	529.9	1662.7	2367.6	3210.4	1642.2
2. Pakistan	21.8	14.4	20.7	41.5	89.8	134.1	157.0	245.5	449.4	511.4	1171.6	1448.0	1796.9	2051.5	1493.3	1896.5	2124.1	2442.7
3. Russian Federation	19.3	23.0	20.6	14.9	14.6	12.3	8.5	35.5	59.9	83.5	114.9	90.6	137.6	189.8	285.7	592.9	862.1	794.5
4. India	16.2	22.5	25.4	16.4	30.9	30.5	22.9	56.8	136.7	169.8	163.2	189.2	255.3	398.5	516.1	432.8	551.8	524.5
5. Kazakhstan	3.2	6.3	9.5	8.4	12.5	63.7	20.0	34.2	54.4	95.0	180.3	194.3	211.8	678.8	449.3	399.1	366.4	421.4
6. Germany	18.3	21.1	17.2	15.7	13.6	16.1	15.9	57.3	103.2	130.0	166.9	275.4	204.0	428.5	340.7	374.9	414.8	403.7
7. Turkey	5.8	2.3	6.9	24.0	0.7	8.9	7.7	22.3	40.1	77.8	124.7	100.2	119.9	150.7	257.0	285.8	303.6	319.0
8. Turkmenistan	10.0	14.2	23.0	22.4	45.0	41.8	24.1	31.4	81.1	106.6	121.8	150.5	186.7	213.2	186.5	236.9	265.3	305.1
9. China, People's Rep. of	34.8	34.4	35.7	26.8	18.3	21.9	19.0	21.9	29.1	62.8	56.3	110.7	186.4	168.0	234.8	192.5	253.1	510.9
10. Thailand	13.4	23.0	17.7	6.8	8.1	2.3	1.7	3.1	11.9	8.9	63.5	68.9	165.4	132.1	156.3	160.4	209.0	157.0
BALANCE OF PAYMENTS *million US Dollars; calendar year*																		
Current account	...	...	...	...	...	...	...	-150	-456	-265	-182	-379	83	92	-347	267	654	346
Balance on goods	...	...	...	...	...	...	...	-1218	-2486	-3443	-4335	-4933	-6002	-6480	-6354	-6303	-7358	-8875
Exports	...	...	...	...	...	...	...	1291	1894	1643	1795	1811	1835	2465	2517	2836	2840	2785
Imports	...	...	...	...	...	...	...	-2508	-4379	-5086	-6130	-6744	-7837	-8945	-8872	-9139	-10199	-11660
Services and income	...	...	...	...	...	...	...	-154	-446	-451	-545	-473	-425	-240	-370	-408	-390	-444
Credit	...	...	...	...	...	...	...	...	...	...	...	...	...	...	...	...	...	...
Debit	...	...	...	...	...	...	...	...	...	...	...	...	...	...	...	...	...	...
Current transfers	...	...	...	...	...	...	...	1222	2476	3629	4698	5027	6510	6812	6377	6978	8402	9665
Credit	...	...	...	...	...	...	...	...	...	...	...	...	...	...	...	...	...	...
Debit	...	...	...	...	...	...	...	...	...	...	...	...	...	...	...	...	...	...
Capital account / Financial account	...	...	...	...	...	...	...	144	149.6	470.2	357	195	25	338	-287	612	234	158
Direct investment	...	...	...	...	...	...	...	50	58	187	271	238	243	300	303	329	315	321
Portfolio investment	...	...	...	...	...	...	...	...	...	...	...	...	...	...	...	...	...	...
Other investment	...	...	...	...	...	...	...	94	92	283	86	-43	-218	38	-590	283	-81	-163
Net errors and omissions	...	...	...	...	...	...	...	161	687	237	223	405	372	541	190	-81	128	–
Overall balance	...	...	...	...	...	...	...	155	380	442	398	220	479	972	-445	798	1016	505
Balance of Payments *percent of GDP at current market prices*																		
Exports	...	...	...	...	...	...	...	30.1	38.4	29.4	27.1	24.1	17.7	22.9	20.0	17.6	14.7	13.9
Imports	...	...	...	...	...	...	...	-58.5	-88.7	-91.0	-92.6	-89.7	-75.5	-83.1	-70.4	-56.8	-52.7	-58.3
Balance on goods	...	...	...	...	...	...	...	-28.4	-50.4	-61.6	-65.5	-65.6	-57.8	-60.2	-50.5	-39.2	-38.1	-44.4
Current account balance	...	...	...	...	...	...	...	-3.5	-9.2	-4.7	-2.7	-5.0	0.8	0.9	-2.8	1.7	3.4	1.7
Overall balance	...	...	...	...	...	...	...	3.6	7.7	7.9	6.0	2.9	4.6	9.0	-3.5	5.0	5.2	2.5

Item	1995	1996	1997	1998	1999	2000	2001	2002	2003	2004	2005	2006	2007	2008	2009	2010	2011	2012
INTERNATIONAL RESERVES *million US Dollars; as of end of period*																		
Total	7.3	7.1	6.6	6.9	6.8	6.4	6.2	6.7	0.6	0.1	0.0	0.1	0.2	3018.4	4278.5	5146.6	6398.8	7142.8
Gold, national valuation	...	...	...	...	...	...	...	...	...	...	...	...	...	587.5	777.2	972.3	1130.4	1160.3
Foreign exchange	...	...	...	...	...	...	...	...	...	...	...	...	...	2430.8	3300.0	3976.7	5071.4	5788.5
Reserve position in the Fund	7.3	7.1	6.6	6.9	6.8	6.4	6.2	6.7	–	–	–	–	–	–	–	–	–	–
SDRs	–	–	–	–	–	–	–	–	0.6	0.1	0.0	0.1	0.2	0.0	201.4	197.7	196.9	194.0
EXCHANGE RATES *New Afghanis per US Dollar*																		
End of period	47.50	47.50	47.50	47.50	46.79	...	47.26	47.26	48.87	48.22	50.41	49.85	49.72	52.14	48.74	45.27	49.04	...
Average of period	36.57	47.50	47.50	47.50	46.62	47.36	47.50	47.26	48.76	47.85	49.49	49.93	49.96	50.25	50.23	46.45	46.75	50.92
EXTERNAL INDEBTEDNESS *million US Dollars; as of end of year*																		
Total debt outstanding and disbursed	...	...	...	...	...	...	...	...	...	...	...	969	2013	2134	2470	2423	2623	...
Long-term debt	...	...	...	...	...	...	...	...	...	...	...	911	1893	1985	2097	1966	2023	...
Public and publicly guaranteed	...	...	...	...	...	...	...	...	...	...	...	911	1893	1985	2097	1966	2023	...
Private nonguaranteed	...	...	...	...	...	...	...	...	...	...	...	–	–	–	...	...	...	...
Short-term debt	...	...	...	...	...	...	...	...	...	...	...	18	21	17	20	102	228	...
Use of IMF credit	...	...	...	...	–	–	–	–	–	–	–	40	99	131	353	355	373	...
External debt *percent of GNI*	...	...	...	...	...	...	...	...	...	...	...	11.8	19.8	19.7	19.6	16.0	...	...
Total long-term debt *percent of total debt*	...	...	...	...	...	...	...	...	...	...	...	94.0	94.1	93.0	84.9	81.1	77.1	...
Short-term debt *percent of total debt*	...	...	...	...	...	...	...	...	...	...	...	1.9	1.0	0.8	0.8	4.2	8.7	...
Debt service *percent of exports of goods and services*	...	...	...	...	...	...	...	...	...	...	3.8	0.2	0.1	0.2	0.4	...	...	...
Debt service *million US Dollars; transactions during the year*																		
Principal repayments on long-term debt	...	...	...	...	...	...	...	...	...	...	...	3.5	1.3	1.3	3.1	1.0	0.9	...
Interest on long-term debt	...	...	...	...	...	...	...	...	...	...	...	5.8	3.2	6.0	6.5	7.0	8.9	...
Interest on short-term debt	...	...	...	...	...	...	...	...	...	...	...	–	–	–	–	1.2	0.6	...

Item	1995	1996	1997	1998	1999	2000	2001	2002	2003	2004	2005	2006	2007	2008	2009	2010	2011	2012
Average terms of new commitments																		
Interest *percent per annum*	...	...	...	...	...	...	...	...	...	...	...	1.2	1.4	0.5	–	–	–	...
Maturity *years*	...	...	...	...	...	...	...	...	...	...	...	39.8	31.6	34.6	–	–	–	...
Grace period *years*	...	...	...	...	...	...	...	...	...	...	...	10.3	8.1	10.0	–	–	–	...
Grant element *percent*	...	...	...	...	...	...	...	...	...	...	...	76.1	69.8	80.5	–	–	–	...

... = Data not available at cutoff date, * = Provisional/preliminary/estimate/budget figure, – = Magnitude equals zero, 0.0 = Magnitude is less than half of unit employed.

a The last census in Afghanistan was conducted in 1979. The population in succeeding years, except for 2004, which came from the Population and Housing Census, Phase 1 (Count), was estimated using population growth rates.

b Includes the population aged 10–59 years. Employed refers to the productive and nonproductive sectors. The productive sector includes agriculture and industry (manufacturing, mining, small-scale industries and handicrafts, construction and geology, and transport and communications); the nonproductive sector refers to other employed, which includes education and health, government departments, and public services.

c Includes wholesale and retail trade; restaurants and hotels.

d Includes finance, insurance, real estate, and business.

e Refers to gross fixed capital formation.

f Includes claims on government and nonfinancial public enterprises.

g In 2002, only three state-owned banks were in operation.

Sources:

Population	Central Statistics Organization (CSO). Official communication, 3 June 2013; past communication.
Labor Force	CSO. Official communication, 3 June 2013; past communication.
National Accounts	CSO. Official communication, 3 June 2013; past communication.
Production Indexes	
Agriculture	Food and Agriculture Organization. FAOSTAT. http://faostat.fao.org/site/612/default.aspx#ancor (downloaded May 2013).
Energy	
Coal	For 1995–1998: United Nations Economic and Social Commission for Asia and the Pacific. *Statistical Yearbook for Asia and the Pacific 2001*; various issues. For 2002–2012: CSO. Official communication, 3 June 2013; past communication.
Electricity	CSO. Official communication, 3 June 2013; past communication.
Price Indexes	CSO. Official communication, 3 June 2013; past communication.
Money and Banking	Da Afghanistan Bank (DAB). Official communication, 1 April 2013; past communication.
Government Finance	CSO. Official communication, 3 June 2013; past communication.
External Trade	CSO. Official communication, 4 June 2013; past communication.
Direction of Trade	International Monetary Fund (IMF). *Direction of Trade Statistics* CD-ROM, May 2013.
Balance of Payments	DAB. Official communication, 1 April 2013; past communication.
International Reserves Exchange Rates	IMF. *International Financial Statistics* CD-ROM, May 2013.
External Indebtedness	World Bank. World Development Indicators and International Debt Statistics. http://databank.worldbank.org/Data/Views/VariableSelection/SelectVariables.aspx?(downloaded May 2013).

Bibliography

Primary Documents

Afghanistan in 2007: A Survey of the Afghan People, The Asia Foundation, Kabul, 2007.

Afghanistan: Post Conflict Environmental Assessment, UNEP, 2003.

Afghanistan's Environmental Recovery: A Post-conflict Plan for People and their Natural Resources, UNEP, August 2006.

"Afghanistan: Children Devasted by War, Afgahnistan's Lost Generation", *Report by Amnesty International*, November 1, 1999, http://web.amnesty.org/library/Index/engASA110131999.

Alexandra Mathieu, "Reaching the Girls in South Asia: Differentiated Needs and Responses in Emergencies", *Report by the United Nations Children's Emergency Fund and United Nations Girls' Education Initiative*, March 2006.

Amnesty International, *Afghanistan. Out of Sight, Out of Mind: The Fate of the Afghan Returnees,* Amnesty International,London, 2003.

An Agenda for Development: Report of the Secretary-General, A/48/935, 6 May 1994; "Supplement to An Agenda for Peace" A/50/60, S.1995/1, 3 January 1995; An Agenda for Democratisation, A/50/332 AND A/51/512, 17 December 1996.

An Agenda for Peace, Preventive Diplomacy and Peace-keeping, Report of the Secretary General in pursuant to the statement adopted by the Summit Meeting of the Security Council on 3 January 1992, A/47/277 - S/24111, 17 June 1992.

An Updated Five-Year Strategy for Tackling the Illicit Drug Problem, The National Drugs Control Strategy (NDCS), Kabul, January 2006.

Annex 1, Principles 24, 25, 26, United Nations General Assembly. Rio de Janeiro, 1992.

ASEAN-ISIS, *Confidence Building Measures in South-East Asia*, 1993,

Ban, K., Secretary-General's statement at open Security Council debate on Energy, Security and Climate, New York, 17 April, 2007.

Building Health Security in Contemporary Afghanistan, Conference Report, May 13, 2009.

'Community Peacebuilding in Afghanistan: The Case for a National Strategy', *Oxfam International Research Report*, February, 2008.

"Ending Afghanistan's Civil War", *Rand Corporation Testimony Series*, Testimony presented before the House Armed Services Committee on 30 January 2007.

From Conflict to Peacebuilding: The Role of Natural Resources and the Environment, United Nations Environment Programme, February 2009.

Human Security Bulletin (www.humansecurity.info).

ICISS, "The Responsibility to Protect: Report of the International Commission on Intervention and State Sovereignty", International Development Research Council, Ottawa, 2001.

James Dobbins, "Ending Afghanistan's Civil War", *Rand Corporation Testimony Series*, Testimony presented before the House Armed Services Committee on 30 January 2007.

Kofi Annan, Millennium Report to the United Nations General Assembly, 2000 and is articulated by Sabina Alkire, "A Conceptual Framework for Human Security", *CRISE Working Paper*, No. 2, 2003, p.14. For details on Kofi Annan's discussion on human security, see Kofi A. Annan, *We the Peoples: The Role of the United Nations in the 21st Century*, available at http://www.un.org/millennium/sg/report/full.htm.

Landmine Impact Survey: Islamic Republic of Afghanistan, Survey Action Centre, 2005.

Manabu Fujimura, *Post-conflict reconstruction: The Afghan Economy*, Report of Asian Development Bank Institute, Tokyo, 2003.

National Development Framework, Government of Afghanistan, Kabul, 2002.

National Drugs Control Strategy (NDCS), Islamic Republic of Afghanistan's Ministry of Counter-Narcotics, Kabul, January 2006.

Post-conflict reconstruction: The Afghan Economy, Report of Asian Development Bank Institute, Tokyo, 2003.

Report of the Secretary- General's High Level Panel on Threats, Challenges, and Change, United Nations, 2004: Boutros Boutros

Ghali, An Agenda For Peace: preventative diplomacy, peacemaking and peacekeeping, New York: United Nations, 1992.

Report of the Secretary-General to the UN Security Council, "The Situation in Afghanistan and its Implications for International Peace and Security", 6 March 2008, A/62/722–S/2008/159.

"The Year in Review", *World Refugee Survey 2003,US Committee for Refugees,* 2003.

UN General Assembly, *Report of the United Nations Conference on Environment and Development.*

UN Secretary-General's High-level Panel on Threats, Challenges and Change, *A more secure world: our shared responsibility: Report of the High-level Panel on Threats, Challenges and Change* (A/59/565).

United Nations General Assembly, New York, 2004.

UNEP and NEPA, *Afghanistan's Environment 2008,* 2008.

United Nations Development Program (UNDP), *Human Development Report, 1994,* Oxford University Press, New York.

United Nations Development Program, "Redefining Security: The Human Dimension", *Current History,* May 1995.

United Nations Development Program (1994): Human Development Report

United Nations Development Programme, *Human Development Report,* Oxford University Press, New York, 1994, p.3. Cited in Sabina Alkire, "A Conceptual Framework for Human Security", *CRISE Working Paper,* No. 2, 2003.

United Nations Environment Programme, *From Conflict to Peacebuilding: The Role of Natural Resources and the Environment,* 2009.

World Development Report 1999/2000, New York: Oxford University Press, 2000.

Books and Articles

A.P. Rana, 'Understanding International Conflict in the Third World: A Conceptual Inquiry", in Kanti P. Bajpai and Siddharth Mallavarapu (eds.), *International Relations in India: Theorising the Region and Nation* (New Delhi: Orient Longman, 2005) p. 16.

Aaron Beers Sampson, "Tropical Anarchy: Waltz, Wendt, and the Way We imagine International Politics".

Adam Pain and Sue Lautze, *Addressing Livelihoods in Afghanistan,* AREU Issue Paper Series, September 2002.

Adil Najam, "The Human Dimensions of Environmental Insecurity: Some Insights From South Asia", http://wwics.si.edu/topics/pubs/najam.pdf.

____, "Living in Fear: Child Soldiers and the Tamil Tigers in Sri Lanka", *Report by the Human Rights Watch*, Vol. 13(C), November 2004, http://hrw.org/reports/2004/srilanka1104/2.htm.

Amitav Acharya, Subrat K. Singhdeo, and M. Rajaretnam, *Human security: from concept to practice: case studies from Northeast India and Orissa*, World Scientific Books, 2011.

Andrew Linklater's works include *Critical Theory and World Politics: Citizenship, sovereignty, and humanity*, Routledge, 2007.

Arnold Wolfers, *Discord and Collaboration: Essays on International Politics*, The Johns Hopkins Press, Baltimore, 1962.

Astri Suhrke, 'Human Security and the Interests of the State', *Security Dialogue*, Vol. 30, No. 3, 1999, pp. 265-276.

Axworthy, Lloyd, "Canada and Human Security: The Need for Leadership", *International Journal*, Spring 1997.

B. Rosamond, *Theories of European integration*, Macmillan, New York : St. Martin's Press, Basingstoke, 2000.

B. Buzan, C. Jones, and R. Little, *The Logic of Anarchy: Neorealism to Structural Realism*, Columbia University Press, New York, 1993.

Barnett, R. Rubin, Humayun Hamidzada and Abby Stoddard, "Afghanistan 2005 and Beyond: Prospects for Improved Stability Reference Document", Centre on International Co-operation, New York University For the Clingendael Institute, Netherlands, Conflict Research Unit, April 2005.

Barry Buzan and Lene Hansen, *The Evolution of International Security Studies*, Cambridge University Press, Cambridge, 2009, pp. 184-85.

Barry Buzan, Charles Jones and Richard Little, *The Logic of Anarchy, Neorealism to Structural Realism*, Columbia University Press, New York, 1993.

Barry Buzan, *People, States, and Fear: An Agenda for International Security Studies in the Post-War Era*, 2nd edition, Lynne Rienner, Boulder, 1991.

Barry Buzan, *People, States, and Fear: The National Security Problem in International Relations*, Wheatheaf Books Ltd., Sussex, 1983.

Bill McSweeney, *Security, Identity and Interests: A Sociology of International Relations*, Cambridge University Press, Cambridge, 1999.

Binoda Kumar Mishra, "Constructing South Asian Security: Breaking Away From the (In)Security Complex", Paula Banerjee and Amrita

Dey (eds.), Security Dilemmas of South and South-East Asia, Frontpage, Kolkata, 2012, pp.31-57.

Brian White, Richard Little, and Michael Smith, *Issues in World Politics*, Palgrave, New York, 2001, p.15.

Burke, Sharon, *Natural Security*, Working Paper, Center for a New American Security, June 2009, p.9.

Charles T. Call and Elizabeth M. Cousens, "Ending Wars and Building Peace: International Responses to War-Torn Societies", *International Studies Perspectives*, 9, 2008.

Charles Tilly, *Coercion, Capital and European States, AD 990-1990*, Blackwell, Oxford, 1990.

Christopher Hill, "Academic International Relations: The Siren Song of Policy Relevance", Christopher Hill and Pamela Beshoff, *Two Worlds of International Relations: Academics, Practitioners and the Trade in Ideas*, Routledge, London, 1994.

Craig A. Snyder (ed.), *Contemporary Security and Strategy*, Macmillan London, 1999

Craig A. Snyder, "Regional Security Structures", in Craig A. Snyder (ed), *Contemporary Security and Strategy*, Macmillan, London, 1999.

David A.Baldwin, *Neorealism and Neo-liberalism: The Contemporary Debate*, Columbia University Press, New York, 1993.

David Mitrany, *The Progress of International Government*, Yale University Press, New Haven, 1933.

____, "The Prospect of European Integration: Federal or Functional", *Journal of Common Market Studies*, 1965.

Douglas Saltmarshe and Abhilash Medhi, *Local Governance in Afghanistan: A View from the Ground*, AREU Synthesis Paper, AREU, Kabul, June 2011.

Dr. Muhammad Aslam Khan, "SAARC: Achievements and limitations", *South Asian News Agency*, www.sananews.com.pk.

E.H. Carr, *The Twenty Years Crisis 1919-1939: An Introduction to the Study of International Relations*, Macmillan, London, 1966.

Ernst B. Haas, *The Uniting of Europe; Political, Social, and Economic Forces, 1950-1957*, Stanford University Press, Stanford, 1958,

Ernst Haas, *Beyond the Nation-State: Functionalism and International Organization*, Stanford University Press, Stanford, 1964.

Frances Stewart, "Development and Security", Centre for Research on Inequality, Human Security, and Ethnicity (CRISE), Working Paper 3, University of Oxford, London, 2004.

Fred Halliday, "The future of international relations: fears and hopes", Steve Smith, Ken Booth and Marysia Zalewski (eds.), *International Theory: Positivism and Beyond*, CUP, Cambridge, 1996, p.318.

Gary King and Christopher J. L. Murray, "Rethinking Human Security", *Political Science Quarterly*, Vol. 116, No. 4, 2001-2002.

Gilpin, *War and Change In World Politics*, CUP, Cambridge, 1981.

Greaves, Wilfrid, "The failure to protect: human security and Canadian foreign policy in Afghanistan", *Journal of Military and Strategic Studies*, Vol. 10, Issue 4, Summer 2008.

Haas, Ernst B., "Regionalism, Functionalism, and Universal International Organization", *World Politics*, Vol. 8, No. 2, Jan., 1956.

Hans J. Maorgenthau, *Politics Among Nations: A struggle for Power and Peace*, 3rd edn., Knopf, New York, 1965.

Hasenclever, Andreas, Mayer, Peter, and Rittberger, Volker, "Interests, Power, Knowledge: The Study of International Regimes", *Mershon International Studies Review*, 40, 1996.

Hedley Bull, *The Anarchical Society: A Study of Order in World Politics*, 2nd edn., Macmillan, London, 1995.

Ian M. Harris, Larry J. Fisk, Carol Rank, "A portrait of university peace studies in North America and Western Europe at the end of the millennium", *International Journal of Peace Studies*, Volume 3, Number 1, 1998.

International Relations: Critical Concepts in Political Science, Routledge, 2000,

J. Mearsheimer, 'Back to the Future: Instability in Europe after the Cold War', in S. Lynn-Jones (ed.), *The Cold War and After: Prospects for Peace*, MIT Press, Mass., pp.141-92 and 'The False Promise of International Institutions' in M.E. Brown *et al.* (eds.), *The Perils of Anarchy: Contemporary Realism and International Security*, MIT Press, Cambridge, Mass., pp. 332-77.

J. Ann Tickner, *Gendering World Politics: Issues and Approaches in the Post-Cold War Era*, Columbia University, 2001, *Gender in International Relations: Feminist Perspectives on Achieving International Security*, Columbia University, 1992, and Columbia University, 1987.

J. Galtung, "A Structural Theory of Imperialism", *Journal of Peace Research*, Vol.13, No.2, 1971.

J. Schafer, "Overview of issues for a research programme on integrating livelihoods and political economy approaches", Overseas Development Institute, London: 2001.

J. Sharp, *Geographies of Postcolonialism*, Sage Publications, Glasgow, 2008

J.E. Dougherty and, R.L. Pfaltzgraff, *Contending Theories of International Relations*, Lippincott, New York, 1971.

J.N. Rosenau, *Turbulence in World Politics: A Theory of Change and Continuity*, Princeton University Press, Princeton, 1990.

James Dobbins, "Ending Afghanistan's Civil War", *Rand Corporation Testimony Series*, Testimony presented before the House Armed Services Committee on 30 January 2007.

Jehan Perera, "Indo-Sri Lanka Relations: Recent Trends", in Deve Raj Dahal and Nischal Nath Pandey (eds.) *Comprehensive in South Asia*, Manohar Publications, New Delhi for Friedrich Ebert Stiftung, Kathmandu and Institute of Foreign Affairs, Kathmandu, 2006.

John H. Herz, *Political Realism and Political Idealism*, University of Chicago Press, Chicago, 1951.

John H. Herz, "Idealist Internationalism and the Security Dilemma", *World Politics*, Vol. 2, 1950.

K.R. Nossal, "Seeing Things? The Adornment of 'Security' in Australia and Canada", *Australian Journal of International Affairs*, Vol. 49. No. 1, 1995, 39.

K. Haq, 'Human Security for Women,' in M. Tehranian, (ed.),*Worlds Apart: Human Security and Global Governance*, I.B. Tauris Publishers, London, 1999.

K.N. Waltz, *Theory of International Politics*, Addison-Wesley, Reading, Mass, 1979.

Kanti P. Bajpai, "Human Security: Concept and Measurement", *Kroc Institute Occasional Paper*, No. 19:OP:1, August 2000. Available at, http://www.nd.edu/?krocinst/ocpapers/po_19_1.pdf.

Keith Krause and Michael Williams (eds.), *Critical Security Studies: Concepts and Cases*, University of Minnesota Press, Minneapolis, 1997.

Ken Booth (ed.), *Critical Security Studies & World Politics*, Viva Books, New Delhi, 2005.

Ken Booth, "Realities of Security: Editor's Introduction", *International Relations*, Vol. 18, No. 1, March 2004, Sage Publications.

Ken Booth, "Security and Emancipation", *Review of International Studies*, Vol. 17, No. 4,

Kenneth N. Waltz, "The Emerging Structure of International Politics", in Michael E. Brown, Sean M. Lynn-Jones, and Steven E. Miller (eds.), *The Perils of Anarchy: Contemporary Realism and International Security*, The MIT Press, Cambridge, Massachusetts, London, 1995, p. 42. For a complete discussion on Waltz's argument on the utility of Nuclear Weapons for ensuring international peace, see Kenneth N. Waltz, "The Spread of Nuclear: The More May Be Better", *Adelphi Paper*, No. 171, International Institute for Strategic Studies, London, 1981. For Mearsheimer's argument on Bi-Polarity and International Stability, See John J. Mearsheimer, "Back to the Future: Instability in Europe After the Cold War", *International Security*, Vol. 15, No. 1, Summer 1990, pp.5-56.

Kenneth Waltz, *Theory of International Politics*, McGraw Hill, New York, 1979;

Kyle Grayson, "Human Security as power/knowledge: the biopolitics of a definitional debate", *Cambridge Review of International Affairs*, Vol. 21, No. 3, September 2008.

M. Horkheimer, *Critical Theory*, Seabury Press, New York, 1982.

M. Hollis and S. Smith, *Explaining and Understanding International Relations*, Clarendon Press, Oxford,1990.

M. Wight, *System of States*, Leicester University Press, Leicester, 1977.

Macartan Humphreys, "Natural Resources, Conflict, and Conflict Resolution: Uncovering the Mechanisms", *The Journal of Conflict Resolution*, Vol. 49, No. 4, *Paradigm in Distress? Primary Commodities and Civil War*, Aug., 2005, pp. 508-537.

Mark F. Giordano, Meredith A. Giordano, Aaron T. Wolf, "International Resource Conflict and Mitigation", *Journal of Peace Research*, Vol. 42, No. 1, Jan., 2005, pp. 47-65.

Michael Doyle and Nicolas Sambanis, *Making War and Building Peace*, Princeton University Press, 2006.

Michael Mann, *Incoherent Empire*, Verso, London, 2003.

Mini Pathak, "Problems of Nation-Building and Inter-State Relations in South Asia", in Gopal Singh and Ramesh Chauhan (eds.), *South Asia Today*, Anamika Publishers, New Delhi 2005.

Mitrany, *A Working Peace System*, Quadrangle Books, Chicago, 1966.

Mitrany *The Functional Theory of Politics*, St. Martin's Press, New York, 1976.

Mitrany, David, "A Working Peace System. An Argument for the Functional Development of International Organization", *International Affairs* (Royal Institute of International Affairs 1944-), Vol. 20, No. 1, Jan., 1944.

Moonis Ahmar, "South Asian Security in the New Millennium", in Rajesh M. Basrur, *Security in the New Millennium: Views from South Asia*, India Research Press, New Delhi, 2001.

Muhammad Jamshed Iqbal, "SAARC: Origin, Growth, Potential and Achievements", *Pakistan Journal of History & Culture*, Vol. 27, No. 2, 2006. Available at, http://www.nihcr.edu.pk.

N. Thomas and W.T. Tow, "The Utility of Human Security: Sovereignty and Humanitarian Intervention", SAGE Publications, Vol. 33(2), 2002.

Nicholas J. Wheeler, *Saving Strangers: Humanitarian Intervention in International Society*, OUP, Oxford, 2000.

Norman Angell, *The Great Illusion*, Weidenfeld and Nicolson, London, 1909.

Paul Collier and Anke Hoeffler, "Economic causes of civil conflict and their implications for policy", Chester A. Crocker, *et al.* (ed.) *Managing Global Chaos*, United States Institute of Peace, Washington, DC, 2000.

Paula Kantor and Adam Pain, *Rethinking Rural Poverty Reduction in Afghanistan*, Afghanistan Research and Evaluation Unit (AREU) Policy Note, October 2011.

Pekka Havisto, 'Introduction', *Afghanistan: Post Conflict Environmental Assessment*, UNEP, 2003.

Peter Wallensteen (ed.), *Peace Research: Achievements and Challenges*, Westview Press, Boulder, CO 1988.

R.O. Keohane, and S. Hoffmann, The New European Community: Decision-making and Institutional Change. Boulder, Colorado: Westview Press, 1991. Inis L. Claude Jr., *Swords into Plowshares*, New York: Random House, 1996.

R.B. Finnegan, 'International Relations: The disputed search for method', *Review of Politics*, 34, 1972

R. Waldman and H. Hanif, The Public Health System in Afghanistan, Kabul: AREU, 2002.

Radhika Coomaraswamy, "The Various Contours of Violence Against Women in South Asia", *Paper presented at the Fifth South Asia Ministerial Conference Celebrating Beijing Plus Ten*, organized by Government of Pakistan and UNIFEM South Asian Regional Office, Islamabad, Pakistan, 3-5 May 2005.

Richard Ullman, "Redefining Security", *International Security*, vol. 8, no.1, 1983.

Robert Jackson and Georg Sorensen, *Introduction to International Relations, 3rd edn. Theories and Approaches*, OUP, Oxford, 2007.

Robert Jackson, The *Global Covenant: Human Conduct in a World of States*, Oxford University Press, Oxford, 2000.

Robert Keohane, *Neo-Realism and Its Critics*, Columbia University Press, New York, 1986,

Robert O. Keohane and Joseph S. Nye, *Power and Interdependence: World Politics in Transition*, Little, Brown and Company, Boston, 1977.

Robert O. Keohane, Nye Joseph S. Jr., Stanley Hoffmann, After the Cold War: International Institutions And State Strategies In Europe, 1989-1991, Harvard University Press, Cambridge, M.A., 1993.

Robert Ornstein and Paul Ehrlich, *New World, New Mind* (London: Methun, 1989) p. 74, Cited in Ken Booth, "Security in Anarchy: Utopian Realism in Theory and Practice", *International Affairs*, Vol. 67, No. 3, 1991.

Roland Paris, "Human Security: Paradigm Shift or Hot Air", *International Security*, Vol. 26, No. 2, Fall 2001, pp. 87-102. Des Gasper, "Securing Humanity: Situating 'Human Security' as a concept and Discourse", *Journal of Human Development*, Vol. 6, No. 2, July 2005.

Roland Paris, *At War's End*, Cambridge University Press, 2004.

Ronald Waldman, Lesley Strong, and Dr. Abdul Wali, *Afghanistan's Health System Since 2001: Condition Improved, Prognosis Cautiously Optimistic*, AREU, Briefing Paper Series, December 2006.

Rubin, Barnett, *Afghanistan and Threats to Human Security*, Social Science Research Council, Speech delivered in Tokyo on December 15, 2001, at the International Symposium on Human Security: "Human Security and Terrorism—Diversifying Threats under Globalization—from Afghanistan to the Future of the World". http://www.ssrc.org/sept11/essays/rubin.htm

S. Dalby, 'Security, Modernity, Ecology: The Dilemmas of Post-Cold War Security Discourse', *Alternatives*, Vol. 17, No. 1, Winter, 1992.

S. Tadjbakhsh, "Human Security In International Organizations: Blessing or Scourge?", *The Human Security Journal*, Vol. 4, Summer 2007.

Sabina Alkire, "A conceptual Framework for Human Security", Centre for Research on Inequlaity, Human Security and Ethnicity (CRISE), Working Paper 2, University of Oxford, London, 2003.

Samuel P. Huntington, *The Third Wave: Democratization in the Late Twentieth Century*, Norman: University of Oklahama, 1991.

Stephen D. Krasner, "Sharing Sovereignty. New Institutions for Collapsed and Failing States", *International Security*, Vol. 29, No. 2, 2004.

Steve Smith, 'The Self-Images of a Discipline', in K. Booth and S. Smith (eds.), *International Relations Theory Today*, The Pennsylvania State University Press, University Park, Pennsylvania, 1995.

Sudhir k. Singh, "Ethnicity and Regional Aspirations In Pakistan", *J&K Insights*, http://www.jammu-kashmir.com/insights/insight 20020101d.html.

Suhrke, Astri, "Human Security and the Interest of States", *Security Dialogue*, Vol. 30, No. 3, September 1999, pp. 265-276.

Tadjbakhsh, Shahrbanou & Chenoy, Anuradha M. *Human Security: Concepts and Implications*, Routledge, London, 2006.

Theda Skocpol, *States and Social Revolutions*, Cambridge University Press, Cambridge, 1979.

Martin Jay, *Adorno*, Fontana, London, 1984.

Timothy Dunne, Milja Kurki, and Steve Smith, *International Relations Theories: Discipline and Diversity*, Oxford University Press, 2007.

Waheguru Pal Singh Sidhu and Jing-dong Yuan, *China and India: Cooperation or Conflict?*,: India Research Press, New Delhi.

Wasbir Hussain, "India's North-East: The Problem - Part 1", *Manipur Online*, May 9, 2006,

William Bain (ed.), 'Introduction', *The Empire of Security and the Safety of the People*, Routledge, Oxon, 2006.

William Odom, 'Military lessons and US forces', G. Allison and G. Treverton (eds), *Rethinking America's Security: Beyond Cold War to New World Order*, W.W. Norton, New York, 1992.

Yosef Lapid, 'The third debate: on the prospects of international theory in a post-positivist era', *International Studies Quarterly*, 33(3), 1989.

Websites

http://data.worldbank.org/indicator/SP.DYN.CBRT.IN (accessed on 12.4.2010).

http://data.worldbank.org/indicator/SP.DYN.CDRT.IN (accessed on 12.3.2010).

http://www.ungei.org/resources/files/unicef_Reachinggirlsinsouth asia.pdf.

http://postconflict.unep.ch.

www.intlhealth.fhpr.osd.mil/MultiMedia/conferencematerials/buildingafghanistanhealth.aspx.

www.humansecurity.info.

http://www.manipuronline.com/North-East/May2006/NEtheproblem 09_1.htm.

http://www.jammu-kashmir.com/insights/insight20020101d.html.

http://www.ssrc.org/sept11/essays/rubin.htm.

Index